Suzy Welch is an award-winning professor of management practice at NYU Stern School of Business and the director of the NYU Stern Initiative on Purpose and Flourishing. A noted public speaker and frequent *Today* show contributor and *Wall Street Journal* commentator, Professor Welch is the author of three previous bestselling books, *Winning* and *The Real-Life MBA*, with her late husband, Jack Welch, as well as *10-10-10: A Life-Transforming Idea*, which presents her acclaimed method for values-driven decision-making. Her values and aptitude assessment tools, the Values Bridge, PIE360, and the Career Traits Compass, are widely used in academic and organizational settings. She received a BA in fine arts from Harvard University, graduated as a Baker Scholar from Harvard Business School, and completed her PhD in organizational behavior at the University of Bristol. The mother of four and grandmother of two, she lives in New York with her three ridiculous dogs.

AF001886

Also by Suzy Welch

Winning (with Jack Welch)

The Real-Life MBA (with Jack Welch)

10-10-10: A Life-Transforming Idea

Becoming You

The Proven Method for Crafting Your Authentic Life and Career

Suzy Welch

ONE PLACE. MANY STORIES

HQ
An imprint of HarperCollins*Publishers* Ltd
1 London Bridge Street
London SE1 9GF

www.harpercollins.co.uk

HarperCollins*Publishers*
Macken House, 39/40 Mayor Street Upper,
Dublin 1, D01 C9W8, Ireland

This edition 2025

1
First published in Great Britain by HQ,
an imprint of HarperCollins*Publishers* Ltd 2025

Copyright © Suzy Welch 2025

Suzy Welch asserts the moral right to be identified as the author of this work.
A catalogue record for this book is available from the British Library.

ISBN: 978-0-00-876969-7

Designed by Bonni Leon-Berman

All rights reserved. No part of this publication may be reproduced, stored in a retrieval system, or transmitted, in any form or by any means, electronic, mechanical, photocopying, recording or otherwise, without the prior permission of the publishers.

Without limiting the author's and publisher's exclusive rights, any unauthorised use of this publication to train generative artificial intelligence (AI) technologies is expressly prohibited. HarperCollins also exercise their rights under Article 4(3) of the Digital Single Market Directive 2019/790 and expressly reserve this publication from the text and data mining exception.

Printed and bound in the UK using 100% Renewable
Electricity by CPI Group (UK) Ltd

For more information visit: www.harpercollins.co.uk/green

To all those who shared their lives and stories to make *Becoming You* ever more purposeful and real, I thank you with love.

Tell me, what is it you plan to do

    with your one wild and precious life?

—MARY OLIVER

Contents

Introduction	The Work of Our Lives	1
1	Becoming You: A User's Guide	19
2	This I Believe	31

Part I — Values

3	Which Tony Is This?	49
4	Taking Our Values by the Reins	54
5	The Bridge to Yourself, and Your Future	76
6	The One and Only Tony	123

Part II — Aptitudes

7	Chloe and the Tao of Aptitudes	129
8	Check Your Wiring	143
9	Your Personality on GPS	166
10	Chloe in the Sky with Diamonds	195

Contents

Part III		Economically Viable Interests	
	11	Open the Aperture, Olivia	203
	12	Your Inner Calling (or Not)	208
	13	All About . . . Industry	220
	14	Magnesium on Mars, and Other Megatrends	228
	15	Olivia, Eyes Wide Open	236
Part IV:		Conclusion	
	16	A Forever Kind of Thing	241
Appendixes			245
Acknowledgments			287

Becoming You

Introduction

The Work of Our Lives

Thank your lucky stars, this is not another book about happiness!

Don't get me wrong, I *want* you to be happy. It's better if you are, of course it is. I would like everyone, everywhere to be happy. Surely that would make the world the better place it's been trying to be since, oh, the dawn of time.

But the achievement of happiness is not my area of expertise, and, frankly, I'm not sure happiness is even possible for prolonged stretches of time, given life just being the way it is, with love and loss, not to mention difficult children, parents, partners, bosses, coworkers, neighbors, friends, and—wait, isn't everyone difficult at some point or another? And happiness is so tied up in personality and genetics, too, isn't it? Also: the culture and the zeitgeist and the economy. Those little things. People with dogs are *said* to be happier, so maybe that's it after all? Or maybe happy people are just the ones who get dogs?

Whatever! Even forget happiness for a moment. I am writing this book to help you answer the question, "What should I do with my life?"

Just that.

Pesky thing, that question, isn't it? Except for the handful of people who are born knowing they have to play in the Super Bowl, belt it out on Broadway, operate on brains, or walk on the Moon—and who actually have the talent, grit, and good fortune to *do* those things—most of us struggle with this question our whole lives long. Some of us even wrestle with it until the very end.

Did I ever do what I was meant to do?

I hope we can avoid that fate for you. I think we can.

Thus, hi, it's Suzy. Welcome to *Becoming You*.

This book presents a methodology I have spent the past fifteen years developing, researching, testing, and teaching, and which has proven—somewhat to my surprise and utterly to my delight—to work very well.

And by "work very well," I mean it appears to be exceptionally effective in helping people discover their authentic purpose.

Sometimes that discovery does indeed *result* in happiness. The poet Mary Oliver famously asked, "Tell me, what is it you plan to do with your one wild and precious life?" And what a relief it can be to finally figure out the answer! And then, over time, to actually do the thing you're meant to do! That's good stuff. That probably feels like happiness. But *Becoming You* is not about that particular emotional deliverable.

It's about teaching you who you are when you're standing still, so that when you get moving, you know which way to go. It's about building the bridge between the life you're living and the life you *want* to be living.

It's about you telling people you actually love, like your kids or your parents or your partner, "Okay, you had your time, and now it's mine, and I know what I'm going to do with it." Or informing your boss that you're moving on to a job for which doing Wordle is not the highlight of the day, although you may put it differently than that.

It's about you waking up, opening your eyes, and thinking, *I. Am. So. Excited. About. Today.*

Can you just taste the possibility of that? The *I am so alive and that is freaking fantastic* of it?

I think we all can.

Because it's a feeling that we, as human beings, have always sought. That yearning is *in* us, somehow, some way. It is. Some scholars believe that the hand stencils that appear in prehistoric cave paintings—we're talking 32,000 BC—suggest even the earliest *Homo sapiens* pondered identity and meaning, along with hunting and gathering. Or consider Homer's *Iliad*, the fifteen-thousand-line epic poem written around 800 BC. Technically, it traces the history of the Trojan War, but if you were forced to read it in high school, as I was, you know it's actually about the warrior Achilles, and his search for purpose amid the chaos of battles, land grabs, plagues, fires, and every variety of treachery under the sun.

Between pride, hubris, and fate, there's probably not a theme on which *The Iliad* does not touch, but in the end, let me just repeat what I told my kids as they marched into their own *Iliad* exams year after year: "Remember, Achilles is trying to figure out what he was born to do. Just like teenagers. Just like all of us. That's why they make you read it."

The search for meaning may be as old as humanity. But today, it also feels newly urgent, doesn't it?

There is an epidemic of purposelessness upon the land, the headlines tell us, particularly afflicting young adults, who are beset with historic levels of anxiety and depression. The renowned social psychologist Jonathan Haidt attributes this alarming phenomenon to childhoods spent immersed in digital worlds that rob us of the ability to connect and cope. He cannot be wrong; we've all seen it with our own eyes. But other factors are surely involved. The general decline of cultural institutions, like houses of worship and bowling leagues and knitting circles, that once gave us instant community and a sense of belonging. The rise of geopolitical chaos. The fact that economic and technological change have accelerated so much that virtually no one works at one company for more than a few years anymore.

If you put all of these ingredients in a pot and stir, you get a sense of what I experience every day as a teacher, mentor, and employer of twenty- and thirtysomethings, and what I hear as an adviser to CEOs at some of the world's largest corporations. You get the synopsis of virtually every piece of research I see as the director of the Initiative on Purpose and Flourishing at the NYU Stern School of Business.

In sum, people are saying: *Things feel broken. Which way is up? Which way is forward? Which way is right? For me, for my community, for any and all of us?*

People are yearning for meaningful lives, at work and outside of it, with an urgency that cannot be denied. We desire flourishing in the here and now. The long-held notion that you work hard and suffer your whole life for a final chapter of freedom and fun where you finally get to be yourself is, to use the technical term, *kaput*.

In my Becoming You class at NYU, I summarize this yearning with a slide showing Proverbs 13:12.

"Hope deferred makes the heart sick," it reads, "but a dream fulfilled is the tree of life."

A dream fulfilled is the tree of life.

As in: Finding and living our purpose *is* life itself in all its glory.

You want that, I want that, we all want that, since time immemorial—and very much right now.

Incidentally, I follow that Proverbs slide in class with a video clip of Disturbed in concert. Yes, *that* Disturbed, the heavy metal band with all the pyrotechnics and quite a bit of screaming in their songs, which have titles like "Ten Thousand Fists" and "Parasite."

In class, however, I skip those cheerful bangers to show a video of the band performing its beautiful, not-screamy-at-all cover version of Simon and Garfunkel's "The Sound of Silence."

"Watch the drummer in this song," I tell my students when the video starts. "Watch his *face*."

And soon enough, they see what I'm talking about.

He looks so rapturous he might levitate.

He is, I hypothesize, the perfect example of a person who has found his purpose.

Or as I put it in the lexicon of Becoming You, he is in his Area of Transcendence (AOT).

He is doing what he wants to do. That is, he's living according to his deepest, most authentic **values**.

He is doing what he's uniquely good at. That is, he's living in alignment with his strongest **aptitudes**.

And finally, he is doing work for which he is rewarded, emotionally or financially or both. That is, he is pursuing an **economically viable interest (EVI)**.

For you visual thinkers, here's what I just said graphically:

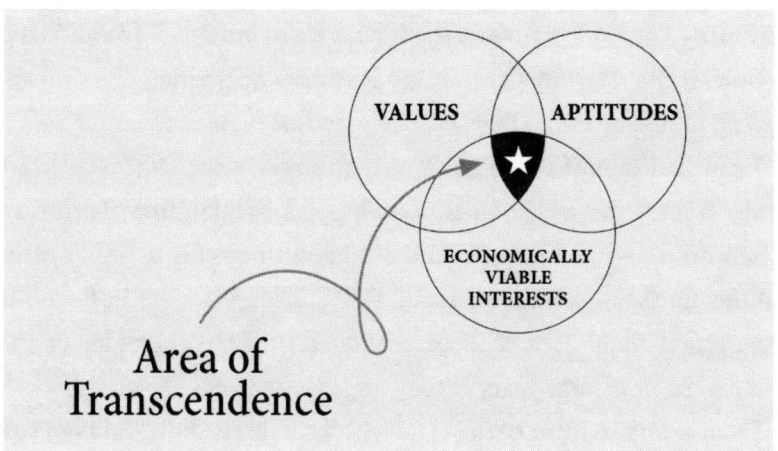

Identifying the center section at the intersection of values, aptitudes, and interests—identifying *your* Area of Transcendence—is the goal of the Becoming You methodology.

Does that sound easy? Of course not! Are you kidding? Indeed, if you are looking for a hack with *Becoming You*, I love you very much, but, as the great send-off goes, "Bye, Felicia." The pages ahead are filled with ideas and exercises that work only if you are digging deep enough and self-examining hard enough that it hurts a little. Or a lot.

But if you can forge through, insight can happen. *Transformation* can happen.

I am thinking of Tachi, a student of mine a few years ago. (Like most of the examples in the pages ahead, Tachi's name and some of his identifying details have been changed for privacy.) Tachi came from a Taiwanese family that directed him into a career in finance before he could even say the words *credit default swap*. Math tutoring starting at age five, a specialized computer-science high school, an undergraduate business degree. It was a straight march from there to seven years as a financial analyst in London before Tachi himself pulled the rip cord to go back and get his MBA, ostensibly to pivot into investment banking.

I say "ostensibly" because why else would Tachi have enrolled in Becoming You, an elective? The last people in the world who need Becoming You are I-bankers, the levitating drummers of Wall Street.

Unless, that is, they have an inner voice whispering, *This cannot be enough*, or maybe even, *They will never find me in Antarctica*.

Tachi had one of those going on, an inner voice. Although, to be totally honest, he was a quiet student who handed in rather cryptic homework assignments, and I did not know about his semester of revelations until the last day of class. That's when students in Becoming You present their Area of Transcendence, and tell the story of their lives for the next forty years as they hope those lives will unfold.

Tachi got up in front of the class with an expression I could not read. Was I seeing a mixture, I wondered, of glee and terror? Indeed, I was.

"So, surprise," he said to begin, "my Area of Transcendence is that I am going to dress Kim Kardashian."

The other students in the class, who knew Tachi by the suits he always wore because he was off to one banking interview or another, broke into laughter and applause. Meanwhile, I was on my perch at the back of the class, imagining Tachi's parents calling the dean of the business school for a refund. *Oh, my God*, I told myself, *I am dead*.

As it turned out, over the course of the Becoming You process, Tachi had realized that wealth was something that mattered a lot to his parents, but not to him. Like, not at all. He didn't care about prestige either. He knew he would likely fail long and hard before he broke through in the fashion business, if he ever did. No, his values were creative self-expression and an expansive life of excitement, even to the point of chaos. The thrill of the runway called him. Beauty and glamour called him. A cocktail dress cut properly on the bias called him.

I mean, hello, *magenta velvet* called him.

There is no magenta velvet in I-banking.

Values are one thing, but what about Tachi's aptitudes, the second part of the AOT methodology?

Tachi shared with the class the results of some of the aptitude testing we do over the course of the semester. He was off the charts on spatial visualization and linear thinking, both essential to fashion design. "And I've always been very good at drawing," he said, recounting that, as a child, he had handed his parents a notebook filled with his fashion sketches, which promptly vanished forever. He kept drawing afterward, hiding the books in his closet, eventually switching over to CAD/CAM software, and then AI tools. He shared a few of his latest designs with the class to another round of applause.

The third sphere of Becoming You is economically viable interests, e.g., the generally stable or growing areas of the economy that call you emotionally or intellectually. We're talking, essentially, about work that you like that can also, hooray, pay you enough.

For Tachi, as noted, "enough" wasn't very much. "I just want to survive," he said. His dream of a life, in other words, did not include a house with a helipad in the Hamptons.

No, his dream of life was Kim K. breaking the internet clad in a design by the House of Tachi. Or as he put it, his AOT was: "To be a part of the creative process of making clothes that make women impossible not to look at."

Just like I-banking, right?

At the end of his presentation, Tachi acknowledged he had some unwinding of his current life to do before he could start the journey and eventually cross the bridge to his new one. There was a finance job he was obligated to muddle through for twelve months, due to a hefty signing bonus he had already spent. There were some fashion design–related classes that he needed to enroll in right away. But as I sat in the back of the room during his presentation, I was the most worried about his family putting a kibosh on this whole thing.

"What do you think your parents will say?" I managed to ask.

Tachi paused for a moment. His classmates gazed at him with a lot of empathy.

After a pause: "I think they'll say, 'At last,'" was his unexpected reply.

Sometimes our authenticity isn't as hidden as we think. We just have to admit it to ourselves.

A dean at NYU once introduced me to a group of alumni, saying, "Suzy has built a factory with Becoming You. Students go in lost and they come out found." He was kind of joking—because schools aren't factories, ha ha ha!—but honestly, I took it as a compliment anyway. And I will add this particularly important observation. Not everyone enters the Becoming You process "lost." Indeed, some people are *this-close* to their Area of Transcendence already. They just need to figure out *why*.

Take Anna.

Anna was a student in one of my executive MBA programs in Washington, DC, where NYU has a satellite campus. She was forty-four and the single mother of an eight-year-old daughter whose father was not in the picture. She owned and ran a collection of med-spas, and was in the process of acquiring more, and was getting her MBA because her company was growing so fast she sensed she needed more CEO skills, such as how to integrate acquisitions and attract private equity. Her résumé was impressive.

Before every semester starts, I ask students to tell me why they've decided to take Becoming You. No answer is ever the same, but usually

I hear some version of "I still haven't found what I'm looking for," to quote the U2 anthem.

Anna's was a bit more fraught than that, to put it mildly.

"I find myself in a constant state of anxiety," she wrote. "If I am good at work, I am a terrible mother, and if I am a good mother, I am terrible at work.

"Because I am in a business that requires regulation, my job involves a lot of politics," Anna's essay went on. "I often feel I am compromising myself too much. Also, I just feel so alone. I wrack my brain for what I can do differently, but nothing comes to me."

"I need this class because I am in a lot of pain," her essay concluded. "Please help me."

Reading this last line, I turned to my assistant and said, "I think we're going to need a bigger boat." With Anna, I felt that I had met my match, or that the Becoming You method had.

Anna showed up to the first class quiet and almost openly despondent. But as the semester went on, and we dug deep into values, aptitudes, and economically viable interests, her mood seemed to lighten. She joined the class conversations more often, and with increasing verve. One day, she stayed after class to show me a photograph of her daughter, who was adorable. We found ourselves laughing so much, I did not want to break the spell by asking her about the pain she had so frankly expressed just a few weeks before.

On the last day of class, Anna was the first to present her final project, by her own request.

Her Area of Transcendence—her answer to "What should I do with my life?"—was, *Exactly what I'm doing now.*

The process had shown Anna not that she needed to upend her life but that she needed to make peace with it.

The truth was, she *was* living by her authentic values: She desired a great deal of wealth, total independence from her parents, and renown. She loved being a CEO. She loved the exotic vacations she got to take with her daughter. She loved meeting new people and running an organization with nearly a thousand employees. She bought herself a BMW every year, and, as she told the class with a laugh, "I guess it turns out a German car is one of my values."

Anna's aptitudes were also aligned with her current work. "I am one hundred percent doing what I am best at," she said during her presentation. The testing was conclusive, she noted, but the success of her company was data enough.

As for economically viable interests: "I love my industry," Anna told the class. "I help women feel good about themselves, and with the aging population, growth will only accelerate in the next ten years."

In other words: check, check, and check.

I will never forget Anna standing in front of her final AOT slide with a joyful smile, while I sat in the back of the classroom, once again thinking, *Wtf?*

Do I just let it go? I wondered, recalling Anna's initial desperation. I felt I couldn't, and shouldn't, because I sensed there might be a teachable moment in the room.

"So Anna," I started in gently, "given where we started this journey together, I'm wondering if—"

"Hold on, Professor Welch!" she interrupted me. "I'm getting to that!"

Well, phew, I thought.

And here's what she said, in so many words.

That pain she had described in her pre-class essay had sprung from how infrequently she saw her daughter, which was sometimes just an hour or two each day. Sometimes she feared her nanny knew her child better than she did.

But when Anna had taken a hard look at and prioritized her values with the Values Bridge, an assessment you, too, will use shortly, she realized that working less and seeing her daughter more was a trade-off she wasn't willing to make.

"I am a good-enough mother, and I will be a better one if I allow myself to live authentically," Anna explained. "I choose to accept my values and let go of my guilt." She went on to describe the "liberation" she had felt after going through Becoming You. Anna didn't need change; she needed self-awareness and self-compassion.

And so Anna's *affirming* experience in class was a complete 180 from Tachi's total reinvention.

But that's the beauty of the Becoming You process.

It's customized to you and for you.

Purpose has to be.

Speaking of purpose, let me return for a moment to something I mentioned in passing earlier, the fact that I am the director of the NYU | Stern Initiative on Purpose and Flourishing. IPF is an academic community, working closely with business practitioners, to advance the discovery and pursuit of authentic purpose.

Leading IPF is a huge honor, but an ironic one, too. Because, as everyone who knows me can attest, it took me long enough to find my own authentic purpose.

Hear now my personal *Iliad*, the abridged edition:

As a little girl, I had no idea what I wanted to be. Watching a lot of TV, as we were wont to do in those days, I became vaguely enamored of the idea of becoming a judge. I think I liked the robe-and-gavel action. Also: ordering everyone around. In this time frame, I also came to realize that I was good at writing, mainly because teachers told me so, and also because it felt easy to do. *So, novelist?* That pursuit, however, struck me as very lonely. Who could go hours on end not talking to people? Definitely not Suzy Spring! Thus, rather randomly, I decided to study art history in college, and that got me thinking, again vaguely, *Hmm, museum curator?*

Luckily, in college I also found *The Crimson*, Harvard's daily newspaper, and, working there twenty or thirty hours a week, I basically just followed along with my classmates as they started applying for reporting jobs. I assure you that I never once pondered, "Should I be a journalist? Does it match my values and aptitudes? Is it an economically viable interest of mine?" No, I just thought, *Wow, it seems I can write and get paid for it. That'll do!*

My first job was with the *Miami Herald*. It was 1981, and the city was beset by riots, drug wars, and boat lifts. It was reporter nirvana, with crazy-big headlines dropping out of the sky on a daily basis. I loved it. *Loooovvvvved* it. The intensity. The *we-are-at-center-of-the-universe!* vibe we all shared, and by "we," I mean the pack of ambitious young reporters I ran with there. We were passionate friends and feral competitors, comrades and warriors. I still get goose bumps thinking about the times we had, exhilarating and terrifying in equal measure. This was Miami, after all.

But.

But journalism can be mean. It can be great—yes yes yes. It can save the world. But it can be *mean*. You have to have a certain skepticism about humanity to do it right. That bugged me from the first day. It wasn't me; I knew that—somewhere deep in my cortex. So deep, in fact, that I just kept plugging away as if the thought didn't exist at all. Eventually, I left Miami and ended up working for the Associated Press in Boston. There, I looked straight ahead and continued to do my job. I liked all the parts except the scolding, righteous indignation of the trade. Well, and the intrusiveness. And, come to think of it, the way we reporters lost sight of the humanity of our subjects while we chased the next big headline. The day I was part of the pack shouting questions at Christa McAuliffe's parents after the Space Shuttle Challenger disaster was the day I checked out of journalism, emotionally at least. Even knowing all the good it can do in the world, I knew, *values*-wise, it was not for me.

So I went to business school. Oh, I know it seems like a wild left turn, and it was, but the facts are, I had been covering business as a reporter for a while at that point, and covering it quite poorly due to utter ignorance. I knew I was out of my depth.

Business school and I got along very well. Who knew? I graduated at the top of my class and marched off to become a management consultant. Once again, it wasn't a particularly well-thought-out decision. I was following the pack, as was becoming my pattern. But how could you complain about a pattern that led you right to gobs of money? And smart people. And shiny offices. And to be honest, at the start, I loved everything about consulting. It was about as far from journalism as you could get. My colleagues actually liked people. They were friendly and kind. They said things like, "Let's have a meeting to discuss alternatives and see if we can come to a shared solution." Very civilized!

But.

But I was not particularly good at management consulting. Oops! I mean, I could get by, and the clients liked me pretty well, but there were better people in the world to be analyzing supply chain economics. It took me seven years to admit that to myself, and even then I didn't really. I just thought, *I can't keep up all this traveling with four little kids.*

Yes, I had four kids by that time, and they were all under the age of six.

And so, quite by happenstance, I became the editor of a business magazine, which was *technically* the perfect "shared solution." I got to be a journalist without being mean, and I got to do work I was particularly good at, writing and editing. And to make matters even better, everyone around me agreed, at least at the beginning, that I was the right person for the job. The world needed me at the helm. No one could do it better!

But then I got fired.

Do not recommend! It wasn't my performance as editor that killed me, by the way, it was that I met a CEO during an assignment, and we fell in love. His name was Jack Welch. Nowadays, I bump into a young person who has not heard of Jack, but in 2001, everyone had. They'd also heard that he was married, with virtually no one also knowing he was separated. Thus, Jack and I created a terrible meshuggaas for the magazine, and a lot of heartache for me professionally, but after the substantial dust settled, we did end up having the happiest marriage in the world. *That* I would recommend.

In the wake of my firing, I forged a new life, not entirely defined by work. My four kids were teenagers by then, and they wanted me around all the time, and one in particular *needed* me around all the time, to pick her up from jail when she and her animal-rights friends got a little carried away at certain protests involving fur. You haven't enjoyed parenthood fully, I like to say, until your child has been fingerprinted!

My husband also wanted me around all the time, mainly because he liked me a lot, but also, later, because his health was beginning to fail. For those myriad reasons, which might be summed up by the word *love*, I bounced between part-time gigs for years. Broadcast journalist on the *Today Show* and CNBC, specializing in careers coverage. Magazine columnist for *Businessweek* and *O, The Oprah Magazine*. Somehow, there were three bestselling books mixed in there, too. And then, through a series of crazy events, I found myself running a music-tech start-up launched by my son and my husband's grandson, plus a small army of Gen Zers.

I loved all these jobs.

I was good at them. They were fun. They had impact. But none of them was exactly right, and I knew it. Because finding that "right" thing was not possible. My life was not my own—our lives are often not our own—and so I was doing the best I could under the circumstances.

In March 2020, late at night, lying by my side at home, my husband passed away. It was peaceful and expected, but utterly devastating, as these things are. What can I say? (Spoiler alert: I will say more later.)

The Work of Our Lives

Two weeks afterward, the pandemic landed in the US. And, oh, the music tech company I was running went into a tailspin. Why? Because our customers were college students, and our business model was based on live events on college campuses. "I've never seen such an existential crisis," as one board member grimly noted.

After Jack's funeral, with my kids and their spouses in tow, I left New York City for the woods of upstate New York. No one knew anything at that time, but I was pretty sure I would never return to civilization. This is called "grief," but at the time, it felt like "logic."

Of course, time passed. In late 2021, the world came back, and my kids returned to it.

I stayed in the woods with my dogs.

I had no idea what to do except walk them. Which I did, a lot. Miles a day, until sometimes they would simply lie down in the middle of the path and look at me like, *Are you effing kidding?* The late Happy Welch, my Great Pyrenees, a dog breed designed by God (and shepherds) to herd sheep on mountaintops for months on end, took to giving me side-eye.

The irony of my aimless wandering, and it's a biggie, is that I knew I could do almost anything. I was fortunate enough to be well educated, well connected, and financially secure, and I had a list of accomplishments it would be hard to sneeze at. My kids were grown and annoyingly self-sufficient. My husband's needs, which had been my organizing principle for years and years, were no more. Heart-achingly gone, but gone.

I was free to answer "What should I do with my life?" any way I wanted.

But *how* would I even know?

I was free to be me.

But *which* me?

A pastor of mine once reminded me that it was okay to not be one big thing in life, but to give yourself the grace to be a "series of commas."

Beautiful and true advice.

Except here's the thing. And once again, it's a biggie. We generally have to go to work every day as *one thing*.

Becoming You is a methodology to help you find that one thing.

Because by probing values, aptitudes, and our economically viable interests, it somehow gets us from "What do I want to do with my life?" to "This is where I'm going with my life."

I say "somehow" because even I don't understand the full alchemy of why the Becoming You methodology works, just that it proves effective more often than I can humbly deny.

I myself am proof.

One day after a long walk in the woods with my devoted dogs, I found myself at my desk staring into my computer, fixated on an email from a friend. I actually unearthed it the other day, just to be sure I was remembering the story right.

He was writing to check in on me, but also, to say this:

"I wanted you to know that I quoted Jack the other day in class to my students. I'm teaching at NYU's business school these days."

I read that last line about sixty times.

Teaching?

At a business school?

Maybe I could do that? Maybe I should do that? Oh my God, I cannot tell you how much I suddenly knew I *wanted* to do that. It was an ineffable feeling, to be honest, but an intense yearning nevertheless.

A few weeks later, I found myself in the office of NYU Stern's then-dean, Raghu Sundaram, explaining the concept of a class I wanted to call "Becoming You."

"I want to teach the class I wish I had taken in business school myself," I told him. "It's a method that helps you make deliberate decisions about your life's work and direction and purpose. It won't save the world, but it could save students a few years on wrong turns and detours."

"But we don't have that class," Raghu said, appearing genuinely disappointed.

"But *I* have it!" I assured him. "It's in my head!"

Long story short, with Raghu's encouragement, I created the class, and in a testament to the goodness of humankind, a bunch of students thought, *I'll take a chance and enroll in this thing!*

To those original fellow travelers in the Becoming You journey, thank you.

It is hard to talk about what happened afterward without sounding like an asshat, so I will be quick. The class was a success. So much so that I was invited to join NYU's faculty full-time. Like, as a professor.

When that happened, tears streamed down my face in a way that reminded me of the weeks after Jack died.

Except these were happy tears.

Happy. There, I said it! Because I was happy. Once I found my authentic purpose. I became me in the process of creating and teaching Becoming You, and the outcome was, well, it was transcendent.

It still is.

Since those early days with the methodology in the classroom, I have taken on teaching other courses in the MBA program, like good old management. But I have also had the joy of bringing Becoming You not just to undergraduates and MBAs but to students of life outside NYU, from teenage coders to retirees in the midst of writing their wills. I have shared the process with moms reentering the workforce and with longtime executives asking, "Is this all there is?"

I have shared it, whenever possible, with anyone who comes around asking, "What should I do with my life?"

I believe that question is the very *work* of our lives. And in a way, it is never done.

That's okay.

Discovering your purpose is a journey. Hard, messy, joyful, exhausting, exhilarating, bumpy, scary, life-giving, and—did I mention—*hard*?

That's okay, too. We will live. It will help us live.

Let's get started.

1

Becoming You: A User's Guide

If you have surmised by now that the Becoming You methodology has three parts, which this book will explicate in turn, then you are correct. Was this seventh-grade suburban soccer, you'd get a trophy! But since it's my book, you'll just get more of me talking, and, more specifically, me talking about how this book is organized and how to approach its ancillary parts. Plus, toward the end of the chapter, I will let you in on the big secret to getting the most out of Becoming You—except it's not really a secret, since I will flat-out tell you.

Here's how Becoming You is organized.

In Part I, we will conduct your values excavation.

In Part II, we will turn to the identification of your aptitudes.

In Part III, we will open the aperture on your economically viable interests.

Along the way, we will meet people of all walks of life, at all stages of their journey, as they put together their values, aptitudes, and interests to create their Areas of Transcendence. I predict that a few of them, or perhaps many of them, will remind you of someone you know pretty well.

And someone who, through this very process, you are getting to know a lot better.

We will spend four chapters talking about values. Maybe that sounds like a lot, but the truth is, most people don't even know what is meant by the term *values*. Chances are, you might not. That's actually entirely typical. Over the course of six months in 2024, I conducted surveys of three tranches of five hundred subjects, professionals aged twenty-five to forty-four. One open-ended question asked respondents to write down their top three values, thus generating forty-five hundred responses. Now, from my work as a journalist covering careers and from my experiences in the classroom, I suspected that there would be quite a bit of vagary in the responses. But, hello, about 80 percent of the answers weren't values at all. They were personality traits, like optimism and curiosity; or virtues, like integrity or generosity; or big umbrellas of needs, like love and respect.

For the record, *values are the desires, motivations, and beliefs that animate our actions and decisions.*

Wanting a very big and interesting life is a value, for instance.

Wanting to be wealthy is a value.

Wanting to be the person who ends world hunger is a value.

A value, to put it in shorthand, is something inside you—a yearning, an intention, a creed—that is strong enough to influence which job you pursue, with whom you decide to spend your life, where you love to live, and even what you love to do on vacation.

Along with delving more into the meaning of values in Part I, we will explore why, even when we *do* know our values, we so often don't live by them. I have dubbed those reasons the Four Horsemen of Values Destruction, to invoke how deadly they can be. *Emotionally* deadly, that is, and unfortunately, I suspect you will recognize them all.

Perhaps most important, though, is that Part I of this book presents a values-identification rubric I created based on empirical and research data and codified as part of my PhD research at the University of Bristol. It posits that there are fifteen core human values, each one existing along a continuum. Every individual, you very much included, has some level of each value—high, low, and in between—and thus, each one of us has a values DNA profile, so to speak. This profile has the power to tell us who we are now, who we want to be, and, drumroll please, the distance between those two points.

Wait, did I lose you at "rubric"? Or was it "continuum" that made your head fall to the side? Look, I promise you are actually going to understand my values-identification tool, which I call the Values Bridge, because it turns out that for many people, when they use it for the first time, they:

1. Actually understand what values *are*; and,
2. Actually find themselves able to fully identify *their own*.

Indeed, by the time you finish Part I of this book, I'm going to further promise that you will have compiled a list of your very own personal values, and it is very likely not the same as the one in your head right now.

You'll also end up with a list at the end of Part II of this book, of your *aptitudes*. As it turns out, people tend to understand the concept of aptitudes better than values, but not by a landslide. In the same research I just mentioned, subjects were also asked to identify their top three aptitudes. Frankly, I could not understand 14 percent of the responses. Another 16 percent were personality traits, which *can* be aptitudes, but usually aren't, and 51 percent of the answers were trained skills, which are not irrelevant but also are not aptitudes. Ultimately, about 19 percent of the answers in my research were technically aptitudes, but most responses were still very generic, such as "creativity," "communication," and "computers."

The Becoming You process abhors such a vacuum. Or more precisely, it vastly prefers when aptitudes are defined in ways that are gritty, specific, and actionable.

Being able to take pieces of seemingly unrelated information and synthesize them into a step-by-step solution is an aptitude, for instance.

Being able to generate a lot of ideas without self-editing and ego-attachment is an aptitude.

Being able to plan out huge, gnarly future projects without losing your place is an aptitude.

There are many more examples, but an aptitude, to put it in shorthand once again, is something inside you, and usually born into you—call it a gift, a propensity, a talent—that comes as naturally to you as writing with your dominant hand.

By the end of Part II of this book, you will know yours better than you do now, or perhaps for the first time.

Part III of this book endeavors to help you uncover what kind of work, job, or industry calls to you emotionally or intellectually, and can pay you enough, albeit in an economic environment that has never been more unsettling. Consider: LinkedIn recently reported that we can expect most jobs going forward to have "50 percent annual skill churn." Translation: In your current job, let's say you need to know how to do ten things to be successful. By this time next year, half of those skills will be unnecessary, and you will need to have mastered five entirely new skills. Wash, rinse, repeat, to the point that, in a few years, everything about the skill and expertise requirements for your job will have changed.

This new reality begs the question, "Why even try to figure out what kind of work calls you intellectually or emotionally? Nothing is staying the same anyway."

It's a legitimate question. When I started as a young reporter, almost everyone read the newspaper every day. Some people read two or three. I thought I could work in print journalism forever if I just accumulated enough mileage, scoops, and awards. And if someone had told me, "Guess what, newspapers are going to die off like dinosaurs before your very eyes, rendering everything you believed about success moot," I would have felt defensive, angry, and flummoxed.

Which kind of sums up how many people feel today about picking a career path.

But the truth is, you cannot be an opportunity agnostic. Even with skill churn, there's still a difference between working in AI, say, and hospitality, between fundraising and game design. There's a difference between pursuing roles in HR, for example, and risk management. Or between operations and sales. Between working in a start-up or a corporate behemoth. Between nonprofit and all-profit-all-the-time. Your interests matter, be they intellectual, emotional, or both.

Thus, in Part III, we will try to sort out those options, and once again, the goal is for you to emerge with an informed list.

There is also a conclusion to this book, but don't expect it to tell you how to construct your Area of Transcendence, because by the time you've arrived at the end of these pages, you will already know. Trust me on this. You will. Your fellow travelers and I will lead the way. (That said, if you think you would benefit from a structured guide for discovering your AOT, please visit the resource hub on my website, www.suzywelch.com, and look for the AOT Catalyst Kit, a workbook I've adapted from my classroom.)

To repeat, however, most people come upon their purpose somewhere in the midst of the Becoming You process. Indeed, it reminds me of the morning I gave birth to my son Marcus. Much to everyone's surprise, we discovered in the delivery room that he was a transverse breech presentation, meaning he was upside down and backward, standing up and facing outward in my womb like a little soldier ready to march off into war. No one wants to hear about my two days of labor, but at hour twenty-three, I said to my doctor, "I cannot do this," to which she snorted, "They all say that. Suzy, there will be a baby in this room."

There was a baby in the room—and with God as my witness, he came out *smiling*.

I promise never to snort at anyone, but to borrow that phrase: There will be an AOT in this room. And I hope it makes *you* smile.

My personal clients and students at NYU partake in a slew of exercises and a few tests to amplify and deepen the Becoming You experience. This book makes it possible for you to do the same.

Do you have to?

The simple answer is no.

This book is written *hoping* you will engage with the exercises and tests, but assuming you may not.

I cannot be disingenuous here, however. I think you will get more out of the Becoming You process if you do at least some of its testing and a few of its exercises. More would be even better, and all would be ideal.

But it's your choice. Honestly, I am just glad you're here, and you can decide how much time and energy you want to put into the Becoming You process without my haranguing you.

I feel compelled to note here, though, that many of the exercises and tests for Becoming You are fun. Like, truly *enjoyable*. I cannot count the number of students who have shared the Proustish Questionnaire with their families, for instance. I've played it with my own family.

More logistics: The exercises for your values excavation appear at the end of this book, in the appendixes. The exercises for the aptitudes are mainly embedded in the chapters themselves. Part III has two resources, also in the appendixes. And if all this is not enough, I also have a weekly podcast and myriad videos on YouTube where I explain and illustrate Becoming You's array of tests and exercises.

Finally, I want to say that I've observed that some people feel inclined to skip the aptitude testing. "I already know what I'm good at" is usually the argument. And I get it. Your life may have already made your "killer apps" abundantly clear. I've known people who are so good at numbers and who love playing with them so much that watching them work is like watching Kristi Yamaguchi perform a triple axel. That said, I have also seen many—I repeat, *many*—Becoming You users have their minds blown by their aptitude assessments. I remember one student coming up to me after receiving her results, saying, "I think I just discovered why I can't do my job. I'm not crazy! This is a great day!" But perhaps my favorite example is Sid, who took Becoming You with a very prestigious consulting firm offer already in hand. Every consulting job is not the same, of course, but most involve a lot of number-crunching, data analysis, strategic planning, and conceptual thinking.

Testing showed that Sid's strongest aptitude, however, was in spatial visualization, a propensity that tends to make people very good with mentally understanding and spatially manipulating *real things*, like structures and products. He also scored highly on the aptitude known as Present Focuser, which is the propensity to live in the here-and-now, often accompanied by an aversion for long-range thinking. For Sid, these results were the final uh-ohs in a growing list. He ended up canceling his consulting offer and starting a restaurant with his brother. He is thrilled to be pursuing a life aligned with what feels natural for him to do.

My guess is that, eventually, Sid would have figured out that consulting wasn't a match for his aptitudes. Testing saved him a lot of time, and probably some agony.

Just saying.

One last piece of navigation.

Each section of this book begins and ends with a story about a real individual facing a real career dilemma. Part I's story is about Tony, whose values call out for clarification, Part II's story concerns Chloe, whose aptitudes are the big unknown in her life, and Part III features Olivia, who is trying to determine her economically viable interests.

Each story exists to specifically amplify its section's respective subject—for example, Tony illustrates the importance and power of knowing your values, and the same is true for Chloe with aptitudes and Olivia with economically viable interests.

In real life, however, Becoming You is rarely about plugging in one missing variable. First of all, we're just too complex for that, and so are Tony, Chloe, and Olivia, each of whom has a smattering of concerns outside their designated "area."

But second, and as important, the Becoming You methodology is not like solving an equation. It's more like producing a Broadway show that just happens to be the story of your life. There are a lot of moving pieces, many of them related. Figuring out your values, for instance, may impact your areas of interest. Understanding your aptitudes might rearrange your values. The three spheres are connected for a reason: they overlap and interact. Indeed, you will see with each section's story that every Area of Transcendence journey is dynamic—it's a living, breathing thing. You, as the director, are getting the right actors on the stage, with the right script, good lighting, great sets, and even the best musicians down in the pit, so that when you shout "Action," as Tony, Chloe, and Olivia eventually do, you can do so with confidence.

We've come to the bit where I tell you the nonsecret secret.

Look, Becoming You is a deeply personal process. It's for you and about you. I love what one student posted on LinkedIn after he graduated. "I was an art major in college and never painted a self-portrait like the one we did in Becoming You." I still want to cry every time I read that.

But that's not my point. My point is less mushy.

For Becoming You to work, it cannot be performative. By which I mean, *you* cannot be performative. You cannot go through the motions, be superficial in your engagement, and still get what you came looking for.

The process requires radical honesty with yourself.

Sometimes that means accepting test results you don't particularly like.

Other times it's about admitting dreams, hopes, expectations, and fears you've worked hard to deny or suppress, for whatever reason.

About, for instance, how much money is enough for you.

Or the kind of partner you really want and need.

Or the amount, say, that outward success matters to you, or not.

Remember Tachi, the banker-turned-designer I mentioned in the Introduction? The one who decided to ditch his banking career to try to design dresses for Kim Kardashian? He'd spent his entire life telling himself he shared his parents' values of financial security and prestige. To say otherwise would have been to renounce people whom he loved deeply and the culture in which he had been raised. But the Becoming You process impelled Tachi to ask, "What do I *really* yearn for? What *really* motivates me?" He could have demurred or balked in his answers, kept with the company line, and carried on. But test by test, exercise by exercise, he began to unsilence his inner voice, until it was ringing in his ears, calling him to an Area of Transcendence he'd never been able to imagine before.

That is the kind of candor I am asking you to access and release.

Anna had a similar experience.

She was the working mother I also mentioned in the Introduction, who started the Becoming You process saying she was in deep emotional distress and didn't know what to do. But during the Values Bridge process, Anna dropped her defenses and admitted that her desire for wealth, status, and self-determination superseded her value of being the "perfect," ever-present mom. Now, if you're getting ready to judge Anna, please cease and desist. To be a working mother is to do daily combat with conflicting cultural messages and the narrative of your own upbringing. It is a never-ending war of values raging in your head. Many of us spend decades with a queasy uh-oh in our guts because we just so happen to passionately love *both* our children and our work, and there are even times we love our work enough to deprioritize our children, and we struggle to admit that to anyone, including ourselves.

Anna finally went there; the tests and exercises helped. That's what they're supposed to do. But let me put it this way. The tests and exercises help those who help themselves.

With their own relentless candor.

Not to bring you down here! True, for some, Becoming You can be an ouch-ridden catharsis. But for many, it's a relatively pleasant ride, a fascinating exploration of your inner workings, with a really cool ending, your Area of Transcendence! But either way—and for anyone in between—Becoming You is most effective when you unleash your most truthful, reflective, nondefensive, open-minded self during the process.

I will be our final exhibit here.

One of my favorite parts of the Becoming You process is the Enneagram, a personality test with ancient roots. To help my students understand their results better, I invite Rasanath Das in as a guest lecturer. Ras became an engineer in his native India, then went to Cornell Business School. Afterward, he became an investment banker on Wall Street, and then, a few years later, found himself called to become a Buddhist monk. There was actually a year during all this when Ras was simultaneously an investment banker *and* a monk. Hollywood, where are you? Eventually, after nearly seven years, Ras left the monastery to start an organizational coaching company called Upbuild, and today, twenty years hence, Ras is one of the world's leading experts on the Enneagram, a visiting fellow at the Initiative on Purpose and Flourishing, and NYU is beyond fortunate that he regularly shares his formidable knowledge with our community.

I did not, however, exactly feel "beyond fortunate" during the class when Ras was describing the unproductive behaviors sometimes demonstrated by my Enneagram type, the Achiever.

Ras is truly one of the nicest people ever put on Earth. I've seen him deliver life-changing truth bombs with such a beatific smile on his face, you would think he was reading a bedtime story to one of his darling daughters. Such was the case when he started reciting in class the script of a show that could have been titled *All the Things Suzy Does When She's Simply Awful*. Not that being an Enneagram Achiever is bad! All the Enneagram personality types contain both "creative" behaviors, which are wonderful and healthy, and "destructive" ones, which tend to come out when we feel stressed or threatened or denied in one way or another.

So there we were, all of us focused on Ras lecturing away at the front of the room about the Achiever's destructive hallmarks, when I felt myself growing vaguely ill.

"And what does the Achiever do when they feel they are not being validated?" Ras asked, smiling warmly. "They exaggerate, right? Sound familiar? They shout louder with their stories. They jump up and down. They need to have the most claps, no matter what the cost . . ."

As Ras continued on, I actually felt my face turn red and toasty. *For God's sake, I'm sixty-four, and fully self-actualized!* I wanted to shout. *I don't do any of those things anymore!*

But.

But then I thought, *Ah, but you do, Suzy. Not often. Not as often as you used to. But you still do.*

Did I hate realizing that about myself?

So freaking much.

Did I benefit from realizing that about myself?

Even more.

Because at that very moment, I was actually being courted to leave the classroom at NYU for a job about which I need to be very vague, sorry. Suffice it to say it was a very high-profile position, one with national prominence. I would suddenly have had a lot of people reporting to me, and a big corner office in the sky.

I knew in my bones I did not want this job, not at all, as it played to exactly zero percent of my aptitudes. Worse, it would draw me away from work that I was good at and that filled my soul with joy.

And yet—I kept taking meetings about it. Because I knew it would make me the girl with the most claps.

Listening to Ras, I had a eureka moment that saved my life. I could not take that job. Because if I was being honest, I wanted that job only to fulfill a need I should not heed.

That is the level of honesty Becoming You asks of us.

It can be fearsome, humbling, and occasionally embarrassing to admit who we are. But we truly do need to know so that we can set out on the journey toward who it is we must become.

I know that is what you want, because all of us do. But the journey there is not always smooth, for it must be paved with revelations of the heart and soul.

2

This I Believe

Not long ago, the alumni office at Stern asked me to be the keynote speaker at an event in New York for recent graduates. The topic was (surprise) the Becoming You methodology, and I was happy to say yes, because in my experience, those first few years after you get your degree can be tough, as reality finally makes itself known to you in all its decidedly uncozy, nonacademic glory.

I was not wrong. The crowd was welcoming and high-spirited, but many people were definitely grappling with the kinds of challenges I had anticipated. In response, I offered lots of specific blocking-and-tackling advice. But sensing that there was an undercurrent of angst in the room, I also made sure to convey something I know to be true, having been to the wars myself.

"Everything is going to be okay," I told the group, "and even if it's not okay, it's *going* to be okay. Just keep going."

After the session, about fifty people stayed to chat with me. I was sorry for their wait, but everyone seemed very cheerful. Except for the last couple in line. They were rather solemn.

By the time their turn came, we were pretty much alone in the room. They introduced themselves: the husband, a banker, and his wife, a consultant. Then they got right to the point.

"We're wondering," the wife asked, "if you think people are fundamentally good or bad?"

I was taken aback. "People-*people*?" I asked, "Or just people in business?"

"All people," the husband answered.

"Because you seem very optimistic," the wife added. "The 'Everything is going to be okay' stuff. You seem terribly upbeat about humanity."

It had been a long night, I was tired, and they were asking a very big question. For a moment, I almost didn't know how to answer.

"I know I can come across as Pollyanna-ish. I've heard that said," I finally replied. "Maybe because I believe in love; I believe in God. I believe the center will somehow hold.

"But you have to remember," I said, "that I was a crime reporter in Miami."

I think I must have squeezed my eyes at that moment, because I was having my least favorite memory again, and Jack used to say that's what I did when it visited. You do not want to know it, or maybe I just don't want to write about it. Let's just say that one morning at three a.m., standing on the front lawn of an apartment building with thirty Miami cops and about as many EMTs swarming around, this girl reporter, age twenty-one, saw confirmation of Joseph Conrad's famous words that man is capable of every form of wickedness.

When I opened my eyes, the solemn couple was looking at me with concern.

I smiled, trying to shake it off. "Look, I've seen people be very bad and very good," I said, "and everything in between. I believe goodness almost always prevails."

The couple suddenly broke into smiles, too, nodding.

"Got it," the wife said. "You fundamentally believe people can make good things happen. We do, too, but sometimes we feel like outliers."

"Well, I believe people can and should take ownership over their lives," I corrected her slightly. "I mean, life is hard, but then you try. And try again, and keep on trying forever. The other option is nihilism, which I don't like very much."

More nodding ensued, and after some small talk, we said our good-byes, the solemn couple and I. Perhaps they thought that was the end of it, but for me, the chatter in my brain was just beginning.

Because they had an excellent point. I do have strong beliefs about how the world works. All of those beliefs undergird the Becoming You methodology. And I *should* share them outright. You should know where I'm coming from, to make sure you want to come along.

This will be quick. First, because this book is not about me. And second, because I promise I won't waste your time with platitudes. I hate platitudes.

How much, you ask?

Okay, I know you aren't asking that, but I have waited twenty-one years to tell this story.

On a sunny day in August 2004, my husband Jack and I finished *Winning*. It is hard enough to write a book alone, but writing a book with your spouse is, well, harder. One of the hardest parts for me, for instance, was having to invent a narrative voice that was a plausible amalgamation of me, Suzy, a hippie nerd from an artsy-fartsy family, and of Jack, a sports-and-business-obsessed, street-raised Irish Catholic kid from Boston. Then I had to write sixty thousand words as that narrator.

To quote the famous meme: "Don't ask me how I did it, I just did it, it was hard."

Which is why, on that glorious summer day when we finished the book, I felt like I had just won an Olympic medal.

"Let's celebrate!" I proclaimed.

But.

Jack had this particular stare when he was thinking. I'm not going to say it was a scary stare, but it was a scary stare.

"Suzy, I have an idea," he said slowly.

It was to take every single sentence of the book we had just finished and put it on a separate index card. Then, we would go through each sentence, one by one, and ask, "Is this banal? Do people already know it? Are we stating the obvious?"

As Jack's idea, in all its logistical horror, settled in, I felt my heart imploding. And not from anger, or frustration, or exhaustion, or any other normal reaction to this outrageous proposal, but from admiration.

"*That* is a genius idea, honey," I said.

We were a fun couple, weren't we?

For the next two weeks, chapter by chapter, I wrote every single sentence out by hand, and Jack and I read each one out loud. Ultimately, we scrutinized more than three thousand index cards. I think we removed fewer than ten of them for not passing muster. But neither of us flagged along the way. And as time went on, with every passing card, I grew to admire this terrible, awful, painstaking, ridiculous, brilliant process more.

No lie.

And *that* is how much I hate platitudes.

Thus, six (hopefully) platitude-free synopses on the beliefs underlying Becoming You.

PEOPLE ARE INCREDIBLY COMPLICATED AND INCREDIBLY SIMPLE AT THE SAME TIME.

You cannot create and teach a methodology designed to discover human purpose without having an underlying opinion about human nature. And my opinion is: *It is impossible to generalize about human nature.* On any given day—in any given hour—somewhere in this world, there is someone who is risking their life to save a complete stranger. Jumping into a rip current. Pulling someone back from an oncoming car. Donating blood or a kidney. A teacher staying late for the new kid who seems lonely. A waitress driving home at one a.m. who pulls a U-turn because she can't bring herself to pass a woman with a flat tire. And in the very same moment that all these people are being good, somewhere in this world there are other people committing senseless, terrible, and tragic acts of villainy.

All the good and valiant people I just mentioned have been bad in their lives at one time or another, and all the bad and villainous people have been good.

Because people are people, and as such, they are big, labyrinthine, tangled jumbles of the love and the hate that has been poured into them by others; of joy and trauma, fear and safety, hope and despair. They are good, then bad, then very good, then awful. They try, then they don't. They are very good, but it is very hard. They are bad, but desperately want to change. They are all these things during just a single Thanksgiving dinner with the family.

Find me one person who is not such a messy mess ball.

At the same time, people are people, and as such, they can be incredibly simple.

Everyone wants to be seen and heard.

Everyone wants to be loved.

Everyone wants to be free.

Everyone wants to be safe.

Find me one person who does not.

I rest my case. That is, I stand firm in believing that you cannot get all lofty about human nature. No one understands it *fully*, and no one ever has. Honestly, people who claim to kind of scare me. They've either got a God complex or they're selling you something.

When I created Becoming You, my underlying tenet was, *Some people interested in this methodology are going to be confident and ambitious, and others are going to be lost and besieged. Some will be eighteen and some will be sixty-eight. Some will be rich and others in debt. Some will have had years of therapy and others not a day. I need to make the process as inclusive as possible.*

Human nature is too expansive for any other approach.

That said, I do have one assumption about you, if you are a person drawn toward the Becoming You journey.

You want a life of meaning. No hard data on this, just my overwhelming experience. Becoming You-ers tend to have hopeful and generous hearts. They are seekers who yearn to make their lives more fulsome and to shape the world into a better place.

It's very beautiful.

In many ways, teaching Becoming You to thousands of people has made me more optimistic about human nature than ever before in my life.

But then again, I don't like to generalize.

LIFE IS INCREDIBLY SHORT AND INCREDIBLY LONG AT THE SAME TIME.

Some people undertake Becoming You because their lives are quietly killing them, and others undertake it because they are pondering.

As in *existentially*.

As in, "How should I endeavor to have my life unfold with purpose and intention over the next several decades?"

Isn't that an interesting coincidence? Because those two ends of the spectrum are simultaneously exactly how we need to think about life all the time. As if it's a house on fire, and as if it's a leisurely stroll through a verdant glen.

At least, that's what I believe.

Now, as you may have surmised already, I've always been a house-on-fire kind of girl. You know that song from *Hamilton*, when Aaron Burr asks, "Why do you write like you're running out of time?" When I first heard that line, I remember thinking, "I was *born* running out of time."

This personality trait has led people to refer to me my whole life as "urgent," and "intense," and occasionally "frantic."

Which makes me refer to them as laggards and slackers. Haha! Jk, jk!

Look, the serious truth is, I've had many experiences along the way that have proven to me that life can indeed give you the richness of time. My very closest friend dumped me when we were in our early twenties. I did not know it then, but her fiancé felt threatened by our closeness and he asked her to choose between us. The loss was as devastating as a divorce to me, with the added pain of having absolutely no idea why it was happening.

After sixteen years, this woman had grown up a lot and so had her husband. Together, they agreed that what happened shouldn't have happened, and she tracked me down. Her email asked if I would be willing to hear her explanation. I wavered, but I had grown up a lot, too—and I was urged on by Jack, who had the benefit of not being Sicilian by heritage.

Today, Sue and I have been best friends *again* for twenty-five glorious, laughter-filled years. Twenty-five! I love her like a sister, and I adore her husband, too. Jack also came to love them both very much.

Who knew? Who knew such a thing could happen?

Life is long.

A year ago, Sue won a Woman of the Year–type award in Philadelphia, where she is revered for her many contributions as a business leader. In her acceptance speech, she pointed me out at the head table and thanked me for all my love and support. Later, I joined her rousing standing ovation, along with the seven hundred other people in the audience.

Two days later, she texted me at six a.m. to tell me about a bizarre numbness in her tongue. Best friends do that kind of thing.

Twenty-four hours later, she was in a coma with viral encephalitis.

As I sat by her bed at the hospital, I wept over the beeping and whirring of the machines, "You just cut this out, Sue. We have only just gotten going."

She did cut it out and went on to have an amazing recovery. She is just like new, and in many ways, better—wiser, softer, deeper. But for a few weeks there, it was very, *very* close.

Sue had always been a card-carrying member of the house-on-fire club herself, but today, we are both piquantly aware that life can be far too short and, too often, is just that.

You have to live it both ways.

Becoming You is built on that paradox. It is designed to give you the self-knowledge, in particular about your values and aptitudes, that you need to plan wisely for your one wild and precious life, and to react as wisely as humanly as possible when no planning can be done.

Becoming You can be a solution, but more than anything, it is a tool you can use again and again.

Because life unfurls—and it erupts. You have to be ready either way.

IN THE END, SUCCESS COMES DOWN TO THREE THINGS.

If you think the first one is luck, sorry! That would be a platitude.

I mean, of course luck matters when it comes to success. It matters in the big-big things, like where and when you're born, your health, your class, your race. But it also helps with the small stuff, like when the person sitting next to you in Row 45 on the Tampa-Chicago flight loves your product and places the order that saves you from bankruptcy.

But aside from luck, which is random by definition, long-term success is a function of . . . PIE.

The quality of your Personal Relationships.

The quality of your Ideas.

The quality of your Execution.

Personal Relationships first. Good news, I am not going to tell you to network. I hate networking. It's mercenary and phony, and it doesn't work. Instead, you should just make friends with all sorts of people, and lots of them, at work and out, with no expectation of anything in return. Such friends may be able to help you someday, or maybe not, but if and when they do, their help will have more impact than any networking contact you made while standing in a vast hotel conference hall, exchanging contact info. So don't bother. Invest that time and energy in genuinely getting to know people and being a good friend yourself.

I gave this anti-networking advice in my commencement speech at NYU one year, and then, right onstage, I asked the dean if I was about to be fired. It got a big laugh, but I knew I was dancing with danger up there . . . because business schools and colleges (and career coaches and parents) incessantly exhort networking, and most people buy into the idea. I had one MBA student proudly tell me that he had made six hundred networking calls in a semester. That's about five a day. He was surprised no one responded. I wasn't.

That's just not how business works.

In 1995, I became fast friends with a brilliant young editor at the Harvard Business School Publishing Company, where we both worked. Over the years, we changed jobs and moved to different cities but stayed close. We just liked each other a ton. We both became runners. She inspired me as I became a vegan. And when I lost Jack, she drove to my house in the countryside at the height of the pandemic, when everyone was in deep plague-like sheltering mode, and insisted on taking me for a walk. She had been widowed, too, five years earlier, and she told me some things I needed to hear.

My friend, my dear friend, Hollis.

She is the publisher of this book.

Would she have acquired my manuscript if she hadn't liked it? No, of course not, and our friendship would have been just fine. Unchanged.

But you've also never seen an easier, faster book deal brokered. The lawyers had nothing to do. Poor them!

Because friends, real ones, are what make business go. And the better the friends you have, the better it will go for you.

More good news on Ideas.

You don't need a lot of ideas to succeed. But I've never met a successful person who didn't have a few really good ones over the long arc of their career—and it is almost always long, by the way. People who succeed wildly in their twenties and thirties are rare, and trust me, all of them will have their share of valleys in time. With careers, as with life, the only game is the long game. But again, a platitude. So onward.

What is a "good" idea? Well, for one thing, it's original. I'm thinking of Jeff Bezos who, as the story is told, was driving his car cross-country in 1994 when it dawned on him that he didn't need to sell just books online. He could sell *anything*. That was one heck of an original idea, wouldn't you agree?

Luckily for the rest of us, an original idea doesn't have to blow up the economy. It can be as small as replacing a bureaucratic process with a nongummy, clean, simple one. Or a marketing activation that bumps sales 3 percent, or a design tweak that makes an industrial product 5 percent more efficient. I know a car salesman who, in his first year on the job, doubled his location's sales by bringing a new *question* to his teammates. When a customer throws a crazy lowball price at you, he said, instead of negotiating off the bat, ask, "Can you help me understand how you came up with that number?"

Killer idea!

He runs the place now.

Good ideas have that effect.

Finally, we come to Execution, the most underrated success-driver of the PIE triad—which is ridiculous, because any manager in the world will tell you they would kill for a team member who actually gets stuff done. They are that valuable.

This I Believe

In my class at NYU, every MBA student must go through an elaborate, in-depth, five-week 360 Feedback process. Some of you have had this experience in the corporate realm, but for those who have not, 360 is an evaluation tool that gathers input from up to twenty of your former and current coworkers, bosses, and employees, and aggregates it into an anonymized report that basically tells you how the world experiences you. (Becoming You's shorter, simpler, DIY version of 360 Feedback, developed by yours truly, is called PIE360 and can be found on my website's resource hub.)

For some students, 360 is a marvelous experience, in which they discover that they are so much better than they ever knew: more innovative, more collaborative, more conscientious. Some find out that they're experienced as lovely and calm and filled with positive energy, despite their anxiety and stress. "Wow," such students often feel, "people kind of love me!"

Sadly, a small minority of students get the opposite kind of feedback. Remember Tachi, the banker-turned-fashion-designer from earlier? He had thought he was showing up at work as a reliable soldier. His 360 Feedback revealed his coworkers at the bank found him sarcastic, hostile, and disengaged.

"I guess they knew the real me," he said, somewhat stunned.

And then there was Sarah, a student who reviewed her 360 results in class, and immediately booked double office hours.

When we met up, she was in tears. "Professor Welch, I need you to teach me how to be a leader," she said, "because my 360 Feedback results are horrifying."

Dear Reader, it was yet another Becoming You *wtf* moment for this professor, for I had also reviewed Sarah's results and my reaction had been, "Nice!"

The issue was that Sarah's 360 results had shown her to be kind of low on leadership traits. But, egad, she was an *operator*! Every single piece of feedback suggested that Sarah was SEAL Team Six when it came to getting projects over the finish line. Her execution was perfect, precise, and invisible. As a leader myself, just imagining this behavior made me feel faint with ardor.

Regardless, I promised Sarah I would try to help her be more of a leader, but I just needed to make sure. Did she actually want to be one?

There was a long pause, then: "Honestly? No!"

Words came tumbling out. Strategy bored her, she told me. Vision statements made her gag. And culture? Snore! Just tell me what needs to be done and get out of my way.

"Why don't you just aim to have a career as a COO?" I asked Sarah. "Every CEO in the world will be in a cage match over you."

"But we're *supposed* to become leaders," she protested. "That's why we go to business school."

Ah, but no, I reminded her. You are in business school—you are in life—to become *you*.

You were hoping I would eventually get to the point, right?

And here it is. The PIE theory, in many ways, drives much of the information Becoming You digs and digs to unearth: how you relate to people, how your brain works, and how you show up in the world.

In that way, Becoming You as a methodology is literally set up to set *you* up to succeed, based on how I believe success actually happens.

Which now you know.

YOU CANNOT HAVE IT ALL, ALL AT THE SAME TIME.

This particular belief is not particularly unconventional, so let me be especially fast.

A major component of Becoming You is ascertaining your values. But there is one little problem with values that most people inevitably bump into during this process.

This I Believe

Values often require trade-offs. At least, I believe they do.
Getting very rich and being a very present and available parent.
Achieving fame and maintaining privacy.
Having boatloads of fun and becoming a Fortune 100 CEO.
These value pairings are inherently in conflict with each other.

It would be a better world, I suppose, if they weren't. If you could simultaneously make a zillion dollars *and* spend unlimited, unfettered time with your kids. If you could be on the covers of magazines and also not have people care when your marriage hits a snag. If you could plan your life around windsurfing, international travel, and raves, and also stick the landing of every earnings call.

But that world does not exist.

I mention this only because I cannot count the times I have heard Gen Z Becoming You-ers tell me that it does and I just don't know it, or, alternatively, that this world will come to be during their lifetimes.

I won't be holding my breath.

Does that sound awful? Geezer-ish? I hope not. I hope it just sounds like the deep sigh of a woman who tried for, oh, about fifteen years to have it all, all at the same time, and discovered it was impossible. Not for lack of good friendships or original ideas or the ability to execute. Not for lack of talent at work, nor lack of being efficient. Not for lack of trying. Oh dear God, I tried.

I could not have it all, all at the same time, because no one can. Not Oprah. Not Candace Bushnell, not Jeff Bezos, not Bill Gates. Not even Taylor Swift, whose album *The Tortured Poets Department* should have been titled *The Tortured Superstars Department* to reflect all the stuff she hates about being spectacularly famous and rich.

Yes, even Taylor makes values trade-offs.

And so, ta-da, Becoming You is designed to help you do the same, because I believe it wouldn't be worth a red cent in the real world any other way.

BECOMING YOU

AN OKAY LIFE IS NOT OKAY.

The Becoming You methodology assumes that Mary Oliver was 100 percent right: we have one life, and it is wild and precious. Further, it assumes that is not to be frittered away, not by fear, or inertia, or doubt. As humans are wont to do.

I call this propensity the Velvet Coffin Syndrome.

The Velvet Coffin creeps into our life insidiously, as our lesser angels always do. You start off by having a dream of a life—big or small, it's your dream. It's everything you want and need, quenching the thirst in your mind, soul, and spirit. Then events come along. We don't get into a certain college. We don't get the job we want, or we don't make it at the one we do. Our partner can't move where we want to live because of their job. One of our kids goes off the rails, so we need to change our work focus. Or our work focus draws our eyes away from our real interests in life. Or we have certain debts and obligations so certain changes just cannot be made.

All of these compromises and accommodations get under our skin. We feel them; they irk us.

But.

But our life is still good enough. It's familiar. Comfortable.

And so we lie down inside our good-enough life's acceptable confines, and slowly its lid starts to close on us.

It's an unpleasant image, I get it. But that doesn't mean it's wrong.

Whenever I speak or write about the Velvet Coffin Syndrome, the reaction tells me that I've hit a nerve. I once posted about it on Instagram and was flooded with comments along the lines of "This is me" and "I needed to hear this."

But I also got this one: "I had this! Had the comfy, enviable corporate job people would kill for in a big city. I called it 'My B+ Life.' Burned it all to the ground. It's super scary, but you have to do it."

You do. At least, that's what I believe, and the Becoming You methodology assumes you do, too.

This I Believe

FINALLY, I BELIEVE ALMOST EVERYTHING GOOD IS HARD.

One time I was walking my dogs in the woods with one of my daughters and we got to talking about the meaning of life.

Every parent has a child like this, right?

Our conversation eventually ended with Eve (lovingly) accusing me of working nonstop and never having fun. I retorted, as usual, that I find my work incredibly fulfilling, and really, what good is fun anyway?

"I guess I just don't believe that people were put on earth to suffer," Eve sighed, "and you obviously do."

"Suffering is the origin of consciousness!" I cheerfully reminded her, quoting Dostoyevsky in *Notes from the Underground.*

"I wish you'd never read that book," she sighed again.

And on we walked. She knew me and I knew me, and I was not headed to a yoga retreat in Tulum anytime soon.

Look, it's not that I *like* suffering. But experience has shown me one million little and big ways that almost everything good comes with some form and amount of struggle—emotional, intellectual, physical, spiritual, you name it.

A marriage you can trust.

Kids who aren't entirely effed up.

A community to call your own.

A friendship that survives heartbreak.

A vague idea that becomes a brilliant reality.

A career that gives you meaning and purpose.

None of that stuff just happens, poof, la-di-dah. No, you go to the mat for it, and sometimes you go to the wars.

Personally, I think that's an acceptable deal. I think it's life.

Which is why Becoming You is not always as easy as a quick game of Solitaire. It's more like an NHL semifinal. Moments of gliding, and moments of face-mask pulling. Oops, blood on the ice! It can happen. Truth and change are messy, messy pursuits.

In the end, though, everyone gets a prize. Their Area of Transcendence discovery, which can sometimes be just what they were waiting for, and what they needed.

It's hard to mention him in the same chapter as Dostoyevsky, but Ringo Starr kind of nailed it when he said, "You know it don't come easy."

It certainly don't, when "it" is anything worthwhile.

And that is what I believe.

Part I

Values

3

Which Tony Is This?

As promised, our values section begins with the story of Tony, or, as his family called him, Little Tony.

Little Tony, it turned out, had a big values problem, although he did not know it the day we met. In fact, back then, Tony really didn't even know what values were, let alone his own.

That very typical phenomenon is precisely why the chapters ahead will do the following:

- Explain the meaning of values, why they matter, and how they impact our actions and decisions in life, work, love, and, well, everything else.
- Identify the four pervasive cultural and psychological dynamics that too often stand in the way of our living our authentic values. Warning: some or all of these may feel painfully familiar.
- Guide you through an interlocking collection of exercises that will help you clearly identify your own values: Six Squared, Whose Life, the Proustish Questionnaire, Alpha Omega, and last but definitely not least, the Values Bridge, my favorite psychometric tool in all the world, and hopefully, soon to be yours.

Let's let Tony be our scout.

Although it probably doesn't matter, I feel compelled to mention there was actually nothing little about Little Tony. Not his actual size—he was six feet five inches—nor his personality. Self-confident, funny, and ebullient, Tony made himself known on the first day of class during introductions. Unlike his classmates, he stood to deliver his. "I'm Tony Caltanisetta, from Jersey," he said with a big grin. "Love the Mets; the Jets; and my wife, Gennie; with a baby boy coming in March." There was applause for this last piece of information. Then he added, "I took this class because it fit my schedule. I already know what I'm doing when I graduate. McKinsey."

I tried to maintain my composure. I already sensed—fifteen seconds in—that Tony did not belong in consulting.

Three hours later, as our first session came to a close, I knew I was right. Because Tony, perhaps not surprisingly, was an active participant in discussions, and all of us had learned a lot about him very quickly.

For instance, that he wanted to be fabulously rich. Like, Elon Musk rich.

Also, that his family came first. He adored his mother—props, Tony!—and revered his wife, whom he spoke of with admiration and tenderness. And, in that first class, he also repeatedly mentioned his brothers, both firefighters in their New Jersey hometown, and happily related that he and Gennie literally lived next door to his sister, about two blocks from their parents. His sister, by the way, was also pregnant. "We're going to raise the cousins like siblings," he said at one point. "That's the way it was for me, and that's the way it should be."

In Becoming You's values language (about which you'll learn shortly), Tony would be said to score very high on two values. The first is what we call Affluence, which measures wealth as a life-organizing principle. The other was Familycentrism, which, as you can likely assume, is the degree to which family is one's life-organizing principle. Neither of those values is in *irreconcilable* conflict with consulting, but they aren't a particularly good fit either.

Which Tony Is This?

But I sensed Tony had other values, too, we just needed to start digging. And we did.

As the semester rolled on, through our exercises and testing, I came to find out that the dark cloud in (Little) Tony's very sunny life was, well, Big Tony, his father. "I look like him, I sound like him," Tony told me early on. "I grew up answering the phone with people saying, 'Which Tony is this?' But I will tell you, I am *not* my father."

I was soon to understand why. Big Tony was quite familiar to me just from broad strokes, coming from Italian stock myself on my mother's side. He was fiercely loving; great with babies; loyal to church, community, and country. Also: opinionated and stubborn.

In many ways, Big Tony was the quintessential American Dream story. He had started his career as a stock boy in a small grocery store. But he wanted more for his family, so he took on three jobs to go back to trade school for air conditioner repair. One thing led to another, and by the time he was thirty, he owned a thriving appliance store. And not just any appliance store. The enterprise brought in more than $1 million almost every year, based on Big Tony's very smart decision, early on, to specialize in the high-margin business of apartment complex installations.

When Little Tony was growing up, it was assumed by everyone that he would go to college, study business, and then follow in his father's footsteps, almost literally.

He complied with these expectations, treading immediately on a land mine. From Day One, Little Tony, with his shiny new degree from Rutgers, started noticing ways his father could and should upgrade operations, especially in marketing. "There are lost opportunities everywhere, Dad," he told him, "We could double our revenues if we change with the times." For instance, when Little Tony started working in the business in 2014, it still didn't have a website.

Did I mention Big Tony was stubborn?

Eight years passed, each one more fraught than the last, as the two Tonys butted heads about everything from pricing to customer service. Finally, after a terrible fight, Big fired Little.

Little Tony, fortunately, had seen it coming. His acceptance letter to NYU's business school was sitting in his dresser drawer, and he went home that day, told his wife about their new life, and sent in his deposit.

"All I knew when I got here was that I had to get as far away from my family and the appliance business as possible," Tony explained to me in office hours. "I knew it was going to be consulting for me. I'm sure I'll have tough bosses and tough clients, but they won't be my dad."

I asked him how his relationship with his father was faring since their professional separation.

He shrugged. "We talk about sports. We talk about . . . other stuff. He's still being an idiot about the store. My younger brother keeps me in the loop on everything going down. I just don't mention it to my dad. But he's being stupid."

At this moment, Tony let out a long sigh. I thought he was about to get philosophical about the nature of family, but instead, he launched into a detailed explanation of advancements in appliance manufacturing, including 3D printing, and an analysis of the industry's growth prospects, which could really change, he told me, depending on which way the government went with import tariffs.

I remember thinking, *I am so excited.*

Not about appliances! About the journey ahead. With Little Tony, I had in my grasp a student whose aptitudes felt prodigious. His intelligence was off the charts, and he had actually helped run a successful business for nearly a decade, with experience in everything from hiring to negotiating to logistics. This suggested a skill base that would make him catnip to employers. And I could be very certain that he knew about his economically viable interests. I mean, he was virtually misty-

Which Tony Is This?

eyed about his old stomping grounds, and how much newer and better they could be. He loved—yes, *loved*—appliances.

What Tony was suffering from was values-itis, the all-too-common affliction of not knowing your values, or not living by them, or both.

In the weeks that followed, he was to get a dose of medicine, as will we, that fixed that.

4

Taking Our Values by the Reins

I'm not going to tell you that Tony was totally ignorant of his values—in his heart, he sensed them—but he was more typical in another way. He'd never articulated those values to anyone, including himself, nor had he connected them with his career aspirations.

Occasionally, though, I do encounter people whose values are as sharp and pointy as a paring knife, which isn't a bad metaphor, by the way, for how values can shape your life.

Molly, a midlevel manager at an enterprise software company, was a private client of mine who started off our session by announcing, "First and foremost, I want an *interesting* life." Her Area of Transcendence ended up being chief of staff for a global tech company, where she could travel from organizational hot spot to hot spot, cooling people off and fixing broken things to her heart's delight. She's on the road to that destination right now.

Vivaan was a Bangalore-born interior designer attending business school to pivot—although to what, he did not know. What he did know was that he needed to "live among beautiful things," as he put it. "And I am *obsessed* with wallpaper," he added. As a person who is also obsessed with wallpaper, I was not freaked out at all by the palpable longing in Vivaan's voice. I just thought, *Wow, now* there's *a defining value I know the name of!* (By the way, that value is called Beholderism. I have it, too.) The thing about Vivaan, though, was that he was at business school to change direction because, he reasoned, surely he wasn't born to choose couch fabric and curtain tassels in a world being turned inside out by AI. In time, his Becoming You process revealed that surely he was, with a twist. He and a group of friends recently launched an app to digitize the often-dreadful experience of turning your rental apartment from a vibeless white box into an affordable little sanctuary.

When I met Kyle, he was four years past a near-fatal biking accident, and perhaps because of it, he was one of the most driven MBAs I'd ever encountered. While many of his classmates were not immune to New York's numerous distractions, Kyle turned every homework assignment into a magnum opus. Concentrating wasn't easy for his brain sometimes. Writing wasn't either. But friendship and generosity came to him as naturally as breathing. I admired him; I admired his clarity about his life's purpose: "I need to lead. I need to work outdoors. And I need to get home to Boise."

If everyone were as clear about their values as these three, I'd still be walking my dogs in the woods upstate.

In reality, though, most people hit default when asked about their values. Which is to say, they simply state the big two—family and financial security. Tony was in this category. I also commonly get a smattering of answers like peace, impact, health, and, of course, my personal favorite, happiness.

Why such vagary around values? I have my theories.

The first is that in recent years, the word *values* has been hijacked by politics. *Family values, American values, liberal values, conservative values, Christian values, progressive values*—we've all heard these terms thrown around like grenades. Never mind that there is limited consensus about what any such designations even mean. Regardless, they incite controversy and discord, with the result being that many of us steer clear of conversations about values altogether if we can help it.

A second, and possibly larger, reason is that K–12 schooling generally does not teach us, anywhere along the way, how to define values or identify our own. Instead, when we're younger, we're taught how to calculate the volume of a cylinder, play the recorder, and reel off the names of Christopher Columbus's ships—although maybe not that last one anymore. College is often no better. As an undergraduate, I read a lot of Greek epic poetry. That's why you heard me raving about the *Iliad* a few chapters back. I learned about art from Japan's Edo period. (That would be 1603 to 1867, in case you'd forgotten.) And I spent a year having my head filled with the intellectual history of early-industrial Europe. It should be against the law for nineteen-year-olds to read Hegel, Kierkegaard, and Schopenhauer, and yet here I stand without an arrest record.

I don't think this is generational either. My own kids took classes just as obscure as I did—I'm so glad my son, a digital marketing specialist in the game industry, spent four years studying Chinese, aren't you? And I have a young woman on my team who once took a full-credit philosophy class titled Nothingness. Which just about sums up what most college kids know about values when they graduate. (For the record, she got an A.)

Now, I am not opposed to a good old-fashioned liberal arts education—there is a great deal to be said for learning for the sake of learning. But I don't believe this education should come at the expense of good old-fashioned instruction on a topic that will affect you every day of your life. I am referring, of course, to your values.

If I could redesign the curriculum of high schools in America, my version would include a class that explains that each one of us has a second spinal cord inside us. Our "real" spinal cord is made up of nerve cells, tissue, and bone, and it controls our bodily movements and functions. The second, figurative one is made up of our intertwined beliefs, desires, and motivations—our values—and it controls our decisions, choices, and actions.

Like, say, whom we marry. What kind of job we end up in. How much money we want. Where we live. How many kids we have. What we do on the weekends. How healthy we feel. Where we spend the holidays. Which car we drive. Even what kind of dog we own.

Destiny Planning 101, anyone?

Since that class doesn't exist, most of us are left to figure out our values over time, sometimes by accident, and often when we have no other choice. Do we move for the new job or turn it down in order to stay near Mom and Dad? Do we forgive our partner's infidelity or walk out the door? Do we punish our son on his third missed curfew or get him help? Do we leave the dysfunctional church we once loved or stay and join the search for a new pastor?

In such crucible moments, we hear ourselves saying things like, "Mom and Dad aren't going to live forever; I would never forgive myself for not caring for them until the end."

Or, alternatively, "I've wanted to run our North American operations for ten years. It would be thrilling, and I've earned it, and I'd never forgive myself for missing the chance to make that happen."

These inner dialogues are how we typically discover our values. In real time. When we can no longer avoid the trade-offs that values tend to involve, or even force. At such moments, we *back into* our values. Which I guess is better than nothing, but it's not much.

There's a third, final, and critically important reason for people not knowing or living by their values, or both at the same time. It's actually a *set* of reasons, which collectively I call the Four Horsemen of Values Destruction: Economic Security, Expediency, Expectations, and Events. These cultural and personal dynamics are omnipresent and totally understandable, but they kill authenticity nonetheless. Let's take a closer look:

Economic Security is the all-too-human tendency to cede to money as a priority, whether it actually matters to us or not.

Carolyn was a thirty-one-year-old Angeleno who came into the

Becoming You process because—hmm, there is no subtle way to put this—she loathed her job. She was an events specialist at a well-known entertainment company, and in our first conversation, she visibly winced when she described how excited she'd been to start that career for herself three years earlier.

"How could I have been so stupid?" she asked.

The answer was soon clear, and not stupid at all. For ten years before joining the corporate world, Carolyn had worked in costume design for movies and TV, jumping from gig to gig, typical for the field. She loved everything about being on a set—the panoply of people, how each day was different, the creative energy. What gnawed at her daily, though, was the uncertainty. Between gigs, she was often forced to go on unemployment, which brought back painful memories of her indigent childhood. Another costume design job always came along, but she could never shake the feeling of living on the edge. *What will I do if I get sick, or my car breaks down?* she would wonder. She found herself staying home more and turning down invitations to weddings and baby showers. It just felt too risky to spend money like that.

The pandemic was the breaking point; Carolyn hardly worked for two years and, at one point, had to move in with her mother because she couldn't afford rent, an experience punctuated by arguments. Then one day, a friend who worked at a Hollywood studio told her about an open events-planning job there. At first Carolyn thought, *I don't know how to do that*, but scanning the job description, she soon began to see what her friend was talking about. The job did seem to play to all her aptitudes—attention to detail, comfort with high-pressure situations, collaboration. And how could she not notice that it was a salaried position with healthcare? For the first time in her career, Carolyn told herself, she might be able to exhale.

Instead, she soon found herself biting her tongue most of the time at work so she wouldn't scream from the tedium. For one off-site, her job was to assemble three hundred swag bags, which, as she told me, "any nine-year-old could have done." Later, her boss complained that the company water bottles she'd packed in each tote were missing lids. She hadn't noticed because she didn't care.

And yet . . .

And yet there was that second coffee or glass of wine she could now order, that baby gift she could now buy, that wedding she could now attend. In a few months, she'd even be able to get a new car.

A year passed, and then another. Carolyn bought a used Toyota, her first car with air-conditioning. She even started thinking about a trip to Hawaii. Maybe she'd invite her mother and they could patch things up.

But at work, every eight-hour shift still felt like eighteen to Carolyn, and time slowed even further after Carolyn's boss was promoted and she applied for the job. "Not enough experience yet," she was told.

Soon after, Carolyn and I met to do Becoming You. Even in our preliminary conversations, I knew values would be our focus, because her aptitudes were so clear, and because she was certain that the only part of the economy that called her emotionally and intellectually was the entertainment business. We had, in other words, two of the three Area of Transcendence spheres already figured out.

And so, we launched into Carolyn's values excavation with my often-recommended first step, Six Squared. (A full description of this two-part exercise can be found in Appendix A at the end of this book.)

In Six Squared's first assignment, it asks you to imagine you've written the story of your life from birth to the present, and then come up with a six-word title for the book.

After fifteen minutes of thinking and tapping out various versions on her phone, Carolyn's was: "It Was Rich, Until It Wasn't."

"Rich?" I asked her for clarification.

"My life," she responded. "Back in the old days, I was poor in my wallet, but I was rich right here." She tapped her chest.

"Ouch," I said.

The second assignment in Six Squared asks you to imagine writing *another* autobiography, this time about your life from the present day to twenty-five years in the future. Furthermore, and more importantly, it asks that this new memoir describe your perfect, unedited dream of a life, the story you would live if you were the *author* of your life, not the editor.

"I hate this," Carolyn said almost immediately.

Not an uncommon reaction. The second part of Six Squared can be agonizing for some of us, because we've spent years *not* allowing ourselves to access our deepest desires.

Finally, after almost a full half hour of thinking and writing, Carolyn showed me her title: "The Oscar Was Worth the Cost."

We both burst into laughter at the clarity of it.

"I cannot tell you how much I love costume design," Carolyn went on to explain, still smiling. "I miss it. I do. I still *dream* about it. I don't think I've ever admitted that to anyone. I dream that someday I'm going to be up on that stage, holding one of the little golden guys, and I'm going to be thanking myself, like Snoop Dogg."

Carolyn was referring, by the way, to a speech the rapper made after he received his star on the Hollywood Walk of Fame, in which he thanked everyone under the sun, and then added, "I want to thank me for believing in me. I want to thank me for doing all this hard work. I wanna thank me for being me at all times. Snoop Dogg, you a bad motherfucker."

The crowd went wild, because who is ever that real?

We had only just begun the Becoming You process, but Carolyn had already decided she, too, wanted to be real. Even if it meant financial sacrifice in the short term, she wanted and needed a life of emotional and intellectual wealth. The kind of life that could lead to fulfilling a value she hadn't even known she had—success seen and acknowledged by the world. (In Becoming You's values language, this value is rather bluntly called Achievement.)

Taking Our Values by the Reins

"I'm giving my two weeks' notice today," Carolyn said. There wasn't a hint of trepidation in her voice. "I can't believe I almost did this to myself. This shitty compromise of an existence."

But I could, because I cannot count the number of times I've seen the Horseman of Economic Security haul people away from their true values. I myself was a management consultant traveling three or four days a week for years, galloping on the back of this very horse, straight away from my deep yearning to be a good mother. Shitty compromise happens all the time because making money makes so much sense—until it doesn't anymore. And at that point we're miserable and asking why.

That's the reason so many Becoming You exercises pick away at your true beliefs and feelings around how much money is enough. For some of us, that answer will be like Carolyn's: not much. For others, it will be way at the opposite end of the spectrum, like another client I had once, whose second Six Squared memoir title read "Riches Beyond, Then Beyond the Beyond." A writer he was not, but that's not the point. The value he placed on Affluence was off the charts. That's an important thing to know about oneself.

And by the way—your Affluence "score," for lack of a better word, is neither good nor bad. It is what it is! I am a 100 percent values agnostic. If you're not hurting anyone, you have a right to your values, whatever they may be. You came to them honestly, through life experience. The bigger issue is whether we know our values and are living by them, and we've not let the first horseman carry us away from them, whether we're holding the reins or not.

Expediency is the second Horseman of Values Destruction. It comes into play when we let comfort, convenience, or the path of least resistance take precedence over our authentic needs, wants, and desires.

I met James when I was in Houston giving a speech to the top executives at his company, an oil rig management firm. My topic that day, somewhat ironically, had nothing to do with Becoming You and everything to do with crisis management, which I also teach at NYU.

I say "ironically" because James was in the midst of his own personal calamity. This fact crept out quietly at lunch, when James and I were seated next to each other, and we got to chatting about our children. He had three of his own, all under the age of ten. But I couldn't help but notice that as he was showing me their photos, he was fighting back tears.

"I'm sorry, are you okay?" I asked.

James was terribly British, so his answer was, "Oh yes, absolutely, just allergies here." But when he quickly excused himself, I found myself thinking, *Too bad, must be divorce.*

Eventually James returned, and we continued talking, this time about my kids. But again, he seemed to be getting choked up. Finally, he dipped his head and whispered to me, "I'm so sorry. It's just that my wife and I are . . . separating."

This is a problem with being old. You get like Nostradamus.

We became friends that day, and in time I was to learn James's whole story. He had grown up thinking he would be a professor. He loved literature and had actually written a scholarly book himself while at Oxford getting his master's—a comparison of two Shakespearean plays. "I've always known what I'm good at and what I love," James explained to me. "School."

In other words, like Carolyn, James's aptitudes and interests were a done deal. It was his *values* that cried out for clarification.

Because I want to do Becoming You with anyone who is willing, James and I ended up embarking on the values-excavation part of the process, which was how we found ourselves staring at his very revelatory Whose Life chart.

By this, I am referring to a Becoming You exercise called Whose Life Do You Want Anyway? You can find the full explanation in

Appendix B, but, to summarize, in this exercise you are asked to come up with a list of people whose lives you love, admire, and/or covet. That's the easy part. The hard part is when you must consider each of these individuals in turn and *honestly* identify what it is about their lives that landed them on your list. Their wealth? Their status? Their fun quotient? Their kindness? Their car? The exercise then asks you to identify what, if anything, you would *not* want from each person's life. Their divorce, perhaps, or their rotten children? Their financial sacrifices? It could be anything. One of my own Whose Life listees is Martha Stewart, for instance, whom I revere for her success, her brilliance, and her relentless ability to reinvent herself. I would, however, leave out her very unfortunate encounter with the US Securities and Exchange Commission. (I suspect she would leave it out, too, although no one has ever handled an unfair imbroglio with more dignity.)

The power of the Whose Life exercise emerges as your list grows longer, because that's when you start spotting the *patterns* that reveal your values.

James was a case in point.

His Whose Life chart included the British literary superstars Ian McEwan and Martin Amis, two Oxford professors, and the editor of *The New Yorker*, David Remnick. For each person, James's What I Love column included phrases like "Ideas and writing all the time," "Life of the mind," and, very poignantly, over and over again, "Taken seriously."

Interestingly, there was extraordinarily little that James said he would jettison from any of his Whose Life selections. Martin Amis was sometimes accused of being arrogant; James wanted none of that. Nor did he want Amis's tendency to be "always in his father's shadow." Both of his Oxford professors were divorced, and James noted, "Hateful loneliness."

"Wow," I said, scanning James's chart, "I think we're staring at your values."

"We are?" he asked, hopeful and incredulous. "What are they?"

I ticked them off with ease.

"You long to live the life of a literary intellectual, teaching and writing at the highest levels, in ways that assure you are taken seriously by your colleagues and your community. You want to be known as a success for your own sake, and no one else's. You value a good, happy marriage and intact family. And I think you want to live in London."

"Where else is there to live?" he answered almost reflexively, and then laughed as if he had been making a joke.

But the situation was actually very serious, and we both knew that. James's life was aligned with none of his values, and he was on the verge of losing the one element he had previously felt secure in: his marriage.

Now, you may be wondering how James had ended up in such a bind, and the answer was simply love. During the summer of 2012, almost a decade before he became my friend, he was in a pub with his friends when a bevy of American women walked in, laughing and chirping away in their insouciant southern accents. They were, he and his friends discerned by eavesdropping, killing time before dinner at the Royal China Club and dancing at Annabel's. "How insanely sexy," was the only thought James's brain seemed able to form in the moment. He picked out the prettiest woman in the group. "I am going to marry that one," he told his friends, pointing at the woman he did in fact marry a year later.

Her name, it turned out, was Elizabeth, and she was the daughter of a Texas oil executive.

When Elizabeth and James married, that oil executive became James's boss.

Some days, James would sit at his desk in Houston, staring out of his fortieth-floor office window, and think, "My God, what have I done?" But other days he truly felt spreadsheets had their own beauty, just as good writing did, and that the history of the oil industry was as good as any novel he'd ever read.

But the real reason he never flinched was Elizabeth. She was the love of his life. Joyful, encouraging, loyal, and dear. The children were just like her. When he kissed them good night, he would often think, *I'm a lucky man.*

Lucky, but flawed. On a business trip to New York, James struck up a conversation with a woman at his hotel bar, and an affair began. Elizabeth came upon their texts two years later.

In true Elizabeth fashion, she didn't rage. She quietly asked him to end the relationship, which he did. She also asked him to attend marriage counseling with their pastor. He did that, too.

And yet, something felt irrevocably broken.

By the time James and I were doing Becoming You together, his marriage had gone from chilly to frigid. He painfully missed Elizabeth—the old Elizabeth—and, worse, he missed his children, whom he felt withdrawing from him on their mother's wordless cue. At the office, he intensified his efforts to stay in his father-in-law's good graces. But James felt him growing aloof as well; surely Elizabeth had confided in him. In short, James found himself being managed out the door of a prison he'd built with his own hands.

This story exemplifies the value destroyer of Expediency in action.

Every decision that James had made since the day he fell for Elizabeth had been made not in accordance with his values but to avoid conflict.

Let's move to Texas.

Okay.

You'll work for my father.

Okay.

I wish you'd put that book down and take up golf.

Okay.

I want you to get baptized.

Um, what? James had always enjoyed going to church with Elizabeth, and he admired her faithfulness. But was he ready to publicly commit to it himself? He knew he wasn't—at least not yet.

Something—*something*—always breaks Expediency's grasp.

At that point we must decide whether we want to live by our values, or live by the glide path of least resistance.

I asked James what his choice was going to be.

"Well, I have two sets of values, don't I?" he asked in return. "I want a happy marriage and family. But I can have that only if I give up all my other values."

I asked if he was sure about that. For instance, I wondered, had he ever asked Elizabeth to live in London, or to support his return to academia? "She would never consider those things" was his reply. "There could be a fight."

Some things are worth fighting for. Like one's self-determination.

"You've surrendered to Expediency without even throwing a single soft punch," I told him.

To this, James dropped his head and his allergies kicked in.

This story has a happy ending that takes place—surprise!—in London. James is getting his PhD, but very slowly, as his new job is running his father-in-law's EU operations. This means a lot of travel to Norway, but no one has ever loved a promotion more or complained less about airplane food.

Are things perfect?

Are they ever in a marriage?

Elizabeth and James are still in a period of rebuilding. They are committed to staying together, but the damage wrought by James's infidelity is still being unwound in therapy. At the same time, Elizabeth has paused her urgency around James's baptism, although James has started to attend a Bible study at their new parish church. Together, James and Elizabeth have started to imagine a future together that is richer and more real—and more shared—than anything they had ever imagined before.

All it took was confronting Expediency's grip on their lives.

When you surrender your values to the anticipation of criticism or judgment, you're taking a ride on the back of the third Horseman of Values Destruction, **Expectations**.

I first met Deidre when she was sixteen. You couldn't really miss her, because she was the only person who wasn't wearing shoes at the very fancy country club wedding that Jack and I were attending.

"I kind of love Deidre," Jack whispered to me as she owned the dance floor during the reception, gyrating around by herself with a huge smile on her face. He had, in fact, known her for longer than I had, as she was the daughter of a top executive he'd worked with for decades.

I think Jack might have been alone in his view. Guests were pointedly not looking at Deidre, and I saw her father actually approach her on the dance floor several times, clearly gesturing at her to sit down. She did, but only when the band took its break.

The funny thing about Deidre is that, as time went on, she also did a lot of things to conform to society's and her family's expectations. She killed it at college and was admitted to medical school. But she dropped out after a year to busk across Europe. That was the last I heard of Deidre until right after the pandemic, when I was at an event in New York. Out of the blue, an elegant woman approached me. It was Deidre's older sister, an attorney at a prestigious law firm. She'd heard about my class at NYU and was wondering if Deidre could meet with me to figure out what to do with her life.

And so it was that I was reunited with a very different Deidre than the free-spirited girl I recalled. She was somber, fidgety, and gaunt, and the light in her eyes was so dull that this time the Nostradamus thought in my head was *Oh no, drugs.*

Sadly, oh yes. Mainly Adderall, it turned out. "It helps with numbing me out," she explained.

Since I'd last heard about her, Deidre's life had been a swinging pendulum of meeting expectations and then defying them. After busking around Europe, for instance, she eventually heeded her parents' call to get a job, entering the buying program at Macy's, an endeavor that didn't last six weeks. After that, she worked as an aide for disabled children in a city shelter for a year but was fired after missing too many days of work. She tried a stint as a paralegal but quit after a few months. When I met with her, she was unemployed, estranged from her parents, and living in her sister's guest room.

How do you do a values excavation in such a fraught situation?

Step-by-step.

Because of its simplicity, I decided to start our process together with what I call the Proustish Questionnaire, a Becoming You adaptation of the Proust Questionnaire, a French parlor game from the 1890s. You can find my more modern and shorter version in Appendix C. It's fun and provocative, but, more importantly, it powerfully adds to your values insights.

Consider some of Deidre's questions and answers.

What is your idea of perfect happiness?

"Dancing in a field of flowers, music pouring down from the sky."

What is your greatest fear?

"Jail."

Who is the greatest love of your life?

"Me."

What is the most overrated virtue?

"Belonging to a country club."

What is your motto?

"Stop asking me to be quiet."

Have you ever seen a raw diamond? It comes out of the earth irregular and knobbly, yellow-brownish in tint. It's actually kind of nondescript; if you spotted one on the beach, you wouldn't bend down to pick it up.

It's only after a whole bunch of cleaving and sawing—technical terms!—with tiny little tools that the perfect diamond buried inside the lump appears.

Cleaving and sawing with tiny little tools is yet another metaphor I like in this chapter. (The previous one being the paring knife, but that was pages ago.) Your values are inside you, usually quite hidden. Exercises like Six Squared, the Whose Life chart, and the Proustish Questionnaire are the cleaving and sawing.

Add to that list now the Alpha Omega exercise, found in Appendix D, and to which I turned with Deidre next.

I have to tell you, I have a special fondness for Alpha Omega. It's so effective! But also because it was the first tool I ever created for values discovery, back in 2009, when I was writing my book *10-10-10*, about values-driven decision-making. I have refined Alpha Omega since then, but—humblebrag—it has aged well.

Alpha Omega is composed of three questions.

The first is crafted to surface our values around character and identity: "What do you want people to say about you when you're not in the room?" Over the many years I've used Alpha Omega, I think I must have heard every possible answer to this question. I've also discovered most answers contain strong hints about each respondent's underlying values. I am thinking of the young teacher I once met who replied, "When I'm not in the room, the minute I walk out, I want people saying that I'm not an asshole like my father."

I was soon to find out that this individual ardently wanted a good reputation in his small town, where he hoped to run for office one day. But more than that, his life was driven by a strong desire to break a generational narrative of abusive men leaving behind broken families. "That story stops with me," he told me.

Remember our friend and guide Little Tony? His illuminating answer to this question was: "When I walk out of a room, I want people to say, 'He did it his way.'" Smiling, he added, "And I made it better."

In my home office that day with Deidre, her answer to the prompt was similarly resolute.

"Who cares?" she said with a sardonic laugh. "People have always talked about me. If I'd listened, I'd be a doctor now."

I told Deidre that I thought her answer suggested strong values of self-determination and individualism, or Agency and Voice, as the Becoming You lexicon calls them, respectively. This dyad is common in nonconformists.

"Yep, me," she agreed.

Alpha Omega's second prompt concerns our values around lifestyle—basically, it gets at how we want to live. It is: "What did you love about your childhood, and what did you hate?"

"Okay, I loved my sister; I loved how she always stood up for me," Deidre quickly responded. "I loved our dog. I loved our summers on the Cape. I loved the sunsets."

"And what did you hate about growing up?" I asked.

"It was one long game," she said. "One long negotiation with my parents to get what I wanted for myself. They always wanted something different." I told Deidre that I was getting strong Agency vibes again; she had a compelling desire not to be bound by the rules or norms of any club but her own.

"Yep," came the reply.

The final prompt of Alpha Omega transports you to the future and asks you to answer: "What would make you cry on your eighty-fifth birthday—from regret?"

When Deidre looked stymied, I tried to paint the scene. "You're much older. You're approaching the end of your life. Put yourself there.

What unlived dream, unaccomplished goal, or unhealed relationship might break your heart?"

She nodded but still said nothing. Finally, she ventured, "I live in the present. I don't think about the future, and I definitely don't care how I'm remembered."

In the language of Becoming You, Deidre's desire for Radius—social or cultural impact—was nil. All she wanted was freedom for *herself*. Tony, by comparison, registered about average on Radius, explaining he wanted to have a massive impact on his family, but had only limited further ambitions to impact the world around him. At his eighty-fifth birthday, he reported, the only thing that would make him cry was being without Gennie and the rest of his brood.

In the end, we never did create an Area of Transcendence for Deidre, as her sister had hoped. She was too at sea in her soul and, frankly, just too mad and sad about her present life circumstances for thinking and planning ahead.

But Deidre was a person for whom planning a life would be the ultimate anathema anyway; that is how I've come to see it. Agency—utter and total independence—was her core value. Becoming You is not for everyone, and I respect the fact that Deidre is among those for whom it isn't.

A last thought about the deadly Horseman of Expectations.

Sometimes the most onerous, values-killing expectations are not the ones that others foist upon us—but the ones we cling to ourselves.

Juan was the son of two successful business owners in Salt Lake City. His upbringing was generally happy and, as even he would tell you, pretty uneventful. His older sister, Stephie, went off to Arizona State when he was fourteen, and he expected to follow her there in a few years. They were a lot alike, especially in their plans to become doctors. Stephie wanted to be a neurologist, and Juan was interested, he told the world, in surgery.

Time would show that Juan didn't actually have the aptitudes to go into medicine. His grades in science were never particularly good. But perhaps more problematic, the sight of blood made him faint. There is actually an umbrella term for this sort of reaction, *vasovagal syncope*, and wooziness at the sight of blood is said to affect up to 22 percent of the population. It definitely makes getting your blood drawn unpleasant, and it's kind of the ultimate nonstarter for a doctor.

For years, though, Juan persisted in his quest. Why? Because he "saw" himself as a doctor in his mind's eye. It was his identity, entirely self-imposed. His parents had actually urged him to consider business. "But that's not me!" he would protest.

I will spare you the details of Juan's career journey over the next ten years, but broadly, he bounced from one medicine-adjacent role to the next. He had stints in pharmaceutical sales, research, and digital marketing for a medical device company. No job ever quite fit, and either he quit or was asked to move on. Finally, one summer, unemployed, he picked up a high school friend from work at Pep Boys. There was a sign on the window for a mechanics-training program. Juan stared at it for a full two minutes before jotting the number down.

Who knew? Who knew he was born to work with his hands, using not a scalpel but a wrench? Who knew how much he'd love it? Who knew how well it paid?

Well, Juan finally found out all those things firsthand, when he let go of the hardest expectations to shake—the ones he had imposed on himself.

The final Horseman of Values Destruction is one that practically carried off yours truly: **Events**.

Events, as in "life stuff." Babies, divorce, death, bankruptcy, marriage, accidents, you name it. These things happen, and sometimes they are so disruptive they essentially force us to veer away from our values. Usually and eventually, things settle back down, but for some reason, we almost never go back and reclaim the values we left behind. Why? Because we're human.

I first encountered Rayna during one of my webinars, when she sent me a direct message ten minutes in. I usually don't look at DMs while I'm speaking, but hers was hard to ignore. "I NEED HELP," it said. We were on a call the next day.

The facts of the case were as follows: Rayna was forty-four and lived in Detroit. She'd grown up in the restaurant business and loved it. Her last job had been her favorite, running a fine-dining hot spot, where she managed a staff of sixty people, from the chefs to the cleaning crew. Included in that roster was her husband, Glenn, a sous-chef.

One night, on a whim, or so he claimed, Glenn swiped several pounds of meat from the restaurant cooler and packed it into the trunk of his car. Security cameras caught the whole thing. The police were waiting for him in the morning, and he was arrested. The owner then fired Rayna.

"I was totally innocent—I knew nothing," she told me. "If Glenn had mentioned one word of this plan to me, I would have killed him." She thinks the restaurant's owner believed her, but "he had to be cautious."

Rayna and Glenn had been having troubles for several years; his burglary was the breaking point. Without children, their split was financially uncomplicated, in some ways, but still filled with recriminations and pain. The fights wrecked her. The loss of her job doubled the damage.

When she typed her DM to me, Rayna had been unemployed for thirteen months. She had moved in with a friend and was getting by working nights at a hotel front desk. At first, she had applied for random restaurant jobs, but, suspecting that word of Glenn's arrest had gotten out, she stopped trying.

She didn't have to tell me she was miserable. I could see it in her eyes.

Together, we worked through the Proustish Questionnaire, with

Rayna's answers coming slowly until we reached the prompt "I will never apologize for ____."

Instantly: "I will never apologize for getting fired. I did nothing wrong," she exclaimed. "I loved being known in the restaurant industry as a success story—that's what they took from me. I'm the one owed an apology!"

The next prompt also elicited a fast reply: "I don't know what happiness is, but I know I'm never sad when ____."

"When I'm the boss!"

"You want to run things?" I asked her for clarity.

"I like being the leader," she said. "It gives me a sense of worth."

"And you were good at it," I reminded her.

She had to be reminded, too, because the firing and divorce double whammy that Rayna had experienced was the perfect example of how events can mute our values. Rayna had been too traumatized—understandably—to turn the sound back on.

Rayna left our conversation with a promise to get her résumé back out there, starting with the owner who had fired her from her favorite job, a very brave step indeed. "I'm going to make my case," she said. And from the sound of her voice, something told me she would make herself heard this time.

Because when we finally reclaim our values from the gravitational pull of events, it doesn't happen by accident. It happens with intention.

I speak from experience. Like Molly, the woman who wanted "an interesting life" whom we met on the very first page of this very long chapter, I always wanted an interesting life, too. And happily, from my early days as a crime reporter, I had no trouble attaining that dream. Then I met Jack. You know that line "You ain't seen nothing yet?" I hadn't.

Jack and I had a life together that was so complicated and chaotic, there were times it was too much for even me. But after a good night's sleep, I was always ready to go again. In our first ten years together, we visited twenty-five countries, giving speeches, meeting new people, exploring castles and ancient cities, trying local food, and going to parties.

So many parties.

Our big life ebbed when Jack started to get sick, and as he got sicker, it ebbed further still, until one day, I looked up and we were on an island whose only other inhabitants were our children; a few of our closest friends; doctors; and our beloved dogs, Happy, Chrissy, and Virginia Woolf. This was the way it had to be for five years, and while I sometimes missed the buzz of our previous life, I never felt even a prick of resentment. I guess you might say I felt nostalgia. But I also knew there was no choice. You can't say no to a terminal disease.

After Jack died, as I've told you, I took to the woods. And then I stayed there in a kind of paralysis—because I'd let events gallop away with my values, and in particular my defining value of wanting a big life. I didn't even think to chase after it. Maybe I had just grown accustomed to the new regime on my little island, of which I was now the sole human inhabitant.

How grateful I am that fate intervened with a call from the *Today Show*, asking me if I wanted to come back on for a segment. The minute I walked back on set, with the pop music blaring over the loudspeakers, and the hustle and bustle of cameras being wheeled around, the big, bright lights, and the director holding up her fingers to count down 3-2-1, I was like, "I have missed this so much."

How did I think I could let go of one of my main values forever?

But that's the thing about the Horsemen—all of them. They can seemingly come out of nowhere and carry us to distant lands.

Unless we grab the reins—and steer ourselves home.

5

The Bridge to Yourself, and Your Future

A quick story for you. It's about the time I dropped my older son off at college.

It was a perfect Palo Alto day—bright sunshine, beautiful campus, parents and kids alike wearing smiles that fairly shouted, *All that hard work and sacrifice—worth it! We made it!*

Roscoe and I had finally gotten him settled in his little dorm room when the announcements started.

"Parents, student orientation will begin in thirty minutes. Please prepare to depart by four p.m."

Depart? Like, leave? Forever?

I smiled wanly at my beloved son, my tenderhearted, fair-haired firstborn. Dearest pal, budding writer, fierce wrestler, emerging leader, utter goofball. "No parent is really going to leave this early," I insisted.

But the announcements kept coming. Parents, prepare to leave in twenty minutes, then fifteen, then ten. Finally, the loudspeaker said, "All parents and students, please go to the courtyard for a required event." At this, Roscoe and I had no choice but to join the exodus down the stairs and outside, where about eighty of us gathered in an awkward circle.

Suddenly, and seemingly out of nowhere, there appeared a group of about twenty bright, shiny kids, clearly not newbies but real Stanford students. They formed a line in the center of the circle. They were smiling at all of us with anticipation, and we smiled back. What was going on? I huddled closer to Roscoe, who had towered over me since seventh grade, and gave his massive shoulder a little squeeze. He squeezed me back. I loved him so much it hurt.

The leader of the students in the circle brought a little pitch pipe to his lips and blew. Ah, they were going to sing.

Then they did. In glorious, flawless a cappella harmony.

"Bridge over Troubled Water."

I am still not over it. I mean, I'm almost crying as I write this, remembering how every word of that song rang true to me, to both of us.

> *When tears are in your eyes*
> *I will dry them all: I'm on your side.*

Roscoe and I had been through a lot together. So much. And obviously that was true for every other parent there, because by the second chorus of the song, we were all sobbing, and I am not exaggerating when I say we were all sobbing *very loudly*.

Life is building bridges, for each other and for ourselves.

Becoming You is one such bridge. It's designed to help you understand yourself in the now so that you are better equipped to design and forge the path to the future you want and need. In the previous chapter, we explored all the reasons and ways our values get mislaid or misappropriated. In this chapter, we turn our attention to the exact opposite. Identifying and claiming our values in their very personal specifics. And we do that with an assessment tool called the Values Bridge.

Our next step together is to learn its language and put it to work for you.

There are fifteen core human values. And you have all of them in you, just to different degrees. I just said we were going to find out your values "in their very personal specifics" in this chapter, and, full disclosure, the work ahead is nitty-gritty indeed. We're going to learn the name and characteristics of each value, determine how much of each one you are expressing in your current life, assess how much of each one you'd *like* to express, given your true self, and finally, begin to understand what all that means for the authentic life you want and need to create.

I'd say, "Fasten your seatbelt," but that's sort of a platitude, or maybe more of cliché? Either way, exciting times are a-coming.

But first a brief overview of context. Like, fifteen values? Where did that number come from?

I've been thinking and writing about values and career choices since 1995, but it was only when I arrived at NYU and started to teach about that very subject that I discovered that no one really had a modern, shared language to describe their values, myself included. That's why I conducted the research I mentioned earlier, which showed that the vast majority of respondents couldn't define values or list their own with any consistency or clarity. *There has to be a way to fix this problem*, I thought, *because you can't really plan your wild and precious life without being able to pinpoint and talk about your values in a way everyone agrees upon and understands.*

Right about that time, I had started to work on something that I should have done in 1988, when a dean at Harvard Business School called me into his office and said, "You're going to be an academic someday. It's so obvious. Why don't you stay here after graduation and get your PhD?" I politely declined, because in those days, I had one value, which was getting out of debt. So off I went to Bain, but that dean wasn't wrong about me, I guess. To make a long story short, I decided to finally get that PhD a few years ago, with the topic being, yep, values and career choices.

It was in the midst of my PhD research, and, frankly, doing so much bitching and moaning about the lack of a modern, actionable language of values, that my thesis advisor, Dr. Graham Abbey, politely told me to shut up and just do it.

The Bridge to Yourself, and Your Future

That is, just do the work to identify and name all the values I had identified empirically, test them with factor analysis, codify them, create a tool to measure them, and then test that tool a billion times.

As you might imagine, that directive felt very daunting, maybe even impossible. But you know, sometimes you want and need something so much, you just shut your eyes and clench your teeth and jump. Not literally, of course, but you get my meaning. Anyway, thus we have the Welch-Bristol Values Inventory and the Values Bridge assessment test.

My inventory, it must be stated, builds on a century-old academic foundation. The German psychologist Eduard Spranger wrote the grounding values taxonomy *Types of Men* in 1928. It was broadened and deepened by the work of Harvard psychologists Gordon Allport and Gardner Lindzey, along with British scholar Philip Vernon, with their Study of Values in 1961. But by far, the most theoretically renowned construct of more recent years is the Schwartz Values Inventory, which Dr. Shalom Schwartz developed at Hebrew University in Jerusalem from 1970 to 1990. It contains ten values, and its findings are very much integrated into my own conceptual framework.

My goal with Welch-Bristol was to enhance the constructs that already existed in a few essential ways. First, I wanted to create a tool that reflected the world today, with changes brought about by the internet and significant cultural trends, especially around when and where we work. I also wanted a tool that would allow people to understand their values relative to each other, e.g., so that they could see which values they had a lot of and which were more peripheral. I also wanted to create an assessment instrument that indicated which of our values are in conflict, and, further, and perhaps most importantly for the Becoming You method, how much of each authentic value we express in our current lives, versus how much we'd express if we could. All of these areas of focus are critical, in my view, to self-discovery and career planning.

But I don't want to get too academic here. (Well, maybe I do, but I won't.) What's consequential is that each of the values in my taxonomy can and should be understood as a "life-organizing principle." You've already heard me mention some of them by name: Tony's Affluence and Familycentrism; Vivaan's Beholderism; Carolyn's Achievement; Deidre's Agency and Voice. As this chapter unfolds, you will learn about all fifteen and, I hope, come to both understand and recognize them with familiarity.

You will also hear that each of the fifteen values I have codified exists on a continuum. Based on validity testing, I use a scale from 1 to 7 to indicate value intensity. But an alert! If you are to use the scales graphically provided in the pages ahead, please read the words explaining them, as the simple summary quotes on each can best be described as "blunt instruments." Values are nuanced and involve trade-offs. For the utmost accuracy of your assessment, again, the interpretative and descriptive text matters too, a lot.

I also invite you, and even urge you gently, to take the Values Bridge assessment test digitally. I think the results are just a bit more accurate than the self-reporting prompted in the pages ahead. A free version of the test appears on my website; it has one hundred questions and will take you about fifteen minutes to complete. You can take it before or after you read this chapter, it matters not. I know that some of you may have already taken it, which is also great. My only goal here is that together, we get you to the list of your values I promised back in chapter 1.

And not just a list, really. But an understanding of your unique values profile, and a sense of how close you are to expressing and embracing your values with your life and career.

How close, that is, you are to becoming you.

The values below are listed in random and nonalphabetical order, simply to underscore that none is more important than another. And here we go:

Radius is a measure of **systemic impact** as a life-organizing principle.

Of course, most everyone wants to leave a mark on this world in some way or another. It's a matter of degree. It's a matter of *how much* having an impact drives, directs, or otherwise spurs your decisions and actions.

If Radius is a very strong value for you—a 6 or 7, for instance—virtually everything you decide and do is precipitated by your desire to change the world. This is not about fame. That desire is captured in the value of Luminance, which we will look at shortly. Radius, rather, is about how big a crater there would be if your life was dropped on the world like a bomb.

People can have Radius as a top value for all sorts of reasons. Sometimes, for instance, people who yearn for impact are healing childhood neglect. Or it can simply be in someone's personality to want to be a "world-changer." I'm not a psychoanalyst, and if you are not hurting anyone, I don't really care why you have certain values. Perhaps *you* should care, but technically speaking, your reasons are irrelevant for the purposes of conducting a Becoming You analysis.

I might also add that some people want a lot of Radius for nefarious reasons. Fictionally speaking, the Joker, from *Batman*, would fall in this category. Historically speaking, so would Attila the Hun and, sadly, too many other profoundly not-good world leaders to name here.

But in my experience, most people who have an off-the-charts high Radius ranking are coming from a noble place, galvanized by a soul-deep yearning to restore dignity to the powerless, aching, and disenfranchised. My friend Bruce Friedrich is a perfect example. Bruce's first job out of college was running a Catholic shelter and a soup kitchen for homeless families in inner-city Washington, DC, which he did for six years during the height of that city's crack epidemic. Over time, Bruce came to believe that the animal agriculture system was at the root of much of the world's hunger and injustice, with incalculable costs to animals as well. In 2016, he founded the Good Food Institute, a think tank devoted to the science of making meat from plants and cellular agriculture (basically, using tissue engineering to make real meat, no live animals required). The goal of the group, which has been ranked as one of the top three climate charities in the United States for impact by Charity

Navigator, is to ensure that as the planet speeds toward a population of ten billion, our human family can afford healthy food that is produced without destroying the planet and harming animals. As Bruce puts it, "A healthy, sustainable and just food system doesn't just happen. But such a system is within reach, if we only make it our purpose."

By the same token, some people care not an iota for Radius. I have a dear friend who believes she's done her job on earth if she's impacted the life of her son and daughter. The rest of the world can take care of itself. In a homework assignment, a student once wrote, "Some people say I should leave a mark on the world or focus on helping others. I have no interest. I do have goals, but they're based on me continuing to live, with actions that don't impact my daughter or wife negatively." Or consider George Harrison. He was the first Beatle to be drawn toward Indian spirituality, and the only one who seemed to stay there, embracing the belief systems of the Hare Krishna and Hinduism, with their tenets of austerity, simplicity, and humility. In 2001, at the age of fifty-eight, as Harrison was dying, a reporter asked him what he hoped his legacy might be.

"Why would I want to leave a legacy?" he said in reply.

Radius ranking: Zero.

How about you? Where are you on the Radius continuum? Like Bruce? Like George? Or somewhere in between?

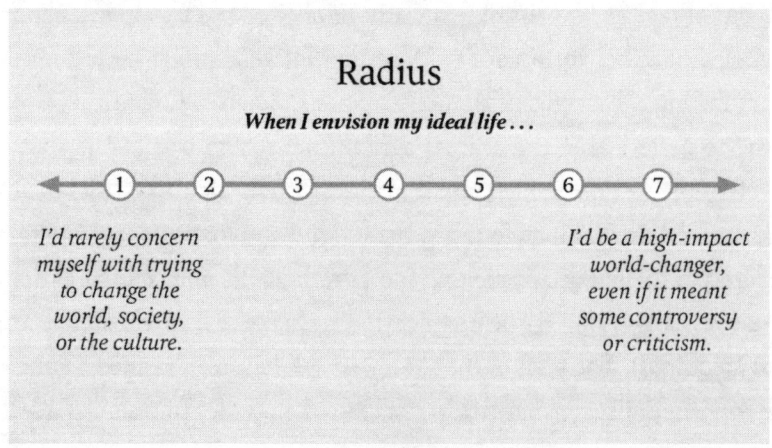

The Bridge to Yourself, and Your Future

Scope is a measure of **stimulation** as a life-organizing principle.

Have you ever had a person in your life for whom it was impossible to buy a gift because they had everything and wanted nothing? Jack was that person for my kids, and it was no end of frustration because they loved him so much, and he himself loved *giving* gifts so much. It was a lopsided, maddening thing.

One year, I found myself Christmas Eve shopping with Marcus, who was probably nine at the time. He had just one gift left to find—Jack's, of course. As the hours went on, and we scoured every store in the mall, I could see tears welling up in his eyes. "This is terrible; this is the worst," he was moaning over and over again.

Then a shout of glee: "I found it!"

I rushed over to his side of the store to see him triumphantly holding up the kind of dish you put on your dresser top for stray pennies—and waving it around. I was like, "Okaaaaay . . ." until Marcus held still for a moment and I could read the decorative text: WHY NOT LIVE A BIG LIFE?

"This is perfect for Jack!" he cried.

He was so right.

Jack was born addicted to what he called "action"—as in, on a Friday night, he'd exclaim, "Let's go find some action!" which would lead to a pub crawl until two a.m., making new friends at every stop along the way. He loved people and parties, and frenzy, and even chaos. Controversy excited him, as did new things, hard things, and different things. Once he was giving a speech to a group of executives. "If you ever figure out you're a bore," he exhorted them, "go slap yourself!" This got a huge laugh, as most people understood that bores don't usually know they're boring. But that truth of the matter was lost on Jack, as he thought people who preferred predictability and calm had a kind of disease that surely caused them pain. He didn't understand that constant stimulation was not for everyone.

Jack would rank a 7 on the Scope continuum, to put it mildly, and one of the reasons that we got along so well was that I am probably a 6.5. As you may remember, I am the girl whose favorite quote is "Suffering is the origin of consciousness." It's not that I want to suffer, but I am willing to, for the learning that comes with having every experience the world can afford you.

But I have to be very clear here. Unlike Jack, I think there is absolutely nothing wrong with ranking a 1 or 2 on the value of Scope. That doesn't make you a "bore" at all. It makes you a person who chooses a life that is a manageable size and moving at a pace you can control. It makes you a person who prefers a sense of emotional or even physical safety. It makes you a person who sees the upside of tranquility. It's a matter of personal preference. It's a matter of what feels right, what feels good, and sometimes what feels necessary.

One of my colleagues ranks herself a 3.5 on Scope. Her voracious love of learning and annual foray into exotic travel might suggest she would be higher—both are common Scope markers—but professionally, she finds herself most comfortable with work that is, in her words, "practically routine." Once, when she had just returned from two weeks on an emu photo safari in Australia and regaled us with photos of herself sleeping in the bush in camouflage pajamas and a *helmet*, I said, "I'm sorry, but this is presenting as Scope-o-*mania*." Her retort: "I like the big life, but in small doses." Thus, her apt dead-center Scope ranking.

My friend Marcia ranks Scope at a 2. "I want to know what I am doing next year on this day at four p.m.," she explains. Her apartment reflects her gestalt. It is an airy, sunlit sanctuary, done simply in shades of white and beige. When I step inside, I feel like a different person. A person who might enjoy yoga and chamomile tea, for instance.

Marcia has spent her entire life in a relationship with anxiety. It stays at bay for years at a time, but it can crop up and wreak havoc at the worst moments, as it did right before her wedding, when it turned what she'd wanted to be a carefree, fun-filled weekend into a battlefield of logistical and emotional stress bombs. Over time, Marcia discovered that the antidote to such anxiety flare-ups is to adjust her world to its right size and pace and level of stimulation *for her*, with planning, simplicity, and orderliness in all things. It works.

And that's the thing about Scope, and all the values, for that matter. There is no right or wrong, just right or wrong *for you*.

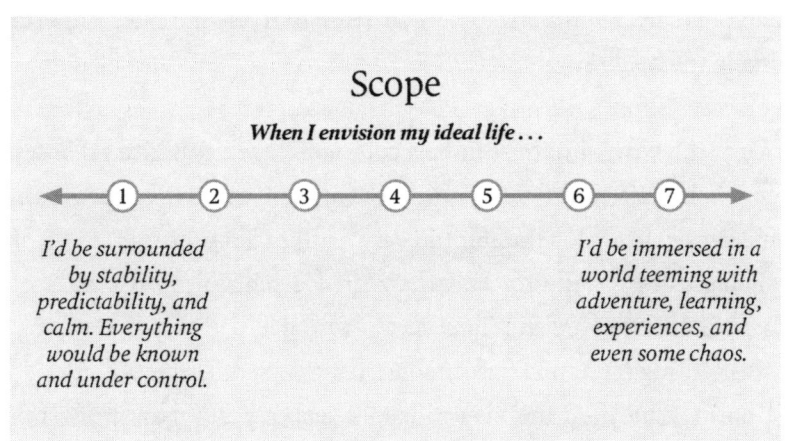

Familycentrism is a measure of **family** as a life-organizing principle.

Over my years teaching Becoming You, I'd estimate 90 percent of all my students have started the Becoming You process identifying family as one of their core values. I've been known to groan audibly at that answer. What does it even mean? That you'd pass up a huge promotion and raise to live near your parents? Or that you love your parents dearly, but one phone call a week and three visits a year are just fine, thank you very much?

Becoming You requires you to understand *how much* you desire your family to drive, design, and impel your actions and decisions, and the Values Bridge measures that.

We all know people who would rank themselves a 7 on the Familycentrism continuum. I have a colleague who married later in life, and then, after thinking he and his husband would never have children, ended up being able to adopt three children within three years. I once expressed to him my sympathy for how hard this must have been. I think my actual line was something like, "Oh my God, how did you survive? What a shit show that must have been! Don't worry, it gets better, eventually." I will never forget him looking at me with mystification. "It was fantastic," he said. "I loved every minute of it. It was when I realized I was born to be a father and that is the most important thing in my life."

Oops.

Over the years, I have seen this colleague repeatedly and relentlessly organize his life to reflect his high Familycentrism. He squeezes all of his teaching into one semester (no easy feat!) to allow himself to be fully available to his family for half the year. He schedules his classes only when his children are in school or at camp. He will stop everything or drop anything for a call from or about his children. Disney vacations are the norm. And if he has ever missed a school performance or parent-teacher conference, I would be stunned.

By contrast, let's return to Anna, the EMBA student I first mentioned in the introduction of this book. She had started the semester despondent, torn with guilt about how little she was seeing her daughter. (Anna ran a growing chain of med-spas, you might recall.)

The values exercises we did in class were revelatory for Anna, however. One by one, they surfaced not that she hated time away from her daughter but that she hated the guilt her absences made her feel. There's a difference.

The truth was, Anna didn't really value family in general. She was estranged from her own parents after years of fighting about how much she worked. She hated how much they tried to control her, and their open preference, in her view, for her older brother. She was hurt by their lack of regard for her accomplishments. As she told me in one office-hours session, "I have a *chosen* family in Washington. People I know from work mainly, people I trust. I don't believe 'blood is thicker than water,' like my mother says. That's old-fashioned. It's about control anyway."

The Bridge to Yourself, and Your Future

None of this meant Anna didn't love her daughter. She did, and she showed it in myriad ways. Fun vacations, a good and caring nanny, a beautiful home to live in, and, yes, time with her every day. But did Anna want to organize her life around her daughter as her top priority? The answer was no. She had other desires, mainly building her business and the wealth that came with that. She also placed a very high value on Scope, which showed up in her desire to travel and socialize. At the end of the day, Anna gave Familycentrism a 3, and she said when her daughter left for college, she would likely lower it to a 2.

You can agree with Anna or not, but you have to admire her candor. Family, and the role it plays in our life, is a loaded question if ever there was one.

So as you place yourself on this continuum, think twice, and then think again.

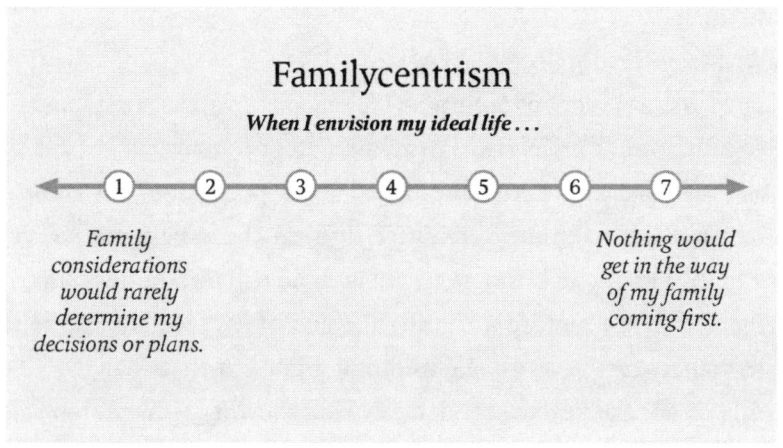

We come now to **Non Sibi**. That term is Latin for "not for self," and as a value it reflects **helping others** as a life-organizing principle.

Some existing academic constructs call this value "altruism." I went with the Latin term not to be different but to be less judgy. The term *altruism* is kind of virtuous by definition, isn't it? If it were a person, it would walk around with a halo over its head. But the point of Becoming

You is not to virtue signal, it's to know the truth about yourself so you can build your life accordingly.

Not surprisingly, lots of people say they want to help others. I mean, who doesn't say it? But a lot of times, helping others can be wildly performative. That's why after every major hurricane, we have Hollywood stars helicoptering in to pass around blankets and ladle out chili. It's why we have rock stars bringing out last-wish, wheelchair-bound fans at their concerts and singing to them on bended knee. God bless them. There is nothing wrong with such camera-ready acts of caring. I don't even care if they're from a real place or not.

But I do care about an authentic Non Sibi assessment when it comes to properly conducting the Becoming You process. Because in truth, not everyone wants helping others to define their *every* word and deed. They don't want helping others to define and drive their careers and personal time.

And then there are people like Jared.

Jared was a student of mine who had happily spent the first four years after college working in HR. Then, in an attempt to round out his skill base and make him better positioned for a promotion, his company moved him into a strategy role. He disliked the experience so much that he quit to attend business school with no real plan besides "making a pivot." When I met him, nearing the end of his second year, he still wasn't sure what he was going to do for a job, but that changed when, during all our class exercises, Non Sibi kept showing up as his top value. For instance, for his first Six Squared memoir, Jared wrote, "Looking for a Way to Elevate," a clever reference to both his work in HR, elevating others, and his journey to business school, elevating himself.

But the aha! came with his second memoir title: "And They All Said Thank You."

Explaining this memoir title to the class, he said, "I don't care what I do in life as long as I am an ally to as many people as possible."

Other exercises told much the same values story about Jared. In the

The Bridge to Yourself, and Your Future

Proustish Questionnaire, he wrote, "I know I'm never sad . . . when I'm helping someone." For the third question in Alpha Omega, "What would make you cry on your eighty-fifth birthday?" his answer was, "Knowing I could have helped someone and didn't."

"Have you ever considered a career in victim advocacy in the DA's office?" I once asked Jared. I was half joking, because that's not the kind of career most MBAs pursue.

His eyes lit up like lanterns. "Is that really a thing?" he asked me urgently.

Anyway, Jared is now happily back in Human Resources at a big company, where the efforts and passion of people like him are a tonic for the sort of cynicism that HR can attract these days. His title, appropriately, includes the words *Employee Care*. As it should for a person with a Non Sibi ranking of 7.

By contrast, I once had a private client named Katie. She was cool in her affect, and even a bit aloof, but her mind was brilliant. She was a serial entrepreneur currently serving as the CEO of her third company, and she described herself in our intake meeting as a "builder," a "visionary," and both "tireless" and "relentless." Everything I knew about her suggested she was right. You do not sell two companies at a profit before age thirty-two by slouching around.

Katie was seeking my help because a major tech company was trying to recruit her into a top executive role, and she was deeply conflicted. On the one hand, she loved the entrepreneurial experience and the wealth it had earned her, but on the other, she could see the benefits of working at a company with a strong infrastructure in place. Plus, she told me, the prestige of working for the tech company in question had its appeal.

In our sessions together, Katie and I spent a lot of time looking at all her values, but it was regarding Non Sibi where our conversation was the most complicated.

One of the things that Katie disliked the most about being an entrepreneur was that it often required her to hire, coach, and motivate people. She just didn't find those activities interesting, nor did they play to her analytical strengths. She lamented the "time suck" of managing a certain SVP at her current company. "She's just so needy," Katie sighed in exasperation. "I can't wait until the new COO comes and he can handle her."

"I think you're pretty low on Non Sibi," I told Katie, and I could see her grimace in her little Zoom box. As I said, no one ever wants to admit that helping people is not their bag. So to further (gently) make my case, I asked her if she volunteered for anything in her free time. "I read industry reports in my free time," she responded, laughing. When I asked her what organizations she belonged to in high school and college, she told me she had played volleyball and run the Finance Club. "No Girl Scouts?" I asked, and getting my drift, she laughed again and said, "Well, I *bought* a lot of cookies."

I don't want to paint Katie as some kind of ogre, because she was a decent person and certainly understood the importance of helping others. She just preferred to do so from a comfortable distance. She donated thousands of dollars a year to two causes she believed in. But when I asked her if she'd ever attended an event for either, the answer was, again, no.

All of this mattered to our Becoming You assessment because the corporate job beckoning Katie had a significant managerial component to it. Katie would be running a team of eight people directly, and thirty-six indirectly. Such a role doesn't demand a huge amount of Non Sibi, but it certainly requires *some*. Katie's ranking on this continuum? She gave herself, a bit sheepishly, an honest 2.

Later, when she passed on the corporate job, I was relieved. Katie's aptitudes and interests made her a great person to quickly conceptualize, operationalize, and sell companies. The people part, not so much. With all her values accounted for, we could see she was already in her Area of Transcendence, exactly where she was meant to be.

The Bridge to Yourself, and Your Future

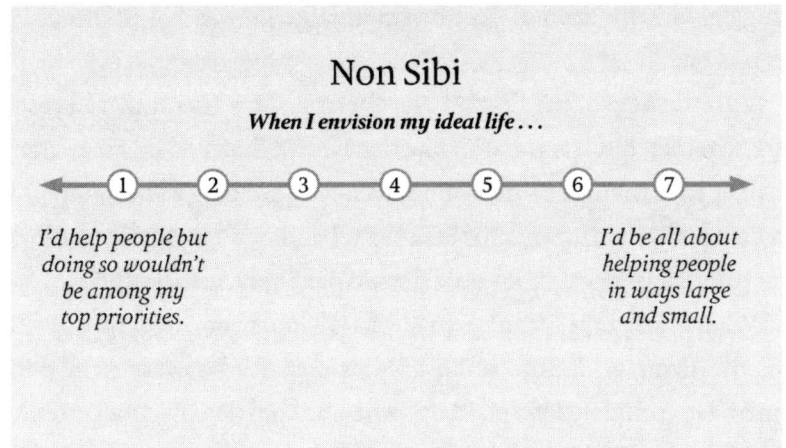

Luminance is a measure of **public recognition** as a life-organizing principle.

Bluntly, this value is about fame. Stardom. Celebrity. Call it what you will, but basically, the higher you are on the Luminance continuum, the more you desire to be a household name.

Perhaps not surprisingly, as with Non Sibi, people aren't particularly good at telling the truth about their Luminance quotient at first try. I think that's because we tend to villainize the desire for fame nearly as much as we tend to canonize the desire to help people.

I get it, but to repeat, that does not work if you want to conduct an authentic Becoming You analysis.

Greg was a private client who answered the Alpha Omega question "What would make you cry on your eighty-fifth birthday?" with a line that nearly made my jaw drop: "Knowing that my obituary wasn't going to be on the front page of the *New York Times*."

That is Luminance on steroids.

Now, in his defense, Greg was no stranger to celebrity. He came from a notable family, with well-known relatives in politics and media. He himself was headed in such a direction, too, with a job in the White House right out of college, but a few years into the role, Greg began to struggle with his mental health. Eventually, he was hospitalized with depression.

With the help of medication and therapy, Greg finally pieced his life back together, but it was hardly the one he had dreamed of. He lived in a small apartment in the same Upper East Side building as his mother. He was not really able to work for long stretches, but a family friend allowed him to conduct research for his firm and paid him a small stipend.

When I heard the "front page obituary" line from Greg, he was fifty-five and living a life that could only be described as very tightly contained. He considered it a good day when he completed a small errand or finished listening to a chapter of an audiobook. Depression is a terrible illness, and small victories such as these are no small matter. If Greg felt proud of them, and it seemed he did, he had every right to.

But the truth was, the chances of Greg's obituary on Page One were slim to none. I gently suggested as much to him, and I mean *gently*. My memory is that I phrased it as a question, as in, "And how might you reach that level of fame?"

Greg immediately caught my meaning.

"Just because you can't have something doesn't mean you can't want it," he said. "You can't just wish your values away."

He was not wrong. You can't wish a value away, but sometimes, if it is simply unattainable and holding on to it causes you angst, you should probably try. Over the past few years, Greg has been slowly working on just that.

"A *medium* Luminance-valuesholder" is the term that one of my workshop participants once used to describe herself. She was already on the way there, too, as a beauty influencer with about 150,000 followers on TikTok. Her goal, she told me, was to hit a half million. That would be enough. "One million is when you stop having any kind of privacy," she opined. "I want to be able to get the reservation at the Polo Bar, but also not have to put on makeup every time I leave the house." She ranked herself a 4, but later, taking the digital version of the Values Bridge, discovered her score was possibly a bit higher, a point she conceded might indeed be true. She is hardly alone. Several recent research studies suggest as many as 70 percent of Gen Zers want to be influencers when they grow up. If you think I am touching that data with a ten-foot pole, you would be wrong, except to repeat what I tell my own students: "I'm sorry, that's just not technically possible."

Of course, some people can and do attain the fame they long for. That was the case with another client, Barry, who ranked himself a robust 6 on Luminance. A celebrity divorce lawyer in Los Angeles, he was known to walk his clients down the red carpet. He loved the spotlight and made no secret of it. Luckily, for the sake of his career and life planning, Barry also had Scope at a 7, and his values around money and work were similarly aligned. As he told me once, "No one in my field gets famous without a strategy."

Please think of Barry's candor as you disclose your own Luminance ranking below.

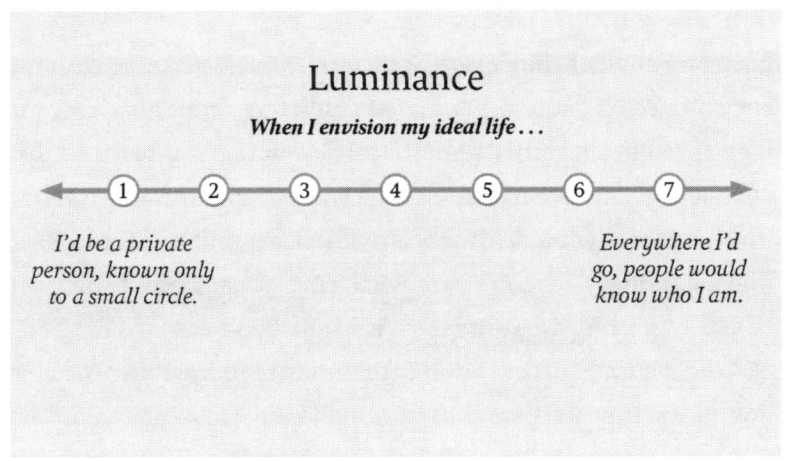

Agency is a measure of **self-determination** as a life-organizing principle.

I'm not going to name names, but I had an uncle who leaned over to me at my grandmother's funeral and asked how it felt to get into Harvard because I was a girl. Charming, right?

Sadly, this comment was not surprising at all, because this uncle had spent his entire life not just saying what he wanted, but more importantly for our discussion of Agency, *doing* what he wanted. He literally never worked for anyone but himself for more than two weeks, because the idea of taking "orders" from another person was anathema to him.

This uncle—and props to me for just laughing him off, albeit not cheerfully—was something of an extreme case of self-determination, and I can't tell you that worked out very well for him in life. But self-determination does work out well—indeed, very well—for many entrepreneurs, who tend to have a surfeit of this value.

Let's take Steve Jobs, whom I often use in lectures as the poster person for this value. I don't have to explain much, either—I just throw up a clip of the speech in which he says, "Your time is limited, so don't waste it living someone else's life. Don't be trapped by dogma—which is living with the results of other people's thinking. Don't let the noise of other's opinions drown out your own inner voice."

In other words, drive your own bus.

Entrepreneurs, of course, are not the only ones out there with high Agency. I once had a mild-mannered student, a former banking analyst, go through the entire semester of Becoming You to stand up at her final presentation with no slide deck to illustrate her AOT journey for the next forty years. This was a first in class, but we were all soon to understand why. "I don't care what kind of company I work at in my life, I don't care what industry it's in. I don't care if I'm head of marketing or run logistics. I don't care if my work is saving the world or not, or making a billion dollars or breaking even," she said. "All I care about is that I make the rules and no one tells me what to do."

Agency can present as a dominant value in some individuals, but this pronouncement felt a bit extreme, so I pushed back a bit. "Are you saying you're not particularly comfortable with consensus and collaboration—"

"Hate it!" she cut me off. "That's how bad ideas and mediocrity sneak through." She nodded for emphasis. "And don't call me a control freak. When I hear that, I know it's coming from someone just like me who isn't getting what they want."

Point made.

Agency, of course, can also show up at the other end of the continuum. I myself have never felt particularly driven to run every detail of every show, except for my son's wedding, and when I did indeed do that, EVERYONE LOVED IT, THANK YOU. But in general, I have always been a pretty big fan of compromise and "shared solutions," as the jargon goes, and if I ever hear myself saying how things *have* to be, I am given to stopping and apologizing for being a blowhard. I'm also kind of a company girl. I serve on boards; I play well with others in meetings. I dig collaboration! Then again, when I am sure I am 100 percent right and time is very short, I can take charge, and do. So all in all, that's why I gave myself a 3.5 on Agency.

Compare that to Zander, to whom Agency mattered not at all.

Zander was a client of mine who signed up to do the Becoming You process after being let go. He had worked for his former company, a podcasting platform, for nearly twelve years, starting as a sound engineer and rising through the ranks to oversee three shows from content conceptualization to guest selection, and all the way through marketing and promotion.

I cannot tell you that Zander loved his job, but he liked it. He enjoyed his colleagues, and he knew many of them very well. And while he wished he were paid more, he felt he was paid enough.

Before he was fired, Zander's job was to guide his programs to success. He needed to understand each show's competitors, form strategies to help them win, and, perhaps most important of all, motivate fourteen people to take the next hill alongside him. But the truth was, Zander didn't like telling anyone what to do. It felt awkward and wrong. Moreover, he just didn't care if things went right or wrong; in his view, life was filled with ups and downs, and luck had a lot to do with everything.

You might say Zander was a follower in a leader's job. In the lexicon of the Values Bridge, I would say he was a very low-Agency person in a high-Agency role. I'm not saying that running three podcasts demands someone who feels driven to act like a dictator, but every leadership role calls for some level of *outcome ownership*.

As a boss, you can't be at a 1 on the Agency scale, where I put Zander after getting to know him better. He argued he was a 2 at first, but then I reminded him of a quirky detail—the fact that he didn't like to drive, because it meant he was the only one holding the steering wheel.

"Oh yeah, that," he conceded.

Regardless, Zander didn't belong in a role where he had to run everything (or anything) because he ardently didn't want to. There's nothing wrong with that—again, values and jobs are a matter of fit. And where is he now? Happily, after a few weeks, and a few revelations about himself, Zander was able to make his case and get rehired by his old employer—as a sound engineer again. He controls a little tiny piece of the whole operation, and that's fine with him. He'd take less if he could.

As you rate yourself on this scale, then, think of how attached you are to things going exactly as you desire at all times. And not just at work—at everything. Who's driving?

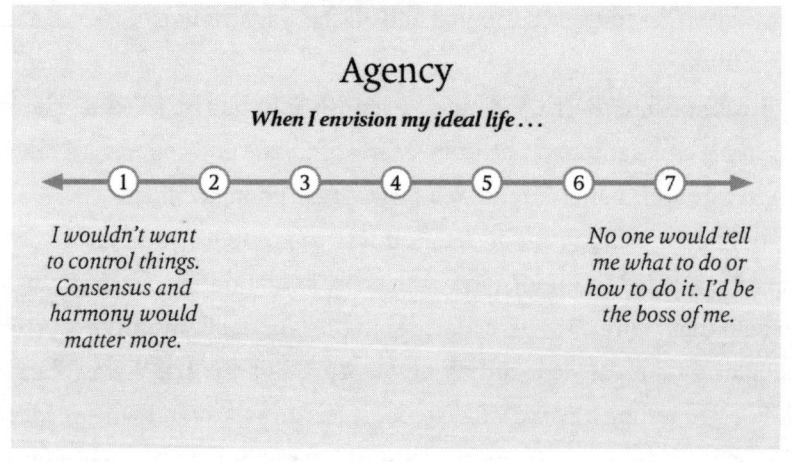

The Bridge to Yourself, and Your Future

Achievement is the measure of **seen success** as a life-organizing principle.

One year after all the fanfare about it, I finally started watching *The Bear*, which follows the travails of an award-winning chef, Carmy Berzatto, who returns home to Chicago to run his brother's run-down sandwich shop after his untimely death. The show is fraught with family trauma and drama, and substance abuse, and it has its fair share of characters living on the edge of a nervous breakdown.

Two episodes in, my daughter texted, "At last you're watching! Hooray! How are you liking it?"

"Terrible! Too intense," I tapped back.

"TOO INTENSE FOR YOU? WTF?"

"Maybe I'm getting old," I replied. "So much shouting."

"Keep going," my daughter wrote, "it's actually about you."

And so I watched another episode that night and then another and another, and what do you know, the show started to grow on me—a lot. There were many reasons, but my daughter was not wrong. I thoroughly identified with Carmy's compulsion to kill it on the big career scoreboard in the sky. To be seen by others for mastery in his chosen endeavor.

Carmy, welcome to the "7 on Achievement Club." It is not always a fun place to be, and like all values, it has its compromises and sacrifices. But if it's in you, it's in you.

To be clear, Achievement is different from Luminance. They can go together, and sometimes do, but Achievement is more about receiving respect from your community, however large or small, for being the freaking best at what you do. That word *seen* is especially important. I'm not talking about the inner satisfaction of killing a long solo run here. I am talking about outward validation, about getting a standing ovation in front of a crowd that matters to you. For instance, there is a moment in *The Bear* when Carmy reformulates every single dish on the menu, a massive task, given the meticulous work that had already gone into them all. His sous-chef comes upon this upending of things and is stunned almost into speechlessness. "What is going on here?" she finally manages to get out.

Carmy doesn't flinch. "Syd, we're going to get a star," he replies, referring to the vaunted Michelin rating system. He might just as easily have said, "We have to be the best because being the best makes me feel alive."

I so get that feeling. I too have thought, "Why do anything half-assed? Why not go for the glory while you can?" But, look, very seriously, I don't want to glorify Achievement. It's a value, not a virtue. The drive for seen success can cause you to deprioritize relationships or your health in harmful ways. It can make you behave in hypercompetitive ways. It can turn you into a hard-charging arse.

And it can lead you to miss things you shouldn't, like fun. Such was the very keen observation of George H. W. Bush, the forty-first president of the United States, right before he passed away in 2018. At that time, his granddaughter Jenna Bush Hager was a correspondent on NBC. She had a new marriage as well, and two young children, and her life was quickly turning into a messy, fraught, daily scramble of trying to be perfect at it all.

None of this was lost on Grandpa, as Jenna called him. One evening when she was visiting him, he leaned close to her on the living room couch. "He could barely speak," she recalled not long ago on the *Today Show* with tears in her voice. "But he said, 'Jenna, don't forget to enjoy the game.' And this . . . this was at the end of his life and the beginning of mine. But he saw what was happening."

I happened to catch this anecdote on-air when Jenna said it, and I literally had to sit down to pull it together. You couldn't extract the desire for Achievement from me with steel forceps, but even I know it has its trade-offs. Like realizing that you have worked 352 days straight, which has happened to me.

This is nothing to be proud of.

Thankfully, many people have a healthy relationship with Achievement; I can think of hundreds of examples, and more power to them!

The Bridge to Yourself, and Your Future

And still others have no relationship to this value at all. I've known Ryan and his wife, Jenny, socially for many years. When we first met through our children, both were working in high-powered jobs in Boston. She was an attorney with a corporate firm, and, with both an MBA and master's in engineering to his name, he was an SVP at an electronics company.

Somewhere along the way, though, I noticed Ryan was the one always showing up at the kids' soccer games. Then, his daily costume went from khakis and a button-down shirt to sweats and hoodies. Finally, it dawned on me he must not be working anymore, a fact confirmed when the couple's kids graduated high school and Ryan bought himself a tract of land in Wyoming to start homesteading there.

Don't worry about the marriage—it was fine and still is. Jenny is still working in Boston, expressing her Achievement value in full force, and Ryan has decided to, well, be himself. She flies out one long weekend a month.

For years, before Ryan went west, he had only pursued Achievement to please or impress other people. His parents. His MBA classmates. Remember Expectations, the third Horseman of Values Destruction? Ryan had been riding that pony right into misery. Until he jumped off.

But the truth was that Ryan didn't care about any of it. According to Jenny, he zoned out when performance reviews came around. He had no interest in getting promoted or managing people. He had zero concern about his title, the size of his office, or, frankly, the company's financial results. The whole idea of winning and losing struck him as wrong. She wasn't mad in the slightest; her love for her husband superseded any hopes she may have had regarding how he operated in the world. "He just wants to work with his hands, and he'd be satisfied if he could build a house for us to live in someday. I miss seeing him all the time, but he's never been happier."

My guess is that Ryan is, at most, a 2 on Achievement. It works for him. And, like all values, that's all that matters.

How about you?

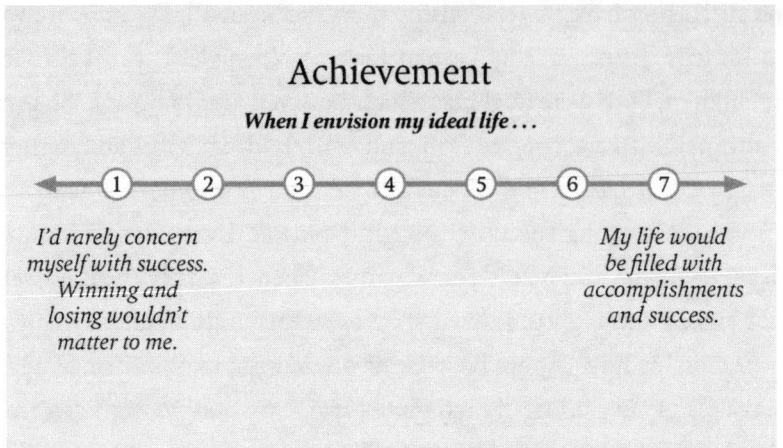

Workcentrism is the measure of, surprise, **work** as a life-organizing principle.

I'm sure you won't be surprised to hear that Workcentrism is the one value that, when most people think about their ideal lives, they say, "Less of this, please."

Even me!

Right now, I'd put my Workcentrism as very, very close to 7. I'm writing a book, after all, but more broadly speaking, my desire to work generally drives every decision and action. How much I see my granddaughter. How often I exercise. How many times a day I walk my dogs. How frequently I get into the garden or pottery studio. Work almost always comes first in my life. It's been that way for a long time, and I don't think it's going to change anytime soon. Right now, that's because I am trying to finish this tome. But to be honest, I just freaking love to work. I think it's fun and interesting. It's one of my most favorite things.

Perhaps as might be expected, many of my closest friends also skew high on this value. My dearest friend, Sue, who was struck by a life-threatening strain of viral encephalitis, as you might recall, was back on her computer, running her company, the day the doctors cleared her to look at a computer screen. A few weeks later, she FaceTimed me to report, "I am putting this incident behind me. It's over. It's history. They're telling me to slow down for a few months. It makes me want to *speed up*. I've got work to do. Everything else is boring."

Bernard and Phyllis were a married couple in their early fifties who were clients of my Becoming Us practice. They weren't exactly on the verge of divorce but definitely struggling enough to seek counseling. During our first session, I asked Phyllis my usual opener: What would success look like for you, if our time together was to be helpful?

"Bernard would be cured of his workaholism," was her sharp and immediate reply, prompting an equally immediate groan from her husband.

I already knew exactly what was going on with this duo, having seen it so many times before, but Bernard quickly confirmed it for me. He was a senior executive at GE and indeed had been there long enough to have met my husband, Jack, before he retired in 2001. Bernard's career had spanned numerous functions and countries and had been a pretty straight shot to the top. Phyllis had been happy to come along for the ride for decades, but with the couple's kids now in college, she was beginning to feel like a widow. "Bernard is married to GE," she said.

"I am," he agreed.

"I tell people, if Bernard could get the GE logo tattooed on his ass, he would," she added for good measure.

"Too afraid of needles, but if I wasn't, yes, I would," Bernard concurred.

"If that doesn't prove he's a workaholic, what else is there?" Phyllis asked me.

"I don't think it proves that at all," I told her bluntly. "All it proves is that he has a high value of Workcentrism."

Bernard took it from there, describing to both of us how much he loved his job. How fun and interesting he found it to be, how much it fulfilled him.

"I'm not sick, Phyllis," he said, "I like my work. I love it. Is that so horrible? It wasn't before."

I expected Phyllis to become defensive, but to my delight, the exact opposite occurred. "I never thought of it that way before. You value Workcentrism very highly, and for a long time, that was good for me, too. I loved raising the kids. But now your high value of Workcentrism is clashing with my empty nest!"

By the end of our first hour together, we agreed that it was a nonstarter to ask Bernard to relinquish a core value. It made much more sense for them to work together to figure out new pursuits for Phyllis that would allow her to live her own values in new and fulfilling ways.

Best of all (for me, at least) was Phyllis coming to see that high Workcentrism is not a disease. It's a value.

As is lower Workcentrism.

I once had a participant in a Becoming You intensive who was about sixty. As was the practice, she stood and introduced herself, and surprised us all with the line, "I've never worked a day in my life, and never plan to." She was taking the class, she told us, to get a better sense of how to spend her retirement, given the competing priorities of grandparenting, volunteering at her local library, and quilting. "I don't need to get a paycheck to feel fulfilled," she said.

Of course, there have always been individuals who have limited interest in work as a life-organizing principle, but Gen Z may be the first *generation* to talk about it with such robust conviction. For many of my undergraduates, Workcentrism is in the 4 to 5 range. I'll be honest, at first this phenomenon shocked me. I literally screamed *"What what what?"* in class the first time I heard one of them blithely use the term *funemployment* to describe the *intentional* taking of leisure time between jobs. Where I'm from, the time between jobs is for feeling terrified and frantic, and for doing everything in your power not to feel that way anymore, because you have a new job.

Kids these days!

But seriously, I get it—lower Workcentrism. I really do. Because the traditional contract between employers and employees is pretty broken. Putting work first doesn't guarantee money or upward mobility. You can give a company 100 percent of yourself for years and get axed in an email. Mergers, acquisitions, and bankruptcies routinely detonate pension agreements. Why bother?

Well, you might bother if you actually love the work. The joy it makes you feel, the excitement, the emotional and intellectual fulfillment. Or you might just love work in and of itself, enough even to get a tattoo testifying to the fact.

In sum—which I am saying to avoid the phrase "bottom line" here after that tattoo reference—there's no crime in any ranking on the Workcentrism scale. There's you, and what you want to do with your days and your life. Mark that values choice on the continuum below:

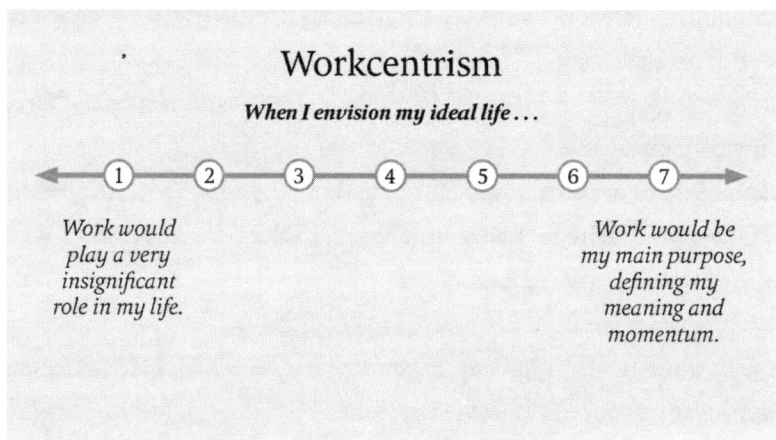

Affluence is the measure of **wealth** as a life-organizing principle.

At last, we've gotten to one of the most important, contentious, and fib-inducing values of them all: how rich you want to be.

One semester, I had a part-time MBA student named Jake who had built an impressive career at an executive search agency, rising to be the CEO's chief of staff, where he essentially ran strategy and HR. And yet, he was enrolled in Becoming You because he was dying to get out of the company and get on with his "real life." When I pressed him for details about what that life might look like, he mentioned a lot of international travel and the kind of success that would regularly land him on the front page of the *Wall Street Journal* for all the right reasons.

"Is this about money?" I probed.

Jake demurred. "Well, I want money, of course. I want financial security."

"Financial security is a very broad term," I pressed. "I mean, when trying to plan your life, to do so in any authentic and meaningful way, it really matters to be honest with yourself about the number that is enough for you."

"The number?" Jake visibly squirmed in his seat.

"You don't have to tell us the exact number," I assured him, "but how about this? Tell us if you want to fly to Europe on a first-class ticket or on a private jet."

"Definitely private," Jake exclaimed. "Private—and not on a charter, on my own plane."

I was just about to ask another question when Jake interrupted me.

"Okay, you want to know how much? Okay, I'll tell you. I want, like . . . I want . . . *ridiculous* money."

"Like a plane *and* a helicopter?" I asked him.

"Like a plane and a helicopter *for each kid*," he said. He was kind of laughing as he spoke, but not really.

I appreciated Jake so much at that moment! Not for his answer, per se, but for his raw honesty. I cannot tell you how many times I have done a Becoming You analysis with clients and students only to find out that the Area of Transcendence solution that we've come up with doesn't really work because, well, they hadn't been exactly forthcoming about how much wealth *really* mattered to them.

Of course, like every value, Affluence has its trade-offs. It's extremely hard to have your Affluence at 7 and your Familycentrism or Non Sibi up there, too. That's just not how life works. You don't usually accumulate "ridiculous money" by visiting your grandmother every weekend, attending PTA meetings, and volunteering in a soup kitchen every weekend. Similarly, it's extremely hard to have Affluence at a 6 or 7 and have Scope at a 1 or 2, or even a 3. And when it comes to dissonance with Affluence, we haven't even talked about the values of personal enjoyment, self-care, and God yet.

To get around its many trade-offs, some people place Affluence squarely at a 3.5 on the Values Bridge scale, which represents a comfortable life, with a bit of surplus. Wealth doesn't drive their lives, nor does the lack of it. I once had a student from Germany who broke the mold of most MBAs because his AOT report noted that he just needed enough money to rent an apartment near his work and go on one beach vacation a year. "I don't want money to own me," he explained to the class, which for many in the room was a new way of looking at it. "Having a rich lifestyle can become like a drug addiction," he said. "At a certain point, everything you do is about feeding it." To be clear, this student didn't aspire for a spartan life, just a simple one. But the only value that came in lower on his Values Bridge assessment was Luminance.

And then there are people like our homesteader, Ryan. When he decided to leave corporate America, his lifestyle with Jenny went from "got plenty" to "just getting by." The couple had four children, all teenagers. Their college tuition bills took a toll on just one salary, and yet all the trappings of wealth meant nothing to Ryan. (Luckily, they also had very little value to Jenny.) The family now lives very minimally, you might even say "austerely." They wouldn't use that word, though. Because for them, very little is enough. And with this value, the definition of enough is exactly what you have to figure out (and admit) for yourself.

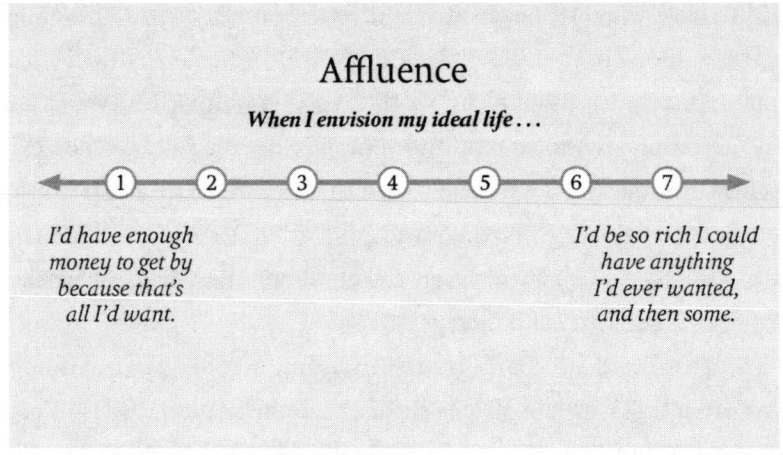

Eudemonia is the measure of **the pursuit of joy, fun, and/or well-being** as a life-organizing principle.

One year in Becoming You, I had a group of students all taking the course together. I could tell they were taking it together because the entire three-hour lecture each week was like their personal party time. Sitting in a cluster, they would cheerfully debate concepts among themselves in stage whispers while I was speaking, cheer whenever a member of the group raised their hand to make a comment, and during class exercises, when I broke students into groups, I would watch them and wonder to myself, *Good Lord, how could it possibly be that much of a hootenanny to figure out your values?*

Well, it can be when your top value happens to be Eudemonia.

You may be wondering why this value is not just called "fun," and the reason is, it's bigger than that. Eudemonia is the ancient Greek word for well-being, happiness, and good spirits. It describes the state of pleasure we get when we are taking care of ourselves, doing what makes us feel good emotionally or otherwise, or living life abundantly in the way we choose. We can experience Eudemonia reading a book by a crackling fire or attending a rave. It can come in the form of a massage or participation in a tennis tournament. You can find it by going for a run, knitting, baking brownies, or taking a long nap. The specifics here don't matter; Eudemonia simply comprises the things that hold *intrinsic pleasure* to you.

Based on nothing but experience and observation, I would make the case that Eudemonia has cultural and generational components to it. This value seems to come naturally to Italians, for instance, and if you've ever done business in Italy as an American (as I have), you need to adjust your expectations about how quickly things happen. This is not good or bad; it just is. Also important: Not being offended when your Italian business partners go on a two-week vacation in the middle of a deal, and then extend their trip a week because the weather in Sardinia is so nice and another friend showed up. The same kind of cultural differences around Eudemonia can even show up between American cities. Just ask anyone who has lived in both New Orleans and, say, Cleveland.

As for generational differences, I am reminded of the time when I spoke to a group of MBAs at another business school. When I was done speechifying not just on career advice but on AI and other economic megatrends, the professor said, "You can ask Professor Welch anything!"

The first question, and the second and the third, were versions of "What do you do for self-care?"

I simply did not know how to answer. I am about a 2 on Eudemonia, and always have been, and Gen Z, to make a grand generalization, is about a 12. I have, in fact, taught sections of forty students where the Values Bridge assessment tool has shown that fully half have Eudemonia as their top value. Indeed, just this week, a student in this category presented her AOT journey, which featured a series of 9-to-5 government jobs punctuated by leisurely vacations around the world. "Nothing is getting in the way of my inner peace," she said to explain her decision not to pursue a job in business. If you are wondering how this student planned to pay for everything, please note that Affluence was a peripheral value for her. Good thing, that.

Please don't get the idea, though, that the generational differential when it comes to Eudemonia annoys or irritates me. Rather, it mystifies me. And, as with Workcentrism, sometimes it even makes me think, *If they are all correct, I have been very wrong about how life works. I hope I don't wake up and discover that someday.*

On another note, sometimes—and definitely not in class—I refer to Eudemonia as the "divorce value," because when partners differ vastly on the relative importance of personal enjoyment, it can be a serious problem. Of course, the opposite is true. I know a couple who has survived painful infidelities by both partners, along with bankruptcy and challenges with alcohol, because, at the end of the day, they both ranked Eudemonia a 7. When the going got tough, they went for a sail, or went dancing, or (once) went backpacking in Ireland. Their shared value of having fun—and the same kind of fun, no less—saved them again and again.

Like people, companies also can place a relative value on Eudemonia. In start-ups, this can be a reflection of the founder's personality, but even big corporations have their "play" and "self-care" quotients. This is yet another reason why it's so critical to know what your own Eudemonia ranking is. To avoid a career-impacting mismatch.

That's exactly what happened to Anthony, an acquaintance of mine in college. I never knew him very well, but he was a legend on campus. His natural intelligence allowed him to skate through classes, devoting all his time (or so it seemed) to the pursuit of merrymaking. Not only was he at every party you wanted to attend, he *was* the party. I was a wonky nerd who lived in corduroys and flannel shirts and so was never invited to many parties at Harvard anyway, but I remember hearing about one famous Anthony fete, and snarking to a roommate, "Maybe he'll grow up to be a wedding planner."

Well, of course Anthony went directly to Wall Street, where, in those days, party people found great success selling financial instruments. For years, or so I heard, he raked in gobs of money mainly for taking corporate stiffs out to dinners and clubs on someone else's dime, and the more effed-up people got, the better he was doing his job. You might call this perfect synchronicity between a high-Eudemonia individual and a high-Eudemonia job description.

Then came 2008.

Like half of Wall Street, Anthony was suddenly out of a job, and the pursuit of happiness in all its forms was replaced by the pursuit of survival. In time, of course, Wall Street revived, and Anthony returned to a sales job at a shell-shocked company that now had approximately zero tolerance for big spending. His term there lasted less than a year. Eventually, Anthony moved to France, where I have heard he runs a swanky club near Cannes. He may have left America, but his Eudemonia went with him, and so it does with all of us, no matter what level we may be.

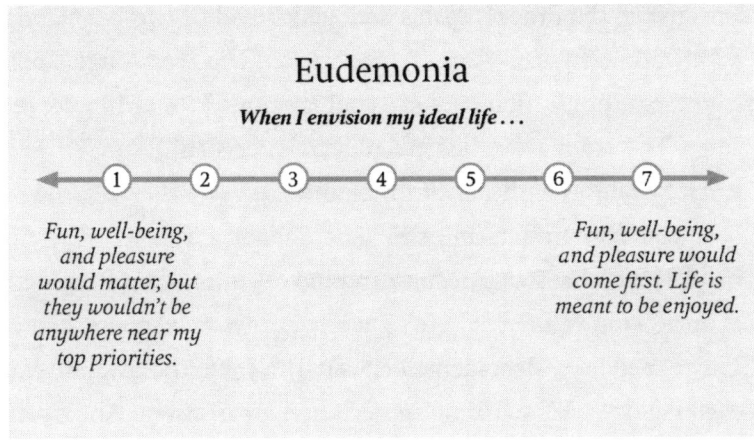

We have come to **Beholderism**, the measure of **appearances** as a life-organizing principle—both how things appear to you, and how you appear to others.

AD subscribers unite! That's *AD* as in *Architectural Digest*, the bible of many people who score particularly high on this value. Like Vivaan, for instance, the interior designer whom we met in Chapter 4, and whom I fondly call "my fellow wallpaper fanatic," for our shared love of wall coverings, especially those made by the House of Scalamandré.

I am fighting off an enthralling wallpaper tangent here. I will stay strong.

Because as a person who is somewhat off the charts on Beholderism, I will admit that how stuff looks is super important to me. I will walk into any room in my home and immediately notice whether a coaster is out of place. But what would bother me more would be if a bouquet of flowers was not exactly vibing with the pillow fabrics. That would be deeply disturbing to my feng shui–ometer. All this makes me a perfect match for my friend Pieter Estersohn, the renowned photographer of architectural interiors and a discerning aesthete if ever there was one. When we go out to play, it is usually to an art opening, like a recent Thierry Mugler retrospective at the Brooklyn Museum, which had us two Beholderism-ites practically levitating from appreciation. "The way Mugler played with structure, proportion, and material is genius," I recall Pieter rhapsodizing. "This is a master class in sculptural precision!"

"What he said!" I enthusiastically agreed.

Look, you may find caring this much about aesthetics superficial, and maybe it is. That's why people can kind of wince when Beholderism shows up as a top value. But here's my very academic response: Get over it! In my experience, Beholderism is usually a profound love of art and those who make it. It's a visceral appreciation for creativity. And, further, it is often a proxy for how much we care (or don't) about harmony and orderliness in our personal environment, which can feel like the only piece of the world we can control. Thus, our attention to aesthetics matters, and can matter a lot, when it comes to life choices about work and life. High-Beholderism people, for instance, can eschew chaotic work settings even if the work itself is right. Or they can avoid relationships that are messy, because messiness, by definition, is unaesthetic. Beholderists (new word!) seek beauty writ large.

As noted, Beholderism is not just about how things look. It's about how we ourselves look and sometimes, by extension, how our family and friends do, too.

The Bridge to Yourself, and Your Future

Remember Tachi, the student I wrote about in the introduction? Following his parents' wishes, he had dutifully pursued a career in finance all the way until the moment when he could no longer, which was when the Becoming You process impelled him to blow everything up to design clothing for Kim Kardashian, or at least *try* to.

As with most people in fashion design, Tachi's score on Beholderism was likely very high. (He took Becoming You before I completed designing the Values Bridge assessment, so there is no way of knowing for sure.) But something he said will always stay with me. "The worst thing about banking was that I couldn't wear what I wanted, and I was basically *forced to live without style*." He said these words the same way someone crawling across the desert might say, "I was forced to live without water."

I hope Tachi is drenched in style now, and living his Beholderism to the hilt.

You can also get a great big eyeful of Beholderism in action at the gym. Or on the streets of Paris or Milan—anywhere, really, that people are demonstrating that they believe that looking good is inherently a good thing. Now, it is certainly true that some people work out for their health, which *technically* falls under Eudemonia. But whenever people spend more than typical levels of time and money on personal, well, *fineness*, you know you are beholding Beholderism. And to quote the famous old shampoo add, "Don't hate them because they're beautiful."

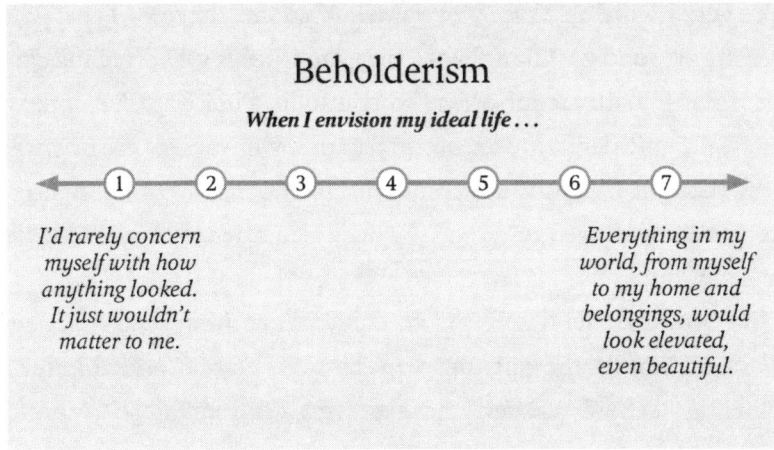

Voice is the measure of **creative self-expression** as a life-organizing principle.

"Why would I watch TikTok? Isn't it just people dancing?"

This was the question put to me by a CEO whom I advise. A bunch of us—myself, the CEO, and his top team—were taking a lunch break between meetings when someone mentioned a hilarious meme that was going around the platform. That launched the usual "Oh, did you see the one . . . ?" chatter. It turned out we were all happy doomscrollers.

Except the CEO. He shook his head at us in deep dismay. "Why do I need to see people dancing—*terribly*—in their living rooms?" he groaned. "Who does that stuff anyway?"

Funny you should ask. Anyone who values creative self-expression does.

One of the smartest women I have ever known was an architecture major at Yale. On the weekends, she and her very artsy-fartsy friends would gather outside Sterling Memorial Library and pantomime vacuuming the air in slow motion. Some fellow students, appreciating this display of creative self-expression—Voice—in all its divine weirdness, would stop and applaud. Other fellow students would walk by in mild disgust or simple confusion. They just didn't get the desire, the yearning, the drive, to let one's freak flag fly.

Almost by definition, artists (and writers, for that matter) tend to score very highly on Voice as a value. Of course they do. Their whole lives are devoted to taking what they are thinking and feeling *inside* and placing it *outside* for others to consume. Rupi Kaur has amassed almost 4.5 million followers on Instagram by documenting her nearly every thought in haunting, epigrammatic poems. "For me poetry is like breathing. I need to do it," she once told *Harper's Bazaar*. "It's the way I am."

But professionals like Rupi, who's had three *New York Times* bestsellers, are hardly the only people with high Voice scores. I know an elementary school teacher who expresses her individuality through her nail art; a vegan activist in Texas who does the same through her tattoos; and a heart surgeon who paints all weekend long, because he feels "silenced" in the OR. People with a passion for social justice also often score very high on Voice, and although their "output" isn't always technically creative, they want and need to be heard for who they are, how they feel, what they believe, and often, how they are unique.

By contrast, people who score lower on the Voice spectrum have less comfort, need, or desire around standing out. At the very lowest end of the spectrum, you would even find people who vastly prefer to fit in to society or a group and will happily sacrifice their own individuality to that end. Indeed, such a penchant brings us to one of our last values, Belonging. But first:

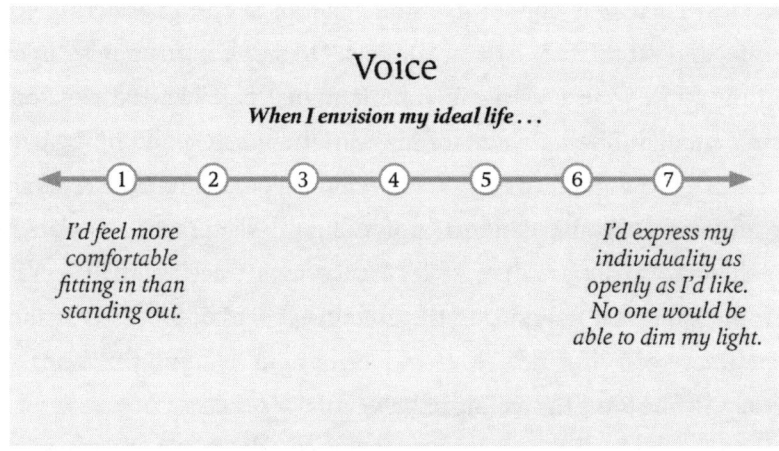

Belonging is the measure of **connectivity** as a life-organizing principle.

I'm convinced there are three types of high school graduates: the ones who never attend a reunion, the ones who show up every five or ten years, and the ones who organize them.

Yes, hi, we're talking about low, medium, and high levels of Belonging, the value that reflects how much of a joiner and stayer you tend to be in life. Or put another way, how much being part of a group of some kind—any kind—calls you and fulfills you.

Consider these three classic hallmarks of people with high levels of Belonging. First, they have lots of friends and/or friend groups. If someone tells you they have eleven weddings in one year, and they're traveling out of the country for six of them, you're seeing a high-Belonging person in full bloom. If someone walks through the halls of your company and appears to know everyone personally, that's typically evidence of high-Belonging. If that same person seems to be on every company committee and shows up at, say, every company volunteer outing, more evidence still.

Second, people high on the Belonging continuum tend to join lots of clubs or organizations, or are extremely devoted to a few of them, or both. Tony, for instance, landed at NYU and immediately joined six clubs. There was one for investors, one for people considering consulting, and yet another one for runners. He didn't want to miss an opportunity to connect with everyone humanly possible; the classroom wasn't enough. Similarly, one of my team members could be crowned "Mrs. YPO America." (By YPO, I'm referring to the Young Presidents' Organization, an international professional development association.) She shows up at almost all of YPO's local events, travels abroad on YPO learning trips, and now sits on the executive board of her YPO branch, sometimes requiring her to attend eight-hour planning sessions on weekends. She loves the feeling of being part of a cadre.

Finally, people who score high on Belonging also tend to feel relatively comfortable operating within institutions, like companies or religious organizations. It's not that they don't see the flaws and idiosyncrasies endemic to such communities. The bureaucracy, the in-fighting, the politics. But they have a higher tolerance for them than most, seeing them as a small price to pay for the joy of belonging to something larger than yourself.

I'm sure from these hallmarks you can infer the profile of people who tend to fall lower on the Belonging continuum. They often prefer having fewer and perhaps deeper relationships; at the very end of the spectrum, you'll find those who want to connect only with their spouse or family. These people tend to enjoy activities of their own design over organized ones. And institutions? Those who rank themselves a 3 on Belonging might tell you, "They make me a little skeptical." At a 1, you'll hear a version of "I don't trust the man."

Every time someone is struggling with where they fall on the Belonging continuum, I tell them the story of Willow, who was a neighbor's daughter. For years, I watched Willow do everything in her power to define herself in contrast to her very straitlaced, conservative family, albeit always within limits. She wore a lot of makeup and very flamboyant outfits, and once she could drive herself to the pharmacy, she changed her hair color weekly. But her parents were rarely mad at her because Willow was, in a word, delightful. Other words for her: hilarious, outspoken, and utterly original.

Perhaps because she had been homeschooled, Willow was dying to get to college and immerse herself in all the classic college experiences, like Greek life. I have to admit, it was a little hard for me to imagine nonconformist Willow embedded in a sorority; nonetheless, I was happy for her when her mom texted me to say that was just what happened. "Willow was their top pick, and she's over the moon," she reported. Come spring break, however, Willow was home with another story, having been unceremoniously asked to exit the sisterhood. When she stopped by to say hi one day, I asked her what had happened.

"Mrs. Welch," she reported, "the bitches are real."

That is low Belonging speaking loud and clear! People like Willow, with Voice and Agency at stun and Belonging on mute, rarely belong to anything for long, of their own volition or not.

In the discussion of Eudemonia a few pages back, I mentioned that company cultures can also fall on any given value continuum, and Belonging is another example. Some company cultures encourage employees to socialize and make it easy to do so, or they reward collaboration and in-person meetings in very clear ways. Those would be signs of high Belonging. Other companies put such an emphasis on individual performance that they actually discourage fraternization, for lack of a better word. I'm not going to opine on which approach is better or worse—okay, fine, I prefer the former—but my main point is: Woe to the person who places a high value on Belonging but works at a low-Belonging company.

Now, I do not want to go overboard here in being a Belonging advocate.

People who are low on Belonging are hardly friendless loners. Willow, for instance, had lots of friends, most of them individualists like herself, united by valuing some things more than being part of a community.

The call is entirely yours to make.

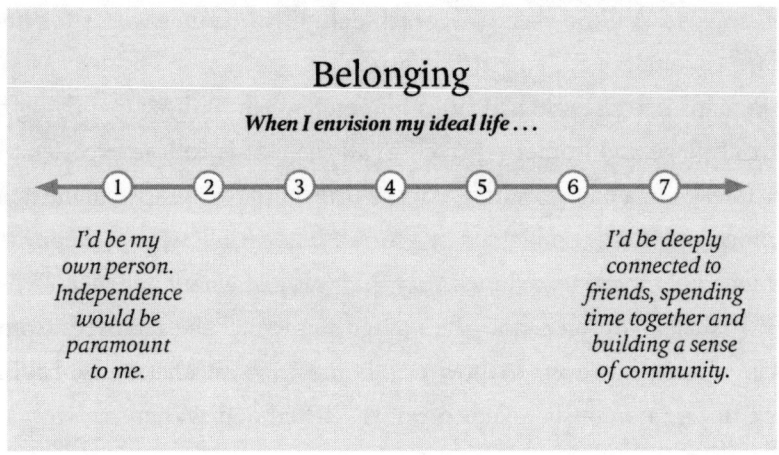

Place is a measure of **location** as a life-organizing principle.

A few years ago, I worked closely with a student named Nelson to create a terrific Area of Transcendence analysis. Not only did Nelson pour his heart and soul into every class exercise, but left no homework stone unturned. And then there were multiple visits to my office. Finally, as we worked together, a seemingly perfect synthesis of Nelson's values, aptitudes, and economically viable interests emerged. He was going to pursue a career in Major League Baseball (MLB) as a data analytics specialist.

There was just one problem. Nelson had neglected to mention along the way that he had one nonnegotiable. He had to live in Indianapolis, where his wife's family was ensconced. He'd promised her.

Say what?

It is hard enough to get a job with the MLB. But to try to get a job with the MLB in a city that does not have an MLB team is . . . not happening.

"Why didn't you mention Indianapolis before?" I asked Nelson with not a little frustration, pondering the hours I would never get back because he hadn't.

"It didn't occur to me where you want to live is a *value*," he replied.

"Of course it is! Obviously!" I said in my defense. But he was right, I had never said that to my students.

I say it now and, as you can see, include it in the Values Bridge.

If you have to live in one place, a *specific* place—be it Indianapolis, Houston, Munich, the Bay Area, or, say, near the mountains or by the sea, rank yourself high on Place. Rank yourself low if you don't care one iota where you live because so many other things matter more, like, say, Radius, Achievement, or Scope.

Just make sure that as you plan your life, you don't forget the one value that has the potential to drive everything: location, location, location.

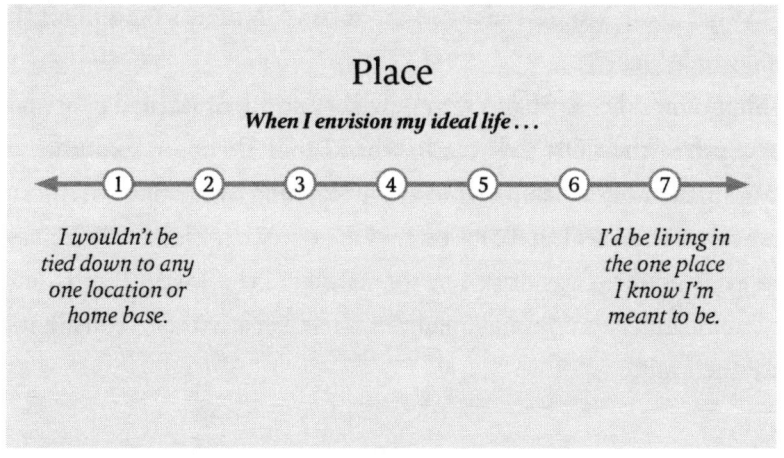

Cosmos is a measure of one's **faith tradition** as a life-organizing principle.

We end our survey of the Values Bridge with the value that almost got away. It can be complicated to talk to students and clients—or anyone—about God. In fact, as a professor, I'm supposed to keep God out of the classroom entirely, and I adhere to that rule, except that sometimes I mention something I heard in church, or something my pastor told me, or oops, how much I love a certain verse from the Bible. But even then, I make sure I bracket my comments by saying something like, "I am fully accepting of any kind of faith system or lack of one entirely," which is the truth. Because my faith system instructs me not to judge anyone but myself.

I don't want to be disingenuous, though. We live in a world where faith has been politicized and weaponized, and frankly, sometimes I do fear being canceled by someone misconstruing my personal beliefs as a directive of any kind.

That is why in early versions of the Values Bridge, I left faith out entirely. Even though it is my own, personal top value. Yep.

But then I started testing the Values Bridge in small groups, one of which was forty former students who came to my house for pizza and agreed to give me the most candid feedback they could muster. It was during one such session that Sharon spoke up.

"What about God?" she asked me softly. "Where is God in all this, Professor Welch?"

Sharon and her husband were Jewish, and I had learned a lot about the depth of their Orthodox faith when I took them out to dinner as a thank-you for her amazing work as my teaching assistant one semester. It was over this meal that Sharon told me every decision in their lives—and every action—was driven by their study of the Talmud, and almost no important decision was made in their lives without consultation with their rabbi.

When Sharon raised her question about the Values Bridge, I will admit, I didn't have a great answer for her.

"I guess my thinking was that your faith would drive all your other values?" I suggested. "Like it would supersede and define all your values?"

"Hmm," she said.

Hmm, I thought.

In the weeks that followed, I reviewed other values rubrics "in the literature," as academics put it, and discovered that few included faith. The Schwartz Value Inventory, for instance, does not, and neither do most popular values tests you can find on the vast internet.

And yet, every single survey of Americans and faith will show you that the majority of people not only believe in God, they try to live according to a faith system. Some studies put this number as high as 70 percent, others closer to 40 percent. Regardless, that's a lot of people.

And so, I decided to add Cosmos, the Greek word for "perfect order," which is the embodiment of the "higher power" in every religion that I know of.

As you think of where you fall on this continuum, please know that your specific faith system does not matter to me, or the test. For the purposes of Becoming You, and the life you are seeking to build, the only thing that matters is how much your faith, like any value, matters to you.

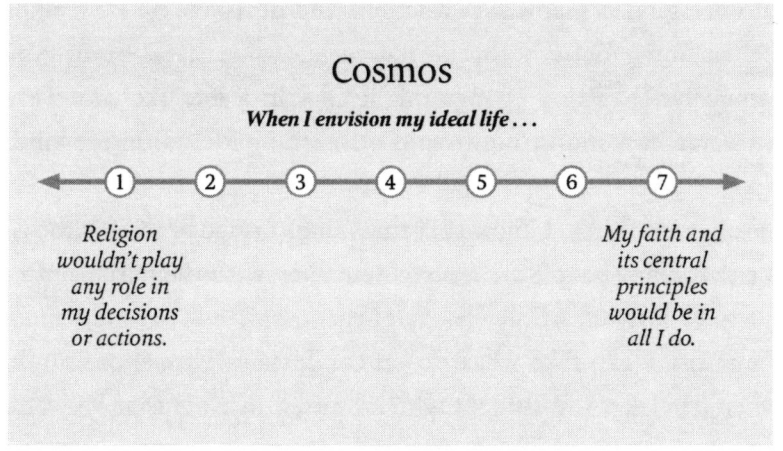

We've come to the end of our exploration of the fifteen values in the Becoming You typology.

That was a lot, right? I get it. Values are a lot.

When we finally sort them out, and see them with clarity, it can be like looking at ourselves in the mirror for the first time.

That can be a wonderful, powerful moment—if you love everything you see. It can be a thunderbolt of happy recognition, as in, "That's who I am! That explains everything! I can't wait to share this news with everyone!"

But.

But more often, seeing your values profile for the first time is complicated. You can, for instance, suddenly comprehend the outsized importance of one value in your life, and you might think something like, *Woah, I knew I cared about Achievement, but not that much. No wonder I keep dropping the ball at home.* Or your thoughts might go to a quandary or conflict at work. *I've been hating on my new manager for being so pushy with me, but maybe I'm just really low on Belonging and the company is really high.* Or you might realize at last, with a Luminance ranking of 7, why you spend so much time on your social media.

Because values are dynamic, we might also discover that a value that once guided many of our actions and decisions no longer holds much meaning for us, or that we have a new value that has only grown in importance. Either change might explain a lot, like why we are drifting apart from certain friends or yearning for a different kind of work.

From experience, I know that the Values Bridge process is the first time that many people are nudged to reckon with their true, authentic expressions of Affluence, Familycentrism, and Agency, among others, and it can take a beat to get comfortable with those eurekas. Remember Jake, the student who admitted in class that he wanted

The Bridge to Yourself, and Your Future

"ridiculous" money? I saw him in office hours more than once after that, as he grappled to reconcile that value, newly unveiled to him, with the narrative he had been telling his longtime boss about why he was leaving the field of executive search. "I kept telling him—and everyone, including myself—that it was about needing to be an entrepreneur," he said. "But the truth is, I don't have an idea for a company, and I actually love search. I love the fun of the work, the meaning of it." His face clouded with dismay. "But it will never pay me what I want and need.

"I have to figure that out," he said.

"You do," I agreed. "To get to where you're meant to be, to your purpose, to that place where you'll flourish."

After all, the Values Bridge is—like all of Becoming You—a *bridge*. Even, if you may recall where we started, a bridge over troubled water.

It shows us our values in the moment, but it also points us toward which values we want more or less of.

When Tony worked through the Values Bridge, for example, his Familycentrism was at a 7. That didn't surprise either of us, but we had a simultaneous uh-oh when he ranked Agency just as high.

"That's your problem in a nutshell," I sighed. "You love your dad, and you hate your dad—for telling you what to do. That's in direct conflict with your value of Agency, I'm afraid."

He nodded solemnly. But we both also knew my analysis was the easy part.

For Tony, and for you, the hard part is what to do next: figuring out how to build that bridge to the future.

It might be a short little foot passage—like a plank of plywood thrown over a stream.

Or it might require a massive construction project like the Golden Gate Bridge, which took 1,604 days to build.

It's beautiful, too, isn't it? Now that it's done.

With values, though, the truth is, we are never done, because we are human, and if we're lucky, we're always growing. My favorite quote of all time is from a letter Emily Dickinson wrote in 1874. "We turn not older with the years," she wrote, "but newer every day."

Oh Lord, I hope so!

If that is the goal, then I will venture to say I know one good way there. It is our journey to our values and ourselves.

6

The One and Only Tony

If you recall, Tony took my Becoming You class on a lark, because he already knew what he wanted to do with his life. Or more precisely, he knew what he didn't want to do: work with his father. He'd been there, done that. A nice, unmessy job in consulting awaited him.

But to his credit, Tony still threw himself into the entire Becoming You values-excavation process, culminating, as I just mentioned, in the collision course between Familycentrism and Agency.

We could have seen it coming.

First, there was Tony's Six-Squared exercise. His original Six Word Memoir read, "Family Forever, Until I Couldn't Anymore." His second told a different story: "We All Lived Happily Ever After." In class, another student commented, "It sounds like a fairy tale," to which Tony replied, "Professor Welch said we should write the book as if our perfect life came true."

Then came the Whose Life chart, which Tony was able to fill out with more ease than practically anyone in class. And when he was done, his patterns popped off the page. Every single entrant was an entrepreneur. Tony explained his pattern as such: "Builders of legacy businesses, inventors, did it their way, bought themselves total freedom." As for the "Um, no thank you," column, on practically every person, Tony wrote, "No family," or "Broken family."

Tony's Proustish Questionnaire and Alpha Omega answers kept the wave coming. His idea of perfect happiness: *Sundays with family, eating dinner together, watching the kids play, talking shop.* His mantra: *If you want it done right, do it yourself.* His eighty-fifth birthday regret: *Alone.*

Along with Familycentrism, Affluence, and Agency at 7, Tony's notable Values Bridge results showed Achievement and Place at 6, and Workcentrism and Belonging at 5. Radius and Scope had no particular appeal for him, showing up around 2, and the other values clustered around 3 and 4.

By the end of the semester, Tony seemed like the least "lark-y" student I'd ever had.

"This has been seriously enlightening," he told me once, and not very happily. He'd come to realize that management consulting, with its constant travel and itinerant dipping in and out of different industries, would have been a detour of notable proportions. Maybe it would have met *some* of his values to *some* degree, but not with the same intensity and fit as a family-friendly, entrepreneurial, New Jersey–based, appliance-focused business would.

When it came time to present his Area of Transcendence project, Tony started by joking, "I knew I should have never taken this class."

When the laughter died down, he explained, "I have to go home soon and do something I never wanted to do, and I'm going to hate doing, and which I dread with every cell in my body."

He was talking about apologizing to his father for his part in their falling-out.

"I didn't respect my dad enough for the courage and perseverance it took to build our family business," he told the class. "Even though I want to blow it up someday, and make it something better and new for the future, I should have started by thanking him for making it possible, and for what he taught me along the way."

Tony then went on to describe the next forty years of his life and career. He would go back to the store and work for his father for two years, slowly re-earning his trust. Then, he would gently try to persuade him to start acquiring other local appliance stores, to achieve the economies of scale needed to take the business to the next level. In time, his narrative went, the entire business would go online. Within twenty years, he estimated, his family's company could come to reinvent and dominate the highly fragmented appliance installation industry in North America.

At the same time, Tony described his family with Gennie growing to four kids. His final slide was an AI depiction of an extended family gathering, on vacation together in Italy.

After the class gave Tony a huge round of applause, I asked him if he'd told his dad of his plans yet.

"Oh no, no!" he exclaimed. "I have to do consulting for a year or two first, just to learn some stuff."

There are still students who remember me shouting, "Nooooooooo!"

But here's the thing. I cannot control anyone who goes through the Becoming You process, nor do I desire to. I mean, I start the darn class by saying, "Becoming You is not a prescription; it is a tool. It's a tool I hope you use for the rest of your life, as you follow your journey, and fall off of it, and get back on."

Even with all his insights, Tony still felt the need to do a stint in consulting. I suspect the Horseman of Economic Security was involved. And the value of Achievement. On any business school campus, you can't do much better than saying, "I'm going to McKinsey."

And so, Tony graduated and went off to consulting with my warm regards. That spring, I received a wonderful note from him announcing the arrival of yet another Tony, who was a cutie. I did not ask him how consulting was going because that would have been obnoxious. I figured I'd be hearing from him in about a year when he couldn't take the PowerPoints and client travel anymore.

He beat my estimate by four months. One morning, I opened my computer to see an email with the subject line: "You can officially say 'I told you so.'"

I wrote back, "I TOLD YOU SO." Mature, right?

Tony has been back working with his father for almost a year now. Ahead of schedule, they have already acquired one appliance store, and are in talks to acquire two others. There have been good days and bad as they work out their differences. His father has not miraculously transformed into a digital convert or a risk-taker, and change is still among his least favorite things.

But Little Tony—Becoming You's Tony—is committed to his plan, because he believes that, with its values infrastructure, it will build the life he truly wants.

Values are like that. They inform us; they warn us; they guide us; they lead us.

Incidentally, Tony has a new title now, just like his dad.

In fact, it was his dad's idea: Co-CEO.

Part II
Aptitudes

7

Chloe and the Tao of Aptitudes

As we open our investigation of **Aptitudes**, let's bid farewell to Tony and his values-discovery journey, and meet Chloe, who could be a mascot for the second part of the Becoming You process.

Because Chloe considered herself competent at many things in life, but not particularly good at *anything*. "Sometimes I hear people talk about their 'superpowers,'" she said to me once, sighing, "and I was like, I'd be happy just knowing my *mini*-powers."

We *all* need to know *all* of our "powers." Or at least we do if we want to figure out our Area of Transcendence. Gathering that information is precisely what this section of Becoming You is about.

First, we'll talk about what aptitudes are and aren't, an area often as murky as the definition of values. Let's clear that up; it matters.

Next, we'll explore how your brain works in eight key cognitive dimensions, and what that information could mean for your career choices. As a heads-up, those dimensions are: Time Frame Orientation, Work Approach, Visual Comparison Speed, Inductive Reasoning, Sequential Reasoning, Spatial Visualization, Idea Generation, and Numerical Reasoning.

Finally, we'll talk about personality, and specifically, the four personality traits that I believe have the strongest implications for what you can and should do with your career. I hate to bury you in lists here, but they are: Nerve, Soundness, Elasticity, and Wonderment. You might notice that the first letters of those terms correspond to the four directions of North, South, East, and West, and indeed, I call this personality mental map the Career Trait Compass. My hope is it will be one more guide for you, and a powerful one, on your Becoming You journey, just as it was for Chloe.

Growing up in the Boston-suburb part of New Hampshire, Chloe was the youngest of three. Her parents worked in tech, and her family was comfortable but by no means well-to-do. She would call her childhood happy, even "normal." She did okay in school and made friends easily. She had a sweet and somewhat goofy personality, and many found her quirky, but in an endearing way.

As time went on, Chloe's two older brothers went off to respected universities, but Chloe never did very well on standardized tests. Ultimately, she ended up going to a small private college. She majored in English, then switched to history. Then she spent a semester trying to major in computer science, but that tanked her grades, so she switched into Classics, where she threw herself into the study of Latin and ancient Greek. The fact that she was becoming fluent in two dead languages was lost on no one, and before senior year, Chloe announced she was going to take a year off.

"Chloe's like a cloud," her mother told me at the time. We were friends, she and I, going back to our own high school days. "She floats through life. I don't know what will become of her. But something will. Everyone finds their place eventually; maybe it will just take her more time."

Although we did not discuss it that day, we both knew that there was a complicating factor in the situation, and that was Chloe's health. Starting in her senior year in high school, Chloe had struggled with persistent headaches and exhaustion. Some doctors thought she might have depression, but eventually, it was determined that Chloe's symptoms were the aftereffects of untreated Lyme disease. A long course of IV antibiotics helped, but if you were to see Chloe, you would immediately observe that she was frail.

Chloe had always tried to make her health a nonissue. From afar, I admired her for being so stoic. She was determined to find a full-time job during her gap year, and when she decided not to return to school at all, that intention redoubled. She found a basement apartment outside of Boston and tried to design a life with minimal expenses. But even with help from her parents, Chloe found that to make ends meet, she needed to work almost more than her body could take, sometimes fifty or sixty hours a week.

Chloe's jobs would surprise no one navigating the job market without a college degree. Waitress, hostess, bartender, babysitter, dogwalker. Also: data entry technician, front desk attendant at a gym, buffet server. Plus, she was a DoorDash driver and an errand runner for an elderly neighbor for $50 a day.

It was in her errand-running period that Chloe tracked me down. By that time, almost ten years had passed since she'd dropped out of college, and she was approaching thirty. "I cannot do this forever," she said. "I need a life. Let's do your thing." She was referring to Becoming You, which her mother had been recommending to her for a while because, well, mothers. And as an aside here, I feel I must mention that in most families, when one member is lost and struggling, as Chloe was, it is an ecosystem problem, by which I really mean: "Everyone hurts." I was so glad that Chloe reached out, and early one morning we began the process together by Zoom.

At my request, Chloe had already taken the Values Bridge assessment, comparing the expression of her values in her current life and how much those values would be expressed if she were to live her "perfect" life. Such variance results show up on an algorithm-adjusted scale of 1 to 100, where, as with cholesterol, you want yours to be low.

"Wow," I exhaled when I saw Chloe's score of 67. I didn't want to be dramatic; the situation was fraught enough. "Chloe . . . are you . . . miserable?"

"That would be one word for it," she replied, laughing dryly. "Annoyed, scared, frustrated, stressed out of my mind. Those would work, too."

I assured her I would do everything in Becoming You's power to change that narrative.

This section of the book is about aptitudes, but a moment on Chloe's values before we get exactly there. Becoming You, after all, is composed of *interlocking* circles.

The Values Bridge showed us that Chloe's biggest individual variance was on Radius, a reflection of how impactful we want our life to be. In her current life, she had ranked Radius as a 2. She ranked it as a 7 in her hoped-for one. "I want my life to mean something, and I'm dropping off milk and eggs, or picking up dog poop," she explained.

Her variance on Achievement was not far behind. "I see my brothers and their work says something to the world," she said. "I didn't finish college, but I want that for myself, too. To actually *do* something that people respect."

Chloe also had a large gap at Belonging, which is the "friendship" value in shorthand, mainly because her life as a gig worker made community activities hard. There was another gap at Cosmos; she had been raised going to church, and she told me she was sad that her faith was drifting away from her. A final variance was around money, with the Affluence of her current life registering a 2, and her hoped-for life a 4. "I'll never be as comfortable as my parents," she said, "and money is not what drives me, but I'd like to own a small apartment one day and not deal with landlords."

For a moment, Chloe and I looked at each other in silence. I wished we were in a room together; I would have given her a hug. I could feel all the varieties of misery she'd mentioned a moment earlier. Her expression was of hopelessness more than anything else.

"Have I stumped you?" she asked. She had a way of phrasing all her hardest questions as quips.

I told her that we had just begun, and that it was time to turn our attention to discovering what she was uniquely good at.

She shook her head. "Good luck," she sighed. "I'm quite worried the answer is nothing at this point."

I have heard this exact sentiment expressed too many times to count, and from people you might never expect, too—people who, from the outside, look perfectly capable, competent, and confident.

That's why my answer to Chloe was so ready.

"You are uniquely equipped to do something. Everyone is," I told her. "We just need to unearth it."

I was also ready for Chloe's response, which was a kind of vulnerable skepticism—agonizing to me, but also familiar. We look around sometimes, and everyone else can seem so dialed in, zooming along at eighty mph on some kind of inner GPS, while our vehicle coughs and sputters in the breakdown lane. I have held workshops with thirty professionals at the seeming height of their powers who are all nevertheless in this shared secret state of angst.

Chloe's angst, I might add, was not so secret.

"I really have no idea what I'm good at," she said, rebuffing my effort to reassure her. "I'm at the point where I don't think I'm good at anything."

We had work to do, but I started with one of my favorite investigative questions, which I put to you also, and ask you to store away for the time being.

"What job have you enjoyed the most in your life?" I asked Chloe. "That can be a great clue in our aptitude-discovery work. I mean, what job did you have where your bosses really loved you? What job did you have that just felt . . . kind of natural?"

Chloe instantly had an answer. "Are you ready for this?" she said. "Hostess—at the Lobster Shack. I did that for five summers. The lines there were always really long, and people would start getting very pissy, and I could calm everyone down. I made waiting into a kind of party. My manager adored me. I made her problems go away."

I asked Chloe why she had quit. I thought the answer might be money, but she told me that with tips, that job was one of the best she'd ever had, financially. "I just hated telling people I was a hostess," she explained. "They were always like, 'Don't worry, you'll find something!' It annoyed me. Or it embarrassed me, I guess."

I asked Chloe to describe a typical night at the Lobster Shack, and she lit up. For five minutes, she regaled me with stories about calming babies, starting sing-alongs, and getting to know customers by filling them in on the area's best beaches. She was like an entertainer, bouncer, and emcee, with a dash of therapist and tour guide thrown in.

"You definitely have a gift for making people feel welcome," I reflected when she was done. "For making people feel seen and heard. Right now, talking to you, I feel that way. You're so present with me, Chloe. That's very rare."

"That's what I'm *good at*?" she asked.

"Honestly, Chloe," I told her, "I don't know your aptitudes yet. But I will. We will. We just have some work to do."

Together, we sighed.

You can sigh now, too. Because identifying your aptitudes almost always does take work. And that's what's ahead for us now. You may be thinking, *Wasn't finding my values enough of a pain in the arse? Now this?*

Please accept my non-apology. I was sixty—SIX OH—when I finally nailed down my aptitudes through decades of trial and error. You just have to make it through three chapters. And don't worry, we will get to the end—and in some ways, the beginning—of Chloe's story, too, aptitudes and all.

How is it, and why is it, that so many of us spend so much time in the aptitudes waiting room, watching the clock, waiting for someone, some expert, some experience, to tell us what's going on inside of us? To tell us our aptitudes *diagnosis*, so to speak?

There's a different answer for each of us, but let's start with mine because, what can I say, this is my book.

And the story I am about to tell is one of the very biggest reasons we are even here together.

As was the style in the 1960s, my parents were very hands off. When I was young, for instance, my three siblings and I spent summers enjoying long, unattended days doing absolutely nothing. We caught frogs, we made puzzles. At night, we played poker. Occasionally, we got a lift to the musty library in the Town Hall building, where we were dropped off for hours at a time.

One of those days, I happened to return a stack of books containing Updike, Freud, and Lessing. This was no big deal to me, but apparently it was to the librarian. "How old are you?" she asked.

"Twelve."

"Did you read all of those books by yourself?"

"Yes."

"Did you like them?"

I cannot, of course, remember exactly how I answered. But knowing me, I can be pretty sure I gave her an earful about Freud, whom I already loathed for being so wrong—I still think he's wrong—and when I was done, the librarian considered me gravely.

"You must be a very smart little girl," she said.

Smart, me? I'd never heard *that* before. That was just not how my family rolled in those days, and not how many families rolled then in general.

By high school, though, I was hearing it more often, mainly from English teachers. But I got A's in other subjects, too. For instance, math. By my senior year in high school, I loved calculus so much it literally made me cry. Not because I didn't get it, but because I *did*. "Forget English," I remember thinking, "math is the most beautiful language in the world."

That summer, I worked as a babysitter and read a lot of books at the same library. I discovered Dostoyevsky, fell in love with the poetry of Mary Oliver, and devoured a ton of Agatha Christie. I headed to college with absolutely no idea what I was good at.

I didn't even know I *should* know what I was good at.

You should.

You absolutely, positively should.

By the end of the chapter, you will understand why this is personal to me—as I keep mentioning!—but for now, suffice it to say that the Becoming You methodology works best when you know what you excel at. What your *brain* excels at, and your *personality* excels at. Those areas of strength are your aptitudes, and sometimes they can elude us our whole lives long. It needn't be that way.

Because the definition of aptitudes often eludes us, too, let's start there.

Aptitudes are not skills, which we acquire by training and practice. Coding in Java. Repairing a faucet. Formulating a high-performing digital ad. Similarly, aptitudes are not competencies or areas of expertise, which are like skills, only amped up with more education, experience, or practice.

Aptitudes *undergird* those things. They're the inborn faculties that make us good or better at certain skills, competencies, and areas of expertise.

Here's one way of thinking about it. We're all familiar with certain *physical* propensities, right? A five-year-old soccer player who can just do crazy stuff with her feet. An eight-year-old gymnast who never misses a landing. When my son Marcus was twelve, he could hit a golf ball so precisely and with such swing speed that it would fly past the *end* of the driving range. The pro told Jack and me, "Your son has something in him we can't teach." He had a *physical* aptitude. Too bad he never learned to like golf, but if he had, it would have been easier for him than for a lot of us.

Musical aptitudes present much the same way. I don't know about you, but I can spend hours going down a TikTok rabbit hole of children performing on *America's Got Talent*. They're marvels. Six-year-olds singing and dancing like Tina Turner or Freddie Mercury! Get out! If you are looking for chills all over your body, do a Google search for eleven-year-old Bianca Ryan singing "And I Am Telling You I'm Not Going."

That's natural talent. Innate. No wonder she won the whole season.

But that's not how it goes for most of us. Our aptitudes don't present themselves to us or the world with kicking, swinging, singing, dancing, or the like. They're in our brains and personalities—they're cognitive, social, and emotional—and thus are often harder to see.

But they're there.

I've been very fortunate that Betsy Wills, an aptitudes expert and the author of *Your Hidden Genius*, is a regular guest lecturer in my class at NYU. We are also very fortunate to have Betsy's expertise on the advisory board of the Initiative on Purpose and Flourishing.

Betsy always starts off her session on aptitudes with my class by asking students to grab a piece of paper and pen and to sign their names with their nondominant hand. Everyone moans and groans; it's hard! Then Betsy says, "Now go ahead and switch, and sign your name with your dominant hand." Immediate laughter and sighs of relief.

"That's so much easier," everyone exclaims.

"*Just like doing anything in life that uses your aptitudes,*" Betsy exclaims back. What an aptitude she has, I might add, for making things beautifully plain.

As a point of fact, I must note that most social scientists define aptitudes just as I just have: natural, inborn tendencies and abilities, physical and/or cognitive. But as you might have noticed, I also include personality traits. That's a little uncommon.

I have two reasons. The first is that some personality traits are inherent—you come loaded with them like preinstalled software, so to speak. Research would strongly suggest this is true, but so would life, wouldn't it? I have a friend who has the most bizarre sense of humor. She's a little dark, you might say, and finds edgy farce much more amusing than most. For ages, we've all just said things like, "We adore Miriam, but *immediately* delete any videos she sends you. They're just so weird." Then one year, we all ended up at Miriam's fiftieth birthday party, and we met her brother, who started in with the discomfiting, dark jokes from hello, and when Miriam said something we all found (as always) oddly off, he burst into laughter. A friend said, "I guess it runs in the family." My point exactly. I could cite umpteen studies here, but we all know that some behaviors—some proclivities—just come with the package, and seem to have a hereditary component. We can tweak them, suppress them, or lean into them. But the facts are, they are there, as much a part of us as, say, our ability to swing a golf club.

The second reason I include personality traits in my definition of aptitudes is that Becoming You is a methodology that is about delivering solutions. I refuse to get too theoretical here; sometimes your main aptitude *is* your personality. My student Bo is a prime example. Bo changes every room he's in with his effervescence. You feel compelled to draw close to him, to hover in his warmth and light. Once, he stopped by my house when he was in the neighborhood just to say hello.

When he left, a colleague who was also visiting said, "Why do I feel like I love Bo?" I told her, "That's what he does. He makes people feel good and safe. That's his personality."

And his defining *aptitude*.

Bo is not yet settled on a career, but he knows that he will thrive where his particular gift is best deployed. With his training as an engineer and his technical skills, he could easily land a job in coding, technology development, or process management. Instead, he is drawn to leadership and chief of staff roles, and I'm cheering him on.

Because aptitudes are all of your strengths, together. The raw materials waiting to help you build the life and career that's meant for you.

Now, you might recall that Chloe's mother said she thought her daughter would find her way in time. "Everyone finds their place eventually," she said. And she was not wrong. The truth is, almost all of us come to know our aptitudes in time because we figure them out the hard way. Just like values. I once had a client named Linus, who had trained at the world's most famous culinary school and then worked for several years in some of New York's finest restaurants. His skills as a chef could not be disputed. I was thinking of him the other day when I was watching an episode of *The Bear* in which Carmy delivers a rapturous monologue about a dessert containing twenty-eight plums, each prepared a different way. Linus could go on like that, too.

But at twenty-six, Linus became a father, and he and his partner decided that a job as a private chef would be a better match for their lives. He quickly landed a job running the executive dining room of a bank downtown. His hours, he rejoiced, were nine-to-five, and his pay was nearly double. He wouldn't be cooking much, true, but he would be managing a great team of chefs. What could go wrong?

A year later, when I met him right after he had just been let go, Linus was still asking that question. I needed only to run him through a few aptitude-discovery exercises to have an answer. It was simple, really: Linus's brain was wired to revel in the particulars. He wanted to know how each plum was prepared, for instance, at which heat; that level of detail obsessed him. You know that old saying, "Don't miss the forest for the trees?" Linus *naturally* missed the forest for the trees; he'd been a trees guy his whole life. That's why he loved working on the pastry line at one of his previous jobs. He could spend the entire night just thinking about the consistency of the icing on the chocolate mousse cake. But his new job at the bank was not about getting one thing perfect. It was about supervising multiple moving parts, as if from twenty thousand feet up. It required a brain that naturally kept its focus on the horizon.

When Linus and I were done with his Becoming You analysis—which was brief, I might add—he finally had the kind of aptitude awareness he needed to avoid another professional detour. Yes, a job's hours matter. Its pay matters. But an aptitude fit can make or break the deal, and your heart.

I realize I'm putting a heavy emphasis on why aptitudes matter so much. So finally, before we dig into the aptitude discovery process itself, allow me to explain why.

By the time I had arrived at business school, I had pretty much accepted the fact that my aptitudes were all linked to my verbal cortex. Yes, I had loved math, but that was long ago. I was a writer, a talker, and an idea synthesizer.

Then an odd thing happened. I fell madly in love with finance, and I started to get really good grades in it.

Now, at that time in my life, I was married to my first husband, Eric, who actually worked in banking. But that didn't mean we talked about my schoolwork very often. We didn't need to. I was doing fine.

Unbeknownst to me, however, there were some classmates who had different suspicions.

These classmates, in particular, were in a second-year advanced finance elective that I was taking. Indeed, the class was among my absolute favorites. Don't get me wrong—it was hard. Most of the other students had a few years of investment banking on their résumés already. And yet I found myself keeping up with them, and occasionally formulating a solution before them. By the end of the semester, I could feel a big fat A coming on. I was even thinking of going into investment banking myself.

The night before our last class, I opened our homework packet to discover the most complicated assignment I had ever seen. I remember thinking, "They're trying to kill us." But my next feeling was relief. Eric was out of town that night for business. I had time.

I inhaled some leftover pizza from the fridge and got down to work.

Four hours later, when I lifted my head to check the clock, I knew I had nailed it. My solution was gorgeous and, most importantly, right. If I hadn't been so exhausted, I might have cried from pride.

The next day, I had a tingling feeling that the professor would call on me to start the class with my homework, and I was right. Off I went. As I spoke for the next twenty minutes, as was the protocol in that class, the professor covered the boards at the front of the classroom with my calculations, until finally there, circled in his red marker, was my final answer. I knew from the expression on his face that it was *perfecto*.

An expectant silence. The professor raised his eyebrows and smiled right at me and nodded. I smiled back.

"Well!" he exclaimed. "Who would like to comment on Suzanne's analysis?"

In my seat, I tried to keep from beaming with jubilation and willed my heart not to pound out of my chest. I had arrived in math nirvana!

In a row way up behind me, in the top row of the class's amphitheater, I heard a small kerfuffle. I turned to see a classmate whom we will call Tom with his hand up.

"Yes, Tom!" the professor said brightly, "You seem to have some thoughts up there?"

A weird expression on Tom's face. Some jostling in the back row. A longer pause than usual.

Then:

"I just want to say . . . I agree with everything Suzanne's husband just said!" Tom bellowed, followed by a huge guffaw.

Did it hurt?

I have to tell you, it still does.

Now, I know such a thing would never happen today. Impossible. No male student would ever dare to suggest a female student's homework had been done by her husband, and probably none would even think it. Further, if such a student did exist, and did manage to say such a thing, the professor would shut it down in an instant. That did not happen in my case. I don't think the professor liked what was happening, but still, there were five interminable minutes of the class laughing and hooting while I sat hunched in my seat staring at the notebook in front of me on my desk, filled with my careful, detailed, grit-and-stamina-laden finance calculations, my whole body vibrating from embarrassment that I should not have had to feel.

The seeds for Becoming You were planted that day, although it took years for them to put down roots. But when people ask me how I developed this methodology, I know in my heart of hearts that it traces back to the moment I realized you have to know what you're good at *and* own it with confidence and pride. All of us do.

And so, here we are.

Aptitudes are our own personal algorithms that unlock the work we should be doing and the life we should be living so that we can thrive and flourish.

Let's go discover yours.

8

Check Your Wiring

Are you done being pissed at Tom?

Yeah, me neither!

Let it go, I tell you and me both; let it go.

It's time to turn our attention instead to the eight archetypal cognitive aptitude spectrums for an assessment on each one.

An important note here: you cannot assess yourself as being "bad" at any of these aptitudes. *There are no good or bad aptitudes in the absolute.* There are only good or bad aptitudes *relative* to what you hope and plan to do with your one wild and precious life.

A quick example. It just so happens that Interpersonal Style is sometimes considered an aptitude. I myself see it as more of a personality trait, but it will do here for purposes of discussion, because it's so familiar, with its continuum from extroversion to introversion. We all know what these terms mean and how they present themselves. For instance, if I were to say, "Sally is extroverted after she warms up, but she can be really introverted when meeting new people," you would get it.

My point is that there is no right or wrong, better or worse, place to be on the Interpersonal Style continuum; this is incontrovertible. We all know introverts whom we love and like, and we all know introverts whom we find impossible to be near. The exact same goes for extroverts. You can make no grand statements about introverts or extroverts being better human beings overall or better performers at work.

But it is only common sense that extroverts perform better and are happier in certain kinds of work, and introverts perform better and are happier in other types of work. The other day on a flight from Chicago to New York, I watched in wonder as our flight attendant spent thirty minutes delivering a stand-up routine over the loudspeaker, much to everyone's delight, and when she was done, she traveled up and down the aisle blissfully making small talk with all takers. I wasn't one of them because I was grading papers, but I felt happy that this extrovert had found such a suitable calling.

Compare her to Carl, one of my favorite students—and as you may have realized by now, they are all my favorites—who emailed me before the semester to say, "As an introvert, I wanted you to know I won't speak much in class, but I assure you I will always be listening."

As the months went on, I was to learn about Carl's aptitudes. His brain, it turned out, excelled in situations where there was a lot of routine. He was wired to oversee processes that had their proper place, like pipes that sat in grooves, and to make sure they stayed there. His happy place, cognitively speaking, was in a rules-and-regulations, by-the-books environment.

So when I saw the first draft of Carl's Area of Transcendence analysis, I balked. It showed him returning after graduation to his old job in business development at a start-up, a role where he had been miserable. Of course he had been! Business development involves cold-calling, chitchatting with random strangers, and presenting audacious pro formas to contentious investors.

"Carl, Carl, we have to talk," I told him. "You are walking into an aptitudes-career mismatch-palooza."

Fortunately, by the time we met for office hours, Carl had caught that problem himself, and he was already looking for roles that played to the data—the data about *himself*, that is.

He ended up taking a perfect job—for his aptitudes—in a process management role at a small logistics company.

Check Your Wiring

As we go over the eight archetypal cognitive aptitudes one by one, don't try to suss out "the best" way to be.

Just focus on where you fall on each spectrum. That's all that matters, so we can do our Becoming You analysis properly when the time comes.

One final comment before we move on to the eight cognitive spectrums: I want to let you know that there is an alternative to this chapter, or, even better, a supplement to it, and that is testing. My students in fact are required to take the eighty-seven-minute YouScience assessment. If the test is within your budget, I urge you to go online and take it (I have no financial relationship with the company. I just think it's a great test). I also would urge you to read *Your Hidden Genius*, coauthored by the aforementioned Betsy Wills and career researcher Alex Ellison. It is a font of detailed wisdom about aptitudes. The next section of this chapter, I must make clear, owes a vast debt of gratitude to Betsy and Alex's brilliant and inspiring work, and to the scientifically validated YouScience taxonomy of cognitive aptitudes.

Let's look at them in turn, although in no particular order, as each is important in its own way.

Time Frame Orientation is the aptitude that reflects the range at which our brains tend to look at events, long distance or up close.

At one end of the spectrum, there are Future Focusers, who are wired to watch the far horizon. Imagine them at the top of the mountain of life or work with binoculars, taking it all in, above, below, east and west, scanning every direction like pathfinders. Or like runners training for a marathon who plan an entire twenty-six-mile route in their head before even stepping into their sneakers, as if they've seen the race as a drone would. This propensity is why Future Focusers are such a good fit doing any kind of work involving Big Hairy Audacious Goals (or BHAGs), to use a phrase coined by management guru Jim Collins to describe complex, long-term projects. These are the kinds of ambitious, multiyear, many-moving-parts gigs that involve a lot of imagination, comfort with ambiguity, and delight in pivoting. Future Focusers come upon such opportunities—or are thrust into them—and think, "Bring it, because I got it."

Anna is a perfect example. As you might recall, when she showed up in my Washington executive education section, she was in the middle of acquiring a slew of med-spas to add to the six that she already operated. She delegated all of the day-to-day operations to each storefront's manager and kept her own attention on demographic and medical technology trends stretching out twenty years. Another interest for Anna was any regulation, either local or national, that might impact her industry. And finally, her horizon-scanning often landed on med-spa-adjacent opportunities for investment. In one of our last conversations, she told me she was meeting with an investment banker about the possibility of acquiring a group of rehab centers. None of this fazed her—quite the opposite. In fact, one of the reasons she was getting her MBA, she told me, was to gain more of a "CEO view" of the world, far enough above the fray to focus on the next big thing, and then the next.

By contrast, at the other end of the Time Frame Orientation spectrum, Present Focusers thrive in environments where the key success factor is, to use the technical term, *getting shit done*. They are the executors of the world, the marathoners who complete one mile before thinking about the next. If you've ever had to lead a BHAG, you know Present Focusers are worth their weight in gold. Without them, things fall apart. While the Future Focusers are soaring up at thirty thousand feet, Present Focusers are in the trenches recruiting the troops, suiting them up, and making sure they are fed three times a day. You've already met a great example of a Present Focuser in Carl, but I'm going to wager that many of the best, most successful managers running Anna's individual med-spas were Present Focusers, too. These two ends of the spectrum balance each other very well; the challenge is to make sure that you are doing the kind of work that aligns with your natural wiring.

Check Your Wiring

At the center of the Time Frame Orientation spectrum is what You-Science's taxonomy calls the Balanced Focuser, a person who moves with ease between long-term envisioning and ASAP executing. Perhaps that describes you. A word of caution, though: with all of these archetypes, it is easy to just place ourselves somewhere in the middle. The truth is, most Future Focusers can be Present Focusers in a pinch, and vice versa, and sometimes life requires that of us. But I urge you to think over the broad expanse of your experiences and to reflect on the kind of work you were doing when you were the most successful and most in your comfort zone. Think, too, about the times where work—or any activity—came with more stress and difficulty.

Now, with that data, consider the spectrum. Where do you really fall?

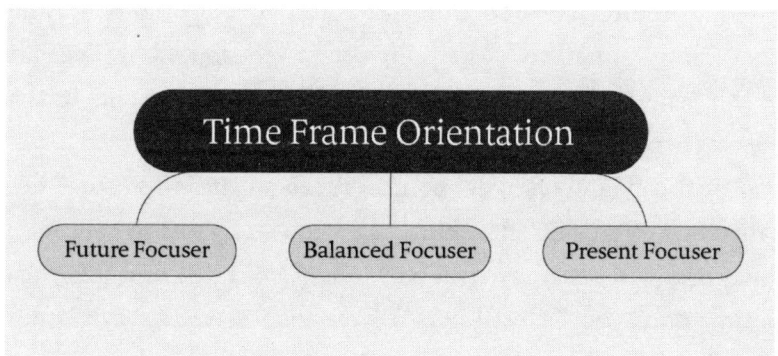

If Time Frame Orientation is the aptitude reflecting the *breadth* of our focus, up close or from afar, **Work Approach** reflects the *depth* of our focus, skimming the surface or drilling below it.

The ends of the spectrum are Generalist and Specialist, with Liaison in the middle.

You can tell Generalists by the impressive extent of their knowledge and, perhaps more tellingly, by their willingness to delegate knowledge collection to other people. "Just tell me what I need to know to run this meeting, thanks," is a classic Generalist line. Or, "Broad strokes only, please!"

I'm not saying Generalists are superficial—not at all!—it's just that we come more naturally to knowing a little about a lot, not the other way around. A perfect example might be the mayor of a small city. In a single day alone, her work may call on her to understand how the sewer system works so that flooding can be prevented when a big storm sweeps in, and to have enough working knowledge of the new federal regulations to make important preschool-enrollment decisions. On the same day, she might also have to have enough information to handle a parking lot dispute, pick the location of an upcoming Fourth of July festival, and fund mental health programming at the community center. All this hop-skip-and-jumping around, topic to topic, cause to cause, issue to issue, might feel maddening to some, but it would feel natural and good—if the mayor was wired to be a Generalist.

In my lecture notes on this aptitude, under Specialist, it simply says, "Funny you asked!" That's my cue to talk about how Specialists are the people who are wired to "go off," as the lingo puts it, when you ask them to explain something. Frequently self-educated experts, Specialists can (and often do) pontificate about stuff in so much detail that you can find yourself asking, "Did you study this in college?" To which they will often say stuff back like, "No, I just find this subject riveting, don't you?" Chef Linus, as you might have already surmised, was a Specialist. I know because I once casually asked him about the challenges of keeping icing from getting runny, and, had I not stopped him, he might still be talking.

If you can recall elementary school geology, you know that the vast rocky pieces that make up the crust of our dear planet are called continental plates, and they comprise the thinnest of the earth's layers. I like to think of Generalists as continental plate travelers, rumbling from place to place with eagerness and curiosity, constantly in motion, never staying still longer than they have to in order to get the lay of the land. Specialists, meanwhile, are moles in their tunnel boring machines, digging through the mantle and heading to the inner core.

Again, the world needs both Generalists and Specialists. And again,

Check Your Wiring

the key is to know which one you are. Because #alignment. Because #fit. Because—no hashtag this time, as I'm very serious—*purpose*.

Eduardo started his career out of college working for his uncle Jorge, who owned a landscaping company in the Virginia suburbs of Washington, DC. With an undergraduate degree in economics, Eduardo wasn't exactly thrilled by the role, but it allowed him to live near his family, his girlfriend, and his church, and the money was pretty good, so after a month of mulling the offer over, he decided to give it a try.

Jorge sensed his nephew's discomfort with joining the company, but he loved him and needed his help. In an attempt to make the proposition seem more attractive to the new graduate, he started him in a pretty senior position, supervising a third of the company's twenty-five teams. The role was about 50 percent logistics, moving the trucks and teams from place to place efficiently. Another 30 percent was people management, with seven foremen reporting directly to Eduardo. The last 20 percent was customer service, troubleshooting calls throughout the day, usually from homeowners who were not exactly happy.

It was soon evident that Eduardo basically sucked at every aspect of his new job. Indeed, he sucked for two long years, making every mistake and annoying every person possible, inside the company and out. Jorge stepped in and tried to coach him, but his efforts were futile. One night, Jorge went home and complained to his wife, "I love the kid, but I give up. I thought he was supposed to be smart!"

And of course, Eduardo was smart, but not in the way he needed to be for the role he was in. His brain was not wired particularly well for juggling a swath of functions simultaneously—operations, HR, and sales—and all their various requirements. It was wired to delve deeply into one thing at a time. Perhaps Eduardo should have known this already. In college, a professor once suggested to him that he pursue a PhD, with the remark, "I've never had a student ask me about a footnote on an academic paper I did not assign." Eduardo remembered thinking, *Sometimes footnotes are the best part.*

There's a good ending to this story.

Eduardo, fortunately, was not oblivious to his shortcomings. He hated failing at his first job, and, on a personal level, he hated letting his uncle down. One day, he started to do something that came naturally to him, researching organic solutions to boxwood blight, which was currently wiping out backyard foliage in the mid-Atlantic states and causing no end of complaints from customers. The more he investigated, the more Eduardo became convinced that he could identify a far better way to treat boxwood blight than the one everyone was using, including Jorge. If he could convince his uncle to invest in the technology to apply this method, it would open up a whole new business. He spent the next two weeks reading every word ever written on boxwood blight and every approach ever taken to eradicate it. He called a professor at the University of Delaware who was said to be the world's leading expert on the subject. He spent two hours interrogating the inventor of the new technology he liked so much, and another four hours reading every word of its user's manual. Finally, he put together a forty-slide presentation to make his case to Jorge.

Guess who's head of R&D at Jorge's new blight-fighting business now?

Eduardo, the Specialist.

Think of him, and the mayor, and how you compare, as you place yourself on the Work Approach spectrum now.

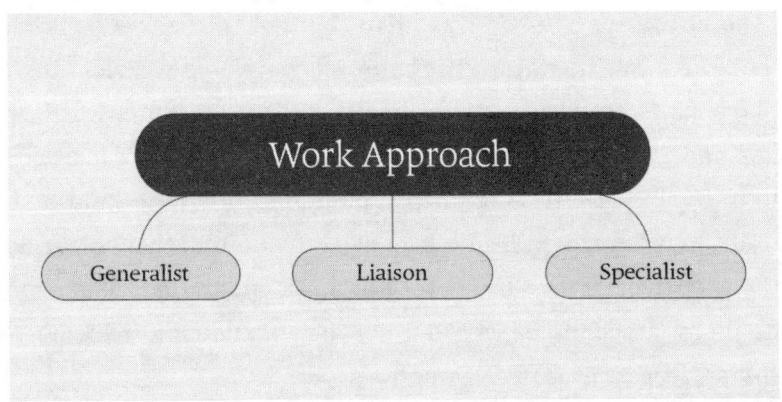

Check Your Wiring

Visual Comparison Speed is the aptitude that reflects how you process detailed information when checking it for accuracy. This one is not a matter of "How smart are you?" It's "How quick are you?" And "How right are you?"

At one end of this spectrum is the Visual Scanner, people who can look at a form or a contract, say, and find any mistake or typo in a nanosecond. People whose brains are wired to think that no detail is too small to care about, no spelling error too small to annihilate. If you have found, repeatedly, that friends ask you to proofread things for them, or seek your input on tax forms, or invite you to scan their résumés for mistakes, the world is already telling you that you're a Visual Scanner. If you love being a notary, for instance, or a clerk who handles massive amounts of paperwork with aplomb, the world is already telling you. If you have caught misplaced decimal points that no one else spotted, the world is already telling you. One of the best copy editors I've ever known once told me that she knew she had found the right career when another copy editor turned to her at work and said, "I didn't sleep all night because I think I left an extra 'the' in Tom's manuscript." Her reply: "I hate that feeling!"

Yeah, not me.

I am the ultimate Double-Checker, way at the other end of the Visual Comparison Speed spectrum. You do not want me near your taxes, or proofreading anything. I immediately hand every contract to a lawyer and say, "Spare me. Just fix it."

Because why? Because details maketh my eyes glaze over.

Oh, had I only known about this aspect of my brain's wiring when I was covering the trial of Claus von Bülow.

That trial, for the non-oldsters reading this, was the absolute news sensation of 1982. An elegant German aristocrat, Claus was accused of having a hand in the demise of his elegant, American socialite of a wife, Sunny von Bülow, in their Newport mansion. I was ecstatic to be covering it.

But oops. Filing my story one afternoon, I wrote, "Von Bülow has been accused of murder and could face..."

Alas—small matter!—Sunny von Bülow was actually still alive, and her husband was accused of *attempted* murder. The AP was forced to issue a rare and dreaded "STOP-KILL" bulletin.

When my bosses tracked me down later, cowering in the corner of the newsroom, they did not particularly appreciate my defense that Sunny was in an irreversible coma. They went ballistic, and rightfully so. Thousands of newspapers around the world counted on the AP for *actual facts*. And thanks to my loosey-goosey relationship with details, I damaged the company's reputation. AP, if you're reading this, I'm still sorry! Personally, I too lost a ton of credibility that day—cred that it took months to claw back. But I did learn that the way my brain is wired means that it is not enough for me to double-check details. I either have to quadruple-check them or outsource this function to people who are toward the opposite end of the Visual Comparison Speed continuum.

Now look, I am not going to tell you that in this day and age, with access to spell-check and any number of other tools that save us from ourselves, Visual Comparison Speed can make or break your career. But it is especially important information to know about yourself and may explain why some of your past jobs have suited you better than others. And further, if you're a Visual Scanner, that may suggest jobs and/or roles where this particular aptitude could make you even more valuable than you already are. Because there is not a company in the world that does not, in some capacity, need to save Double-Checkers from themselves.

Pause here for a moment, if you would, and reflect if you've ever had a killing-off-Sunny-like experience, or quite the opposite, or if your experiences suggest you're somewhere in between, a cognitive type called a List Checker. Then go ahead and make the assessment for your own brain.

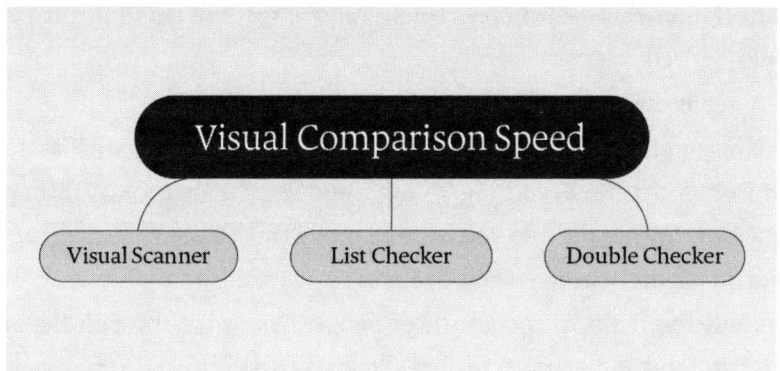

We now turn to **Inductive Reasoning,** the aptitude that relates to our ability to see relationships in seemingly unrelated pieces of information and rapidly draw conclusions. I consider this one of the most impactful of the archetypal cognitive spectrums, especially when it comes to one's fit with certain types of professional work. TL;DR: listen up.

At one end of this spectrum, there's the Diagnostic Problem Solver. Such a person just seems to have a knack for finding solutions. They hear about a problem, absorb facts and ideas and information from here and there, sprinkle in some intuition perhaps, and then, without any obvious or stated method, produce an answer. It usually happens pretty quickly, too, with all the machinations happening naturally and invisibly in the Diagnostic Problem Solver's head. In a way, Artificial Intelligence is (or aspires to be) one big Diagnostic Problem Solver for the universe, smushing together every bit of information and data out there and spitting out an instant "If so, then."

At the other end of the spectrum is the Fact-Checker, whose brain is not wired like a black box that produces insta-solutions. It is wired like a laboratory device that tests inputs repeatedly. Give Fact-Checkers a problem to solve and you will often hear two things: "I need more data" and "I need more time." It's not that Fact-Checkers don't want a solution. They just want a solution that can be reasonably and logically explained to all.

In the broken-record department, please see: the world needs both types.

It needs both types in their proper roles.

Not long ago, I was at a party and ended up chatting with a brain surgeon about the Becoming You methodology. When I was through, he asked, "What data do you have to prove this thing works, and what data do you have to show how the process works?"

Now, the truth is, thousands of people have gone through Becoming You, and if I wanted to, I could collect data on how many have made positive life changes. But I am a Diagnostic Problem Solver by nature, so I replied, "We just have the experience of all the people who have gone through the process. I don't keep track of the numbers. I just know empirically that it works. I'm not exactly sure *how*, except that I see it happening. There's a preponderance of anecdotal evidence. Frankly, I think it wouldn't be a great use of anyone's time for me to unpick any of that. Why bother?"

To which the surgeon scoffed. *Openly*. I mean, we are talking "harrumph" territory.

"With my patients, we have data on their outcomes going out five to ten years, meticulously recorded, cross-checked, and verified by two outside labs," he said. Ah, but that was just the beginning. I was then to learn, for several minutes, in even more detail about the testing and verification of all of his data. Fascinating!

When he was done, I just kind of threw up my hands. "Well, life can't always be measured like the results of a craniotomy," I said. "People get fired. They lose their jobs. Their values change. There's no real way to measure Becoming You's precise efficacy except anecdotally and empirically."

He scoffed—again. "I just don't buy it," he stated.

Oh, you don't?

"You're just a stinking Fact-Checker," I muttered.

"Excuse me?"

Check Your Wiring

"Nothing," I said lightly. "Understood!"

And that was that, really, because the good doctor had a point, and more important to this discussion, he had *his* aptitudes, and I had mine.

Diagnostic Problem Solvers are a great fit for certain kinds of work—for instance, jobs or roles in which you have limited time and access to information, but still need to make decisions quickly based on experience and available insights. Certain companies and cultures also welcome more intuitive decision-making of this sort. It's okay if a mistake is made with the best intentions, as long as the process is fast. It's okay if a decision is not fully backed with data, as long as it is better than doing nothing. And some jobs—almost by definition—simply require Diagnostic Problem Solvers, like hospital emergency rooms and airplane cockpits. In such settings, asking for more data or saying "I'm not ready to decide" can literally be fatal.

By contrast, I'd like my craniotomy done by a Fact-Checker, thank you very much. I'd like it done by a person who has reviewed the research umpteen times and pinpointed the exactly correct, proven, data-backed way to fix my noggin. I should have kept that guy's card.

More seriously though, as a leader, I'd like a Fact-Checker on every team, pushing back against the Diagnostic Problem Solvers, adding more data to the mix when possible, and asking questions like "What are you basing that assumption on?" Fact-Checkers can slow things down, and their meticulousness can drive some people crazy, but if you are building a tech project with only one shot to get it right, bring them on.

Bring. Them. On.

Time for your self-assessment again.

At the center of this spectrum are what YouScience calls "Investigators," people who have traits of both the Diagnostic Problem Solver and the Fact-Checker. Do you think that's you? It's odd. Most people do, right off the bat. So on this spectrum, I suggest you poke around and ask people who know you well if you're more likely to jump to conclusions too fast or consider options too slowly. It's not a perfect measure, but their answers could give you a good directional sense of your place on this important spectrum. (And again, allow me to note you can take the YouScience test online for an accurate reading.)

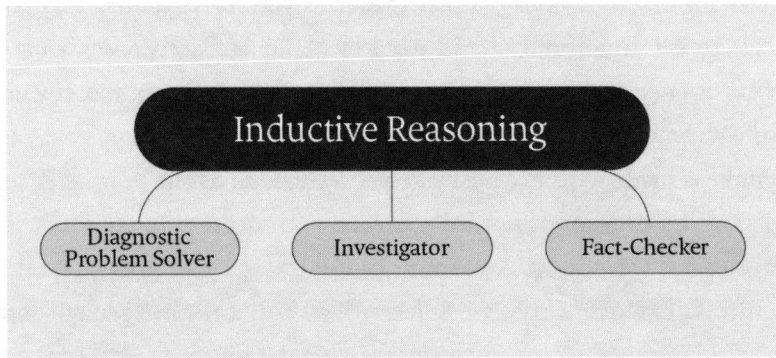

We now turn to **Sequential Reasoning**, the aptitude that describes how our brain is wired to manage, organize, and sort information. This may sound a bit like Inductive Reasoning, and indeed the two aptitudes often track together, but not always.

I will do my best to unpick the two aptitudes, but please know, there is overlap. Here we go.

At one end of this spectrum, there are Sequential Thinkers, who relish complexity and even chaos; you can often spot them by what they don't need to do, which is write things down to figure things out. (They also don't need to organize their desks a certain way, a hallmark.) Because they simultaneously think and act with such ease, and can abhor "how it's always been done," Sequential Thinkers often present as smart and innovative. They can make certain kinds of work—especially on-the-spot analysis—look effortless.

I'm on a corporate board filled with Sequential Thinkers. But let's take just one, Mark, as an example. Mark is a JD-MBA who runs a large tech company. When he opines on anything, it becomes blindingly obvious that he has organized scads of information, and even whole systems, in his head, which he will now synthesize in a cohesive way to reach a logical conclusion about what we should do. Should somebody interrupt Mark with an opposing view or new data, you can practically see the gears in his brain reprocessing and revising in real time, and then he seamlessly carries on, taking the new information into careful account, even if it's major. This is not dissimilar from what a Diagnostic Problem Solver does, but a Sequential Thinker is usually operating with much more information. And they're often much more comfortable explaining their thought processes.

It's actually kind of frightening.

At the other end of the Sequential Reasoning spectrum are Process Supporters, who are in their comfort zone when they can be guided by procedures, rules, and regulations. They're determinedly organized and prefer practical plans to ambitious ones.

I have been insanely lucky to have the ne plus ultra of Process Supporters by my side for twenty-three years. Rosanne Badowski was Jack's longtime executive assistant when he was at GE, and then when he retired in 2001, she stayed on to help Jack's business and our new family. I can fairly say that without Rosanne's obsession with process and her practicality, we would have been able to do only a fraction of what we did in our wild run. She planned and executed our trips around the world with four children; she moved us from house to house; she made sure our big old Great Pyrenees never ran out of treats, because she made them herself, and at the end, she coordinated the scheduling of Jack's hospice care nurses so that I could devote all my time and energy to abiding him. The world would grind to a halt without Process Supporters, which is why it was incredibly hard for me finally to heed Rosanne's pleas to retire last year. Honestly, it still pisses me off. But now I just get to have her as a friend. A friend whose vegetable garden is *very* organized.

Before leaving this spectrum, I feel compelled to tell a story about a client who was a successful Process Supporter, but then, with great fanfare by her organization, was promoted into a role that called for a Sequential Thinker.

By trade, Julie was a painter, and what a gift she had in this arena, with her work appearing on many popular Instagram feeds. Her specialty was near and dear to my own heart—she painted dogs. I still hope that one day, she will have the time to paint mine.

Unfortunately for Julie, a factory accident left her partner, Earl, unable to work. He received a good settlement for his care, but for a variety of reasons, the couple decided afterward that it made sense for Julie to return to her previous job as a nonprofit administrator, if only for a few years. Her employer welcomed her back with a party—literally. That's how good Julie had been at managing the Byzantine paper-pushing systems that undergird most large philanthropic institutions that rely on grants. Everyone loved her because, as one colleague put it, "Julie makes all our problems go away." She was the master bureaucrat, you might say, able to understand, work, and "grease" the system like a true insider.

For two years, Julie was actually not unhappy to be back at her old stomping grounds. She knew she was terrific at what she did, and she felt a lot of pride at being the first person called during any kind of hullabaloo or crisis. She was painting dogs on the weekends, which wasn't enough, but it was something.

Then an interesting thing happened. Julie's boss was poached away by another nonprofit organization, and before he left, he suggested to Julie that she apply for his job. He actually did one better, too. He went to the CEO and recommended Julie for the position.

Skipping to the chase, Julie got the job, and it thrilled a lot of people no end. It's a great story, isn't it? The inner-office administrator who makes it to the top floor of HQ? Who goes from herding staffers to managing her own team, plus overseeing twelve department administrators? Isn't that the kind of opportunity that good organizations are all about?

They are, except the *work* part of it all has to work.

As a Process Supporter, Julie managed the system. She knew its idiosyncrasies and byways; she knew who to call to fix things when they broke. Like Carl, she was great at keeping pipes in their grooves. I love that image. It reminds me of the time Julie said to me, "It makes me happy to send someone an email to remind them that they need to do something tomorrow."

Julie contacted me about two months into her ill-fated new role, and after that conversation, the first thing I did was call an old friend of mine who was a nonprofit CEO for twenty years. "Explain your job to me," I asked. It took me all of ten minutes to know Julie was now in the land of Sequential Thinkers, where a person does not oversee the grooves. A person engineers the route of the grooves pursuant to the route of all the other grooves in the system.

In our second call, I suggested Julie ask for her old job back, and I think I used the term *aptitude-misalignment hellscape*, to explain why. She did not disagree. "It's embarrassing, though," she sighed. "Everyone will wonder what I did to get myself demoted."

"For five minutes," I reassured her. "After that, everyone will be happy again, especially your old department. And you."

To this, Julie agreed. She moved her stuff back to her old office and got back to doing what her brain was meant to be doing.

How about your brain on this spectrum?

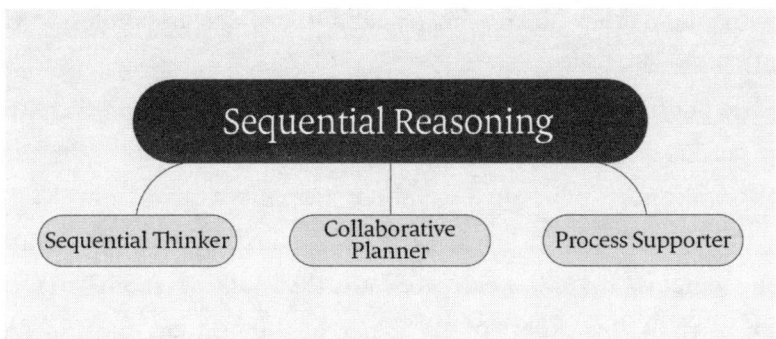

Spatial Visualization describes the aptitude that allows us (or not) to mentally translate two-dimensional images into three dimensions. Or, as I like to tell my students, Spatial Visualization is a measure of how well you can do origami in your head, which matters significantly in some jobs, like, say, architecture and product design.

People with these abilities are called 3D Visualizers, and they're wired to be good at so much more than just mental origami. They can rotate buildings in their minds to see if a different site plan would be better. They can look at a chandelier in a showroom in Paris and know if it will fit in a bedroom in Albuquerque just by squinting at it. They can think of the most functional, efficient, and attractive way to package a product. They have an innate sense, often, of what colors and textures belong in a room. They can imagine creative solutions to screwed-up spaces. They are very good at designing or envisioning stuff you can touch, and that process gives them visceral pleasure.

Often the first presentation of our placement on this spectrum shows up very young. We've all seen some kids gravitate to LEGOs like an addiction. I used to think this was consumerism run amok. Nowadays, I think these kids are 3D Visualizers just being their natural-born selves. Similarly, there are kids who want to play with clay; kids who obsess over every new sneaker, and just have to touch them to feel alive; kids who draw what they see all the time. Other aptitudes might explain these predilections, but none as neatly as Spatial Visualization.

As much as Spatial Visualization facilitates some careers, it matters not an iota in others. Like being a poet. Or, say, a college professor who teaches self-discovery.

The poets and I—we're at the other end of the spectrum here, the one labeled Abstract Thinker. I've been tested for this aptitude, but it was unnecessary, honestly. I could not assemble a chair from IKEA if my life depended on it. I find even *looking* at chair-assembly instructions agitating. *What, what, what* are they talking about? But I've known about this aspect of my brain for a long time. Back in high school, I fancied I might be good at architecture like my father, so I signed up for a class. One of our first assignments was to build a bridge out of toothpicks. My project was not just plain ugly, it was a complete functional fail. I didn't understand it, and by "it," I mean anything—space, mass, perspective, proportion. *Nada*. But words? Yes, thank you. Concepts? Those, too. Love them. Abstract ideas? Let's move in together.

Because of the chasm between the 3D realm and the abstract, it can be frustrating (or infeasible) for an Abstract Thinker to serve in a 3D Visualizer's role, and vice versa. Kyle was not a client, but he was the boyfriend of one, and I got to know him pretty well. He was a polisci major three years out of college, working in marketing for his dad's company because he couldn't come up with anything better to do.

It is not unusual for clients to urge their significant others to take some of Becoming You's tests, and that's what happened in this case. This was how, quite by accident, we all discovered that Kyle, who was down the center on almost every other aptitude, was a 3D Visualizer of epic proportions. (He took the digital YouScience test.) Interestingly, his result may have surprised me and his girlfriend, but it did not surprise him. After receiving it, Kyle regaled us with stories of his childhood, where his favorite class in school was shop and his favorite after-school activity was, yep, LEGOs. He thought about studying engineering in college so he might get into construction, he said, but his parents didn't like that idea, and he found many of the math classes too hard.

After that, he just bumped along, knowing a job at his dad's company awaited. As did the boredom and frustration of a 3D Visualizer doing an Abstract Thinker's job.

In the end, I'm sorry to say, nothing changed in Kyle's life. He had other reasons not to leave his marketing role, like stability and financial security. I get it. I just hope that someday he builds a work shed in his backyard and starts making himself a wooden toolbox or two or three.

Of course, as with every spectrum, you can be a mixture of 3D Visualizer and Abstract Thinker, which is called a Space Planner in the YouScience lexicon, and, coincidentally, I would say my father happens to be the perfect example. He was an architect by training, and a philosopher by avocation. I've never known a person who read more books, and even after he lost his sight in his seventies, he would listen to an audiobook every day. Maybe that is why his career as a practicing architect so quickly morphed into being a teacher in architectural programs.

But the data would suggest Space Planners are rare, at only 9 percent of the population. The time has come for you to assess which end of this spectrum you're at or close to, and here's the thing, I bet you already know.

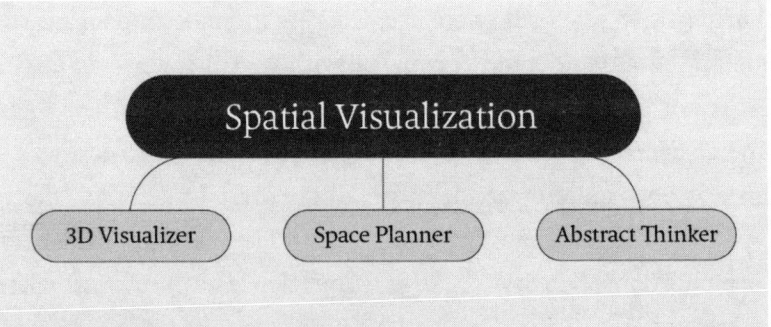

Idea Generation is the aptitude that reflects our natural ability to conjure up ideas in a limited period of time.

Or put another way, imagine someone asks, "What would you do differently if you were seven feet tall?" and gives you exactly sixty seconds to produce a list of answers. Idea Generation measures how *many* ideas you produce. Not how good they are. How numerous.

Is this just a test of creativity? Yes, to some degree. But not necessarily, because there can be wildly creative people who have very conscripted, careful output. The late, very great John Updike wrote only three pages a day. No more, no less. He rejected the notion that creative people were fonts of verbiage and concepts and stories, explaining, "I try to be a regular sort of fellow—much like a dentist drilling teeth every morning—except Sunday. I don't work on Sunday, and of course, some holidays I take. A solid routine saves you from giving up."

And yet, something tells me Updike still would find himself at the end of this aptitude's spectrum labeled the Brainstormer. Because all things being relative, a man with twenty novels, a dozen short-story collections, eight volumes of poetry, and two Pulitzer Prizes had ideas, and a lot of them.

Miranda was a stay-at-home mother whom I met in Central Park one day; it was during the pandemic, when those beautiful eight hundred acres became every Manhattanite's saving grace, and conversations with strangers, even with masks on, became somehow easier to come by. We started off by admiring her new puppy and ended up discussing how she might reenter the workforce when life returned to normal.

In her previous life, before three children, Miranda had been a court stenographer, a job she'd never liked much anyway. Now, she told me, she wanted a profession that took full advantage of something she loved doing, and did naturally: idea generation.

"I have no self-edit button," she informed me, and I agreed this was an excellent trait for someone who wanted a job big on creativity.

I wish I could tell you I saw Miranda again! But let's just enjoy her story for its laser-like identification of what distinguishes true Brainstormers—the ability to spout ideas without ego attachment. I imagine her today in a field like party planning, or social media, or any kind of content creation, really, where a lot of ideas go a long way, as long as just one of them is good.

At the other end of the Idea Generation spectrum is the Concentrated Focuser. These are individuals who don't spout ideas, but often have a gift for getting excited about other people's ideas and, in some cases, implementing them. Sometimes, Concentrated Focusers are just introverts—they like to take things in and process later, in private, at which point they may have a lot of ideas. But sometimes Concentrated Focusers just aren't big idea producers. That happens, and it's fine—as long as your life, work, or career doesn't need you to be. Julie, for instance, rarely needed to generate a slew of ideas, especially once she was back in her rightful and right-fitting role as a Process Supporter extraordinaire. Indeed, part of what irked her about her promotion was all the ideas her new job required her to produce on a regular basis.

"That's just not how my brain works," she said, and I could not say it better myself.

In the center of the Idea Generation spectrum are Idea Contributors, people who may not spout one unedited idea after another in brainstorming sessions, but who stay in the mix, sometimes with their own ideas and sometimes building on someone else's.

Where on this continuum are you?

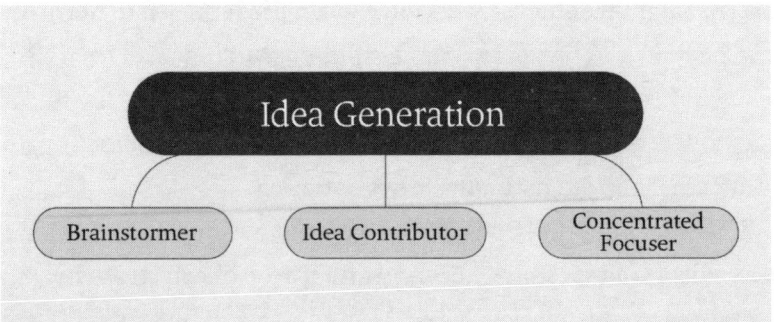

And so we come to the final aptitude of the eight archetypes, my old friend **Numerical Reasoning**, the ability to understand and make inferences from numerical information, including numbers, statistics, probability, and mathematical patterns.

At one end of this continuum, there is the Numerical Detective, able to see not just information and trends in numbers, but also stories. Most people know whether they have this ability by the time calculus rolls around in high school. I certainly did. (Although apparently not well enough to tell anyone!)

At the other end of the Numerical Reasoning spectrum is the Numerical Checker. These individuals are most comfortable using formulas that they have repeatedly applied and have little interest in the theory or process behind the development of those formulas. I know so many brilliant people in this category that it seems pointless to point out, but for the record, how good you are at math has nothing to do with how smart you are, full stop.

Check Your Wiring

However, it is important to make sure that, given your Numerical Reasoning aptitude placement, you are in the right job for it.

I might have been a banker. I guess I could have been.

I'm not sorry I wasn't. I love my life and where it's ended up, right here at the heart of my Area of Transcendence. And to be honest, sometimes I wonder if my encounter in that fateful finance class happened for a reason: to give rise to Becoming You, as it eventually did.

If so, Tom, I actually love you very much.

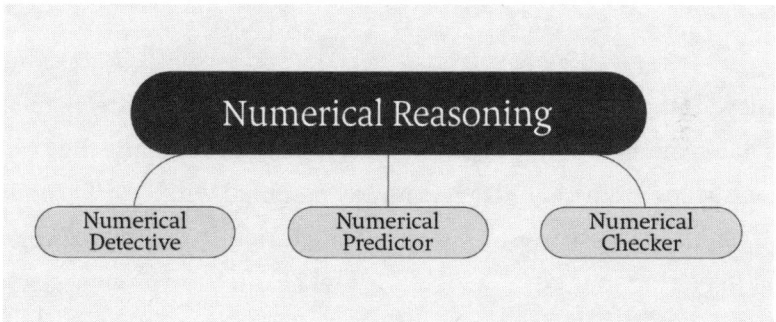

Now, any expert in the field of aptitudes will tell you that there are about two dozen aptitudes that I haven't described in this chapter. There's a reason for that. Most of them are very specific—like glare factor, which measures how you react to light, and which only really matters if you're a pilot, or a truck or race car driver. Another is hue detection, the ability to see the difference between, say, three similar shades of blue. This aptitude is important for people in the design fields. But for the rest of us, we'll just say, "They all look blue to me," and leave it at that.

Regardless, just know that you can be tested on almost every aptitude that exists. You don't have to guess. And you shouldn't. Because when it comes to aptitudes, information is power—the power to claim your natural talents as your own, for you to live into—and for all the world to see.

9

Your Personality on GPS

I know authors aren't supposed to talk about their favorite chapters. It's like a mother talking about her favorite child, I suppose. But we're now turning from cognitive wiring to emotional wiring in Becoming You's aptitude work. Yes, personality! Such rich stuff, and so important to getting your purpose right. As I said earlier, too often neglected when we think about career planning. The reason is beyond me. Maybe it's the specter of my longtime nemesis Sigmund Freud, who taught that personality was a mysterious and nefarious thing, never to be fully unlocked, and when it couldn't be avoided, was to be accessed only by experts.

Please.

Now, there are plenty of widely available ways to help us understand our own personality more deeply. Therapy, for one. But so too dozens of assessments that can be found online or in academic or organizational settings devoted to personal and professional growth. Some of these tools are famous, such as the Myers-Briggs Type Indicator, which has stood the test of time for a reason. If you haven't taken it, I recommend you do. I even more highly recommend you take the Enneagram, which does have a small cost associated with the excellent RHETI version. I find the Enneagram's results about personality so important, I require it of all my students. And indeed, if you are able to add its findings to your journey of self-discovery, please don't miss my interview in Appendix E with Rasanath Das, the acclaimed Enneagram expert I have referenced earlier in these pages.

In my Becoming You class at NYU, every student is also required to take what is commonly called a 360 Feedback assessment, with aggregated, anonymous feedback from former and current colleagues—bosses, colleagues, and subordinates, thus the name—who rate them on multiple personality dimensions. We obviously cannot simulate that process here. It takes five weeks and it's very costly; that's why such 360 assessments usually happen only in big corporations and university settings. But as I mentioned in Chapter 2, I developed a DIY version of this very thing as a proxy for the participants in my Intensive and workshops, and yes, those reading this book. It comes nowhere close to the depth and sophistication of more elaborate 360 assessments, but the tool is very fast, pretty darn cheap, and aggregates feedback from up to forty raters. It's called PIE360, and you can learn more about it on my website if you're interested.

You may be wondering why I went to the effort of creating a more accessible 360 tool, and I'll tell you, although you may not like the answer. The truth is, most personality tests are self-reported. And, sure, we know ourselves. But there is much to be gained from hearing how we show up in the world. From learning, that is, how others experience us. Gaining that knowledge can take our whole lives. And maybe it should. But if you seek a shortcut, and you really want to accelerate finding your purpose, sometimes you have to go looking for data. That's what 360 is all about.

But even with my mentions of PIE360, the Enneagram, and even Myers-Briggs, surely you suspect I have some other personality assessment up my sleeve. And indeed I do. It's called the Career Traits Compass, the focus of this chapter, and a central pillar of Becoming You's aptitude data gathering process.

The Compass is based on my belief that four particular personality clusters can be—and often are—very influential in identifying the correct career path. I have no scientific evidence per se, just forty years of empirical data and several years of anecdotal evidence that the construct is valid. (Incidentally, you can take the Career Traits Compass assessment test on my website; it is free, and if you like getting scores on things, it will certainly meet those needs.) I mentioned the Compass's traits by name earlier: Nerve, Soundness, Elasticity, and Wonderment. Shortly, we will delve deep into each of them in illustrative detail.

For you visual learners, here's the Compass graphically:

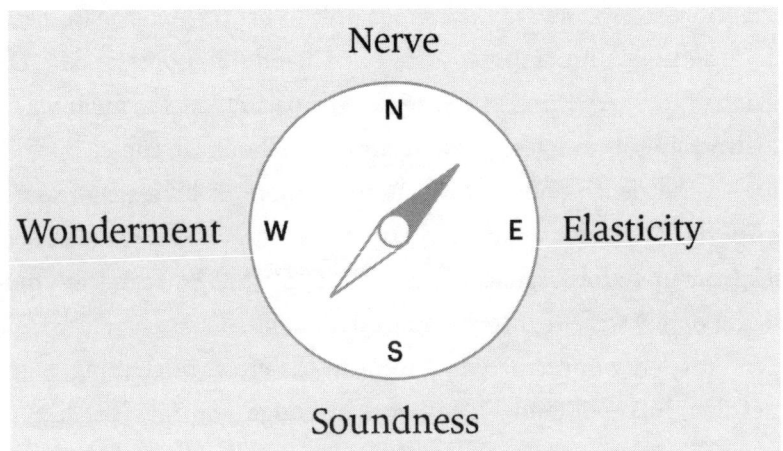

Now, for full disclosure: I happen to like the four traits that comprise the Compass. I like it when I see them in myself and in others. I think more of each and every one of them is generally better for you in life, because such plenitude increases the number of your career options.

But you are you and only you. I am also not one of those career advice bloviators telling you how you *have* to be. It's nonsense to ask someone to change their personality, and in a book no less. Instead, my goal in this chapter is to describe each of the four Compass personality traits and discuss what having more or less of each one suggests for the kind of work and life that's right for you. In that way, exploring the Career Trait Compass parallels the approach we just took to cognitive aptitudes. There is no right or wrong way to be on any Compass coordinate, just right or wrong for you *and the career you are in or considering.*

Although, a caveat! Everyone—everyone—should have as much of one particular trait as possible; it's a component of Soundness. This particular quality has no disadvantages. In the pages ahead, we will meet the fifteenth-century Japanese shōgun Ashikaga Yoshimasa to identify which one, and understand why. Admit it, you're intrigued. And I've done my job.

Sāikō! (Onward, spoken by a shōgun.)

Because I am a writer and a teacher, I am always looking for clever, memorable ways to package information. That's why these traits are organized as a compass. Thank goodness the English language cooperated!

And so let's start with the Compass's "northern" coordinate, **Nerve**. It encompasses a pulsating and often related bundle of personality traits: stamina, candor, and decisiveness. Together, these traits add up to a certain way of showing up in the world: boldly, alive, and with confidence in your actions and decisions. In a word, we're talking about *guts*. And perhaps I could have used that term instead, if it had started with *n*.

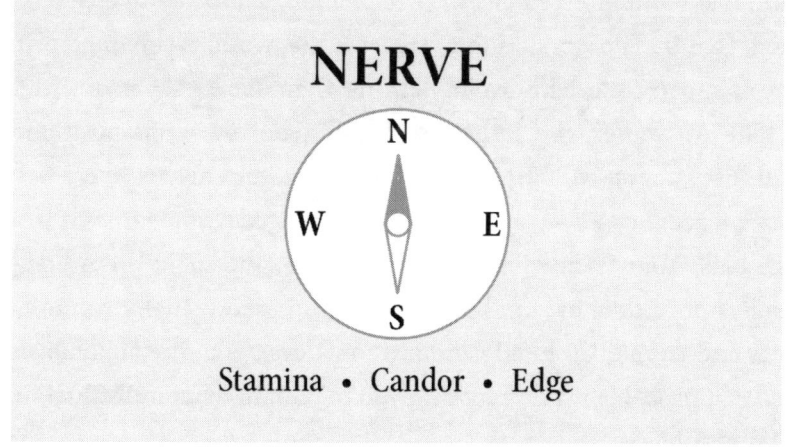

Some degree of nerve is important in almost any job these days, given the pace of change and the universe's general complexity. Sure, there are routine jobs that kind of leave you alone. But somehow, these days, even yoga teachers get the blues. (Just ask one.) I once counseled the handyman at an old-age home who was on the verge of quitting because of all the drama and strife in his job due to warring factions among the staff. An old-age home! And on a little island, no less! And remember Julie? She was the nonprofit administrator who was promoted to a more strategic position, and then voluntarily demoted herself. She missed her old job, with its structured systems and rhythms. But—and here's my point—even that role had its stressors. Julie told me once, "Each week has a mini-crisis." And for those, even with her job's relative calm, she needed some degree of stamina, candid straightforwardness, and decisiveness.

But without a doubt, the need for Nerve definitely increases the higher you move up in most organizations. The responsibilities get heavier, the work more complex and ambiguous, the decisions more fraught and with steeper consequences. For speed, especially in highly competitive situations, you need courageous levels of honesty and decisiveness to cut through the usual organizational BS. You face the prospect of failure more often, and you must accept that with preternatural equanimity. You just have to be more *out there*—in order to be good, that is. The worst kind of leader in the world is the fingerprint-less one: someone who avoids leaving their mark, a person utterly lacking in Nerve, who refuses to commit to any single position or plan, uses jargon to obfuscate real meaning, and hedges every bet. I mean, leaders can *try* this approach, but at decent companies it never lasts long. Your team will end up hating you, and so will your bosses. Leaders have to show up, keep showing up, and actually commit to ideas and people. So in all candor, I must urge you, if you are low on Nerve, it probably makes sense for you to remain in an individual contributor role.

Chloe, with whom our Aptitudes exploration began, was a person who self-identified as low on Nerve when we were working on her Becoming You process. First and foremost, there were her health challenges, which significantly diminished her endurance. But as she put it, "I'm not so sure I ever had a lot of stamina. I'm a mellow girl." Then there was her mixed relationship with candor, which she chalked up to being conflict-averse, and also, "super nice." Her desire to please everyone was one of the reasons she did so well calming the crowds at the Lobster Shack, right? She was the first to admit that she was not boss material. "I could never fire anyone," she said, laughing, adding that the worst performance review she could imagine herself giving would include feedback like, "Well, maybe you're a little less than perfect. Are we still okay?" Finally, Chloe was a person with almost zero edge, unable to make decisions without a deadline or her back up against the wall.

All of these aspects of Chloe—her low Nerve, essentially—did not detract from her wonderfulness as a person or, as you will eventually see, from her ability to get a great job matching her purpose to a T. But they definitely suggested she stay away from leadership.

And from entrepreneurship.

Nothing, nothing, nothing demands Nerve like a start-up, because nothing takes it out of you like a start-up. Mentally, emotionally, financially, spiritually, physically. Nothing. It takes every ounce of your endurance, every bit of your courage and candor, and every iota of your speed.

It's like that old saying, "Most founders run out of steam before they run out of money." That's because being a founder is a grind of epic proportions—if you care. And you have to care; otherwise, you're dead at the starting gate.

We cared at Quadio. That was the name of the start-up founded by my son Marcus and Jack's grandson, Joe, before the pandemic, and which I got deeply drawn into as the resident adult. We believed in our product, a streaming app for college musicians. We believed it could change the world for young artists. You may not think that's a noble goal. We did. I remember coming in one morning at six and seeing our head of marketing sitting at her desk, pounding away at her keyboard, black circles under her beautiful eyes. She hadn't been home for two days, and many others were working in similar charettes. No one was complaining. We were in start-up mode.

Because we were a music app, we often had a soundtrack booming in the office, and our theme song was by one of our earliest believers, a freshman who thought he might make a career in music, thanks to Quadio. It was called "Belly of the Beast," which perfectly described where we all felt we were. And for the life of us, for the love of us, we were going to get out.

We couldn't. The pandemic hurt us, too many strategic changes hurt us, too many bells and whistles on our earliest product offering hurt us, but so did a litany of just plain dumb beginner's mistakes, many made by yours truly. We ran out of steam and money at about the same time, but sometimes I wonder what would have happened if one of us had had an ounce of Nerve left in the tank. Could we have made it work then?

I don't know. I just know that all of us were running on empty at the end.

A few days after we closed shop, I called a friend to vent. He was a successful serial entrepreneur whom I knew from business school, and along the way with Quadio, he'd been an invaluable source of advice and encouragement to me. But when I started in on my tale of woe, he offered zero sympathy.

"Welcome to start-up world," he said. "I'm not sure you were ever enough of a lean-mean-fighting-machine over there at Quadio."

I asked him if he meant we lacked Nerve, as I've defined it here.

He agreed, and then said another interesting thing: "I think I may have too much of it." He ticked off the three corporate jobs he'd taken between his various stints as a founder. I hadn't realized he'd been fired from each one. He explained why. He'd worn his people out with his always-on, twenty-four/seven go-go-go; he'd spoken out too often and bluntly without concern for the humanity of the peeps on the receiving end of his candor, and he'd made too many decisions too quickly and unilaterally. In a word, he was what is often called a good old-fashioned "asshole."

Nerve is great, until it isn't.

I'm not saying you shouldn't lean into this trait if you have it. Au contraire. Stamina, candor, and edge will help you in almost every job. Chaos loves (and needs) a commander.

But only you know if chaos-taming, BS-slaying, distance-running Nerve is in you, and how much.

And then it's a matter of making sure your life's work aligns.

At its best, **Soundness** is a splendid mix of positive energy, self-awareness, integrity, and resilience—basically, Soundness means behaving like a grown-up, emotionally healthy, dependable, and decent.

SOUNDNESS

Positive Energy • Self-Awareness • Integrity • Resilience

Unfortunately, in the workplace—and just in real life, period—Soundness has some complications.

First, introverts too often get mislabeled as having negative energy.

Second, self-awareness is brutally hard.

Third, everyone thinks they have integrity.

And finally, resilience requires something rather radical to get right.

Mingze, an engineer by training, wrote me an email about a year after he graduated from Stern. He'd never taken Becoming You, but he had been a star student in my management class. Now, I must add that Mingze had never actually *spoken* in class. He was too shy. But he shone in all of his homework assignments, and his final exam was *chef's kiss*. I'd also met with him a few times in office hours, and, once relaxed, he was perfectly delightful, teeming with insights about himself and the world. He struck me as wise beyond his years. *Who knew, I remember marveling, that this guy was filled with so much Soundness?*

Unfortunately, at work, bosses need to know this kind of thing, at least in most jobs. Mingze was reaching out to me by email because he'd been passed over for a promotion once again. "I don't want to sit at my desk tweaking algorithms for the rest of my life," he explained, "but they won't put me into management because they say I have *negative energy*." The term clearly pained him.

I suggested to Mingze that he try the direct approach, speaking with his superiors about his introversion, explaining it as a work style, not a personality deficit. At first, he demurred. But Mingze desperately wanted to move up in his company. Achievement was one of his defining values, as was Affluence—as in, he wanted to be rich and successful someday. Both required he shed the label that was hovering around him like a shadow, and that he acquire a new, more accurate one for the person he truly was just below the surface.

I cannot report a miracle here, but Mingze did eventually convince his bosses to let him run a team, perhaps intentionally filled with introverts like himself. This was a small step forward, but a real one, and the kind that "subdued energy" (read: introverted) people need to be willing to accept if they desire leadership positions.

For better or worse, the truth is that the working world tends to favor extroverts. It reads their outgoingness as positive energy. They're seen as more can-do, more in-the-conversation, better with clients, more fun to work with. While this bias has lessened in recent years as the world has generally opened up to difference, the onus remains on introverts to explain themselves to their teams. Or to adjust and/or design their career paths for work that accommodates their "energy" authentically.

Time was when corporate America was surprised to learn that emotional intelligence (EQ) mattered as much as IQ in boosting the performance of individuals and, thus, their companies. I remember, in fact, publishing one of the first articles about EQ in the *Harvard Business Review* in 1998, written by EQ's great early and foundational proponent Daniel Goleman, and hearing pushback from readers that the whole concept was too soft and fuzzy. But the research was so persuasive that such resistance faded pretty quickly, because—can I be blunt here?—*duh*. EQ is the ability to perceive, interpret, demonstrate, control, evaluate, and use emotions to communicate with and relate to others effectively and constructively. How could anyone not know those behaviors are essential to personal and organizational success?

I was very lucky to be one of Dan's editors myself, and I once asked him which aspect of EQ was the most important. His answer was immediate: self-awareness.

Too bad it's so hard. So hard to have—and so hard to know about ourselves.

Take Ben, who graduated from a small college near Philadelphia. He'd always been drawn to nursing, and, with his natural empathy and kindness, everyone agreed it was his calling. Fortunately, Ben's school had a nursing program, and he entered it with the highest of hopes.

He hit a wall almost from the start. He could not find his way past a C in virtually any class involving science. Ultimately, thanks to tutors and repeated classes, Ben got his RN, but the whole process was a struggle.

The nursing shortage in the United States is no joke, however, and Ben was still able to land his first choice of jobs. He ended up in the NICU at a big-city teaching hospital.

Almost immediately, the nursing supervisor in the NICU was all over him about mistakes. He was great at making patients feel comfortable. But when it came to crisis situations or understanding a doctor's rapidly changing instructions, he felt like he was back in school all over again.

To make matters worse, while Ben was flailing, other nurses were excelling. His hospital had recently started a fast-track program for its RNs to elevate their careers by becoming nurse practitioners. Ben's mother urged him to apply, which he reluctantly did, only to be rejected, while three fellow nurses, all about his age, got in.

One evening not long after, Ben went home and composed a resignation letter, and he started applying for nursing jobs in hospice, where the pace was slower, the medical demands less complex, and his tenderness an asset.

"I don't know why it took me so long to figure myself out," Ben told me when I met him three years into his thriving hospice career, which he loved. But I didn't think it took him long at all. Many of us spend our whole lives pinpointing our strengths and weaknesses through trial and error. It's all up to us—because too often no one tells us. The worst offenders can be the people who love us most, not wanting to hurt us. Ben's mother is a case in point! I am a case in point! And in a moment of dreadful feigned humility, I must say that's why I love the whole Aptitudes portion of Becoming You so much. It's designed to *manufacture* self-awareness.

We never have as much as we think.

The same goes for integrity.

Please, stay with me! I know the minute people hear the word *integrity*, they can zone out.

Because everyone thinks they have it.

Your Personality on GPS

Am I right? I am so right.

But do they? Well, no. Of course not. Because integrity is not just the blunt instrument of knowing right from wrong and acting accordingly. Although it *contains* that.

Integrity is also about execution. It's about (cliché alert!) walking the talk, closing the loop, dotting the i's and crossing the t's, and finishing what you started. Failure to execute is probably the leading cause of termination out there in the world of work, and if not that, it is certainly the leading cause of frustration. If you don't fulfill your responsibilities, your colleagues eventually loathe you, and so does everyone else your work touches.

But that's not all. Integrity is also the ability to apologize to those you've hurt and say thank you to those who've helped you. It's about being able to say *I was wrong*. It's about accountability.

Ah, now integrity is getting a little wince-inducing, right?

I have a theory about why we all think we have integrity but often have less than we think.

When I was a girl reporter in Miami, a police detective named Joe Lodato took me under his wing. He thought I was a promising newbie because I did not walk in the door hating the police, as some of my colleagues did. But he was worried I didn't hate criminals *enough*.

One day, Detective Lodato cooked up a plan for me to come to a county jail so I could interview a man accused of attempted murder who was going on trial the following week. The detective thought it would be interesting for me, he said, to hear the suspect's side of the story.

And what a story that suspect had to tell, in his bright orange jumpsuit! Not only did he persuade me he was totally innocent, he had me practically sobbing in sympathy. I could not wait to cover the trial to see him exonerated!

Yeah, so, surprise, the suspect was a complete pathological liar, and at his trial the prosecutors made quick work of him, armed with fingerprints and a parade of witnesses.

I'd been snookered! By the criminal, but also by Joe Lodato, who was trying to teach me a lesson.

"Everyone writes the story of their life," he told me pointedly, "with themselves at the center as the hero."

I have invoked this line of courthouse poetry roughly one million times in my life. It explains bad behavior almost every time.

We all have our defenses; we all have our excuses.

Forget attempted murder! I'm talking about our little daily transgressions. The white lies, the minor exaggerations, the late projects, the unfinished assignments, the blame cast on others or circumstances for our own screw-ups, the credit-stealing, either by omission or commission.

These are all matters of integrity.

And how does this matter for Becoming You and your career planning? Let me count the ways.

Some career paths are quite integrity-independent. There are companies that don't value it, and some entire industries don't either. I'm not going to name them, because there are exceptions to every rule. It's more accurate, however, to say that some *roles* don't require integrity because you couldn't cheat if you tried. For instance, thanks to our friends at the SEC, it would be hard to break the banking system now, given all the controls built into every procedure.

But sometimes, our Area of Transcendence is pointing us toward a destination where integrity *does* matter, and matters a lot. Where the only thing standing between good and evil is our moral compass. Any job centered around the elderly or children, for instance. Teaching, coaching, law enforcement. The same is true for many jobs that involve animals, who can never speak for themselves.

Other jobs require heightened levels of responsibility. If you don't deliver your goods on time, or you're prone to lateness, exaggeration, or lone-wolf behavior, the whole kit and caboodle comes crashing down. One of the brightest, most creative, and most appealing people

I've ever known was fired from his job at a consulting firm after he got promoted to team manager. The clients loved him, and his insights as an individual contributor always took the conversation to important and unexpected places. But as soon as people had to rely on him for things like performance reviews, goal-setting, culture-building, and mentorship, it was a disaster. He just couldn't get things done if those things were not about himself.

If your Becoming You journey is leading you in such a direction, that is, toward a career where integrity *writ large* is going to measurably impact your success, taking the pulse of your integrity is going to be essential.

But how? How, if "everyone writes the story of their life with themselves at the center as the hero"? I guess you must ask the hero-slayers in your life, the friends and family who might interrupt your narrative with a dose of the truth. (Small plug: the aforementioned PIE360 is another reasonable way to get unvarnished *outside* feedback, especially about your ability to execute.)

But most of the time, as with self-awareness, an integrity assessment is up to us. Do Detective Lodato a favor, and bring yourself in for questioning.

The final part of Soundness is resilience, the trait that I alluded to before, which has no downside. The more you have, the better, period.

And I am not talking about grit—or not grit alone.

To my mind, resilience is actually kind of useless without the key that unlocks it: forgiveness.

Hear me out.

When do we need resilience at work? At our lowest moments, right? When we've been fired or passed over for a job by a boss we thought was a friend. When we've lost a client for whom we'd given our all. The same is true in life. We need resilience at our nadir. When our cancer has come back; when our kid has dropped out of school for all the wrong reasons; or our beloved wanders off and, after long and agonizing waffling, decides not to come back.

In such moments, the common refrain on resilience is that we are supposed to light our inner fire and draw from our depleted well of courage and forge ahead. *It's up to us.* We're supposed to make ourselves strong.

That is very, very hard.

Because when the world comes down on us in any number of ways, we are weak, and, often, we are mad. In fact, one of the most human things we do in darkness is go blame-hunting.

When Jack died, I had all the feelings we normally assign to widows. Grief, longing. But, oh my God, I was ripshit too, to use a charming regionalism. Why did this happen to me? Why did the end of his life have to be so painful? Why did we have twenty years together instead of thirty? I was also incredibly, irredeemably angry at myself, because on the last day of Jack's life, he told me he saw his Aunt Theresa in the room, and I thoughtlessly replied, "Theresa's not alive, honey."

Why couldn't I have just given him that simple comfort of knowing he was not going to be alone?

So. Much. Self-loathing. *For months and months.*

But here's the thing. It finally subsided, indeed it *only* subsided, when I told my pastor about the incident, and he said, "Suzy, you have to forgive yourself. A heart filled with anger or blame or regret never heals."

I was thunderstruck; he was so right. I knew it instantly, but still, it launched me into a little mission of studying resilient people. Some I knew personally; others I'd just read about. Of course, in almost every case, the company line was that these individuals had "grit." But when I spoke with them, or read detailed accounts of their actions, I realized that almost invariably they'd forgiven those who had broken them, or forgiven themselves for screwing up, or both.

Your Personality on GPS

I don't have a handy story here of a student or client whose forgiveness-laden resilience made their Becoming You story come true. I just know my own new life was made possible by the fact that I forgave Jack's illness, I forgave myself, and I forgave the universe for what had happened, and I replaced the anger and the blame and the regret with gratitude for all the love that I experienced on my way to grief and back.

My heartbreak made me better and stronger. I'm not happy it happened, but I'm not sorry either. It made me who I am. That's how grit plus forgiveness work together as one, equaling resilience.

A year ago, I was thinking about a way to teach the "grit + forgiveness = resilience" concept to my students when it dawned on me that the time had come to share something wonderful that I'd had in my head for forty-seven years but hadn't been able to use, even at cocktail parties: familiarity with Japanese art of the Sengoku Jidai period.

Yes, we have at last reached the rumored reference to the fifteenth-century shōgun Ashikaga Yoshimasa. We made it.

Lore has it that one day, despondent over dropping and breaking his favorite tea bowl, Yoshimasa, a military leader, ordered the piece sent to China for repair. When it was returned with simple metal staples, Yoshimasa was not pleased, and he ordered the Japanese artisans under his command to invent a better-looking method of repair.

That must have been some special tea bowl, I think we can all agree.

Anyway, the Japanese artisans, fearing for their lives for all we know, came up with a brilliant solution: they filled the bowl's cracks with resinous urushi lacquer mixed with powdered 14-karat gold. In such a way, the bowl's imperfections miraculously became its most valuable parts.

The art form of kintsugi was born.

Over the centuries, kintsugi has come to represent the concept that heartbreak and failure are inescapable in life, but that our scars are what make each one of us beautiful, precious, and unique.

It's the perfect metaphor, isn't it?

So perfect that I became obsessed with the idea that I had to teach kintsugi in class. And I mean *teach*-teach. Like, I came to believe I needed to have my students break little ceramic pots at their desks with little hammers, and then get out their little brushes and fill their little cracks with urushi lacquer.

It is one thing to *hear* about kintsugi, I thought. It is one thing to *show* my students slides of the world's finest kintsugi vessels. But for them to really, really, really *understand* that resilience is to be embraced as the discipline of forgiveness and rebirth, they must *act it out*.

They had to crack their pots, pick up the pieces, and slowly, deliberately meld them back together with a gold-flecked bond. Brilliant, right?

Thank God in heaven I had the presence of mind to try kintsugi at home for myself first.

I still have lacquer stuck to one of my nails. And apparently, you should not so much strike your pot with the hammer as tap it.

Now I know.

When I was done cleaning up the mess, another metaphor came to me, though. Kintsugi, as an art form, is also about teaching us how hard it is to turn our scars into our strengths. We do not gain resilience by accident or serendipity, or by willing it upon ourselves.

We gain it by insight and practice—and not by trying to muscle our hurt and anger to the ground, but by giving that pain away.

The world has always been daunting. How else can we explain that kintsugi has become such an enduring metaphor?

Perhaps the future will be more daunting still—and if that's true, I wish lots of resilience, in all its glory, very much for you.

The east coordinate of the Career Traits Compass is **Elasticity**, the eager and willing propensity to continually expand our collection of skills *and* our collection of friends.

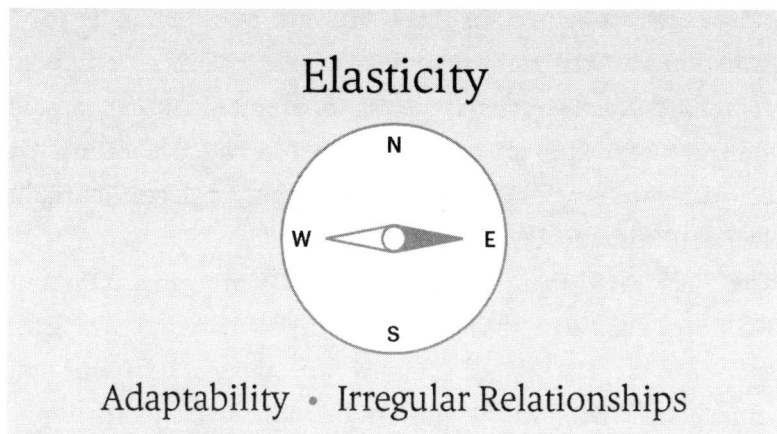

Elasticity

Adaptability • Irregular Relationships

Very hard! Both of these things!

Take the first, which is commonly called "reskilling" in corporate-speak.

Um, thanks, I'd rather not.

I mean, who would *want* to reskill all the time? It's enough just to do your normal job, which is typically bigger and harder than you'd like. Sure, some people are hungry for a bit more challenge. But no one is ever saying, "Wow, I wish my job would be totally reinvented right underneath me!" No one wakes up in the morning and thinks, *I can't wait to throw out skills I'm good at so I can replace them with brand-new ones I've never seen before!* Or, *Bring on the new software, systems, tech, and procedures! It's fun to keep rebuilding my brain with no instruction manual!*

Personally, I get exhausted just thinking about reskilling.

And yet, the need for such adaptability is here to stay. In fact, according to LinkedIn, adaptability happens to be the number one aptitude employers say they are looking for right now.

So do you have it?

My favorite example of a person demonstrating adaptability in extremis is, coincidentally, Dan Roth, the editor in chief of LinkedIn.

Dan was raised in Kentucky, and from a very early age he knew exactly what he wanted to be when he grew up: a business journalist.

In those days—way back in the 1980s and '90s—the route to that destination was well marked, and with college, Dan set off upon it. He attended Northwestern's journalism program and, upon graduation, got a reporting job at a little paper in North Carolina. Over the next several years, he worked his way up the business journalism ladder with stints at *Forbes* and *Fortune*.

But there was distant thunder. The first clap of it came at the end of 2008, when Bob Cohn, the number two in command at *Wired*, left the magazine to run TheAtlantic.com. Everyone thought he'd gone nuts—Dan included. "Bob had the greatest job in magazine journalism," he recounts. "We all thought he'd lost his mind."

But while his print comrades remained incredulous, Dan soon shifted his stance. Maybe Bob wasn't crazy, he thought. Maybe Bob was the canary in the coal mine.

Dan decided to join that flock. With very little actual knowledge about digital journalism—by his own admission—he wrote a passionate memo to the CEO of *Fortune* outlining a bold vision for Fortune.com, and soon he was put in charge of creating an online version of one of journalism's most iconic brands.

Two years in, however, Dan realized the economics of Fortune.com were not going to work. The problem was Google, which could serve any given ad to many, many more people in a more targeted way than Fortune.com ever could, and for much, much less. "Digital is probably the future," Dan decided, "but not how we're doing it."

Fortunately, Dan had already met the executive team at LinkedIn, when he talked to them about an API collab. They must have sensed his adaptability mindset, and next thing you know, he was hired to turn the company—then a place mainly for networking—into a content site.

In the early days, at home at night with his wife, Lisa, their two little boys sleeping close by, Dan would rationalize his leap into the unknown. "I'm just giving this thing two years," he would say. "Worst case, it all blows up, and we figure it out. At least I've gained some new skills and developed a new network. Best case, I learn some new things about technology that I need to know to stay employed as a journalist from now on."

Hilariously—in retrospect—Dan took a pay cut to go to LinkedIn. The opportunity to reskill was worth that much to him. I mean, he got equity, too, but he recalls thinking, *What's that ever going to be worth?*

Dan Roth for the win!

And not just because of the equity, but because Dan bet on the power and potential of his own Elasticity.

I'll ask again. Do you have that? Are you adaptable *like Dan*? If so, that has significant implications as you build your Area of Transcendence, in that it opens up the possibility of pursuing work in industries awash in change. You can even feel comfortable entering a brand-new industry, like quantum engineering, space mining, or AI, or taking a role at a company in the middle of a merger, say. Your Elasticity will keep you afloat.

If you're a person for whom change and/or reinvention is something of an anathema, on the other hand, it's helpful to acknowledge your lower Elasticity. There is no need for self-recrimination. Indeed, I applaud your self-awareness.

But for you, the goal should be to steer away from rocket-ship or roller-coaster jobs, companies, and industries. My dear friend runs a little home design shop in Brooklyn, which she specifically created to keep life slow and simple, inured from the topsy-turvy world just outside its doors. It's a beautiful sanctuary of a place, timeless in its vibe, and has ardent fans, who, like its owner, know that Elasticity is not really in them. And they're happier that way.

As they should be, and will be, with a purpose that fits.

Elasticity also encompasses your comfort level with what I referred to earlier as "irregular relationships."

To back up a little: as I explained, I'm not a big fan of networking.

I think it's mercenary and transactional. No one achieves long-term success because they glad-handed with strangers at faceless schmooze-fests. I've yet to meet one person who has ever said, "I owe it all to an acquaintance."

No, when people succeed because of people—which they often do—it is because of *friends*. Real friends. Regular friends. People who have a reason to help you when you need them. They like you. They love you.

But if you want a big, high-achievement career in our brave new world, you also need *irregular* friends, people from outside of your immediate circle. Why? Because, Young Grasshopper, when companies and industries go down, they go down together.

Yes, that was a *Karate Kid* reference. Not on your bingo card? Mine either, until I typed it.

Also not on anyone's bingo card usually—being laid off or fired.

But it happens, and it is likely to happen ever more frequently in a world that is being constantly upended by tech, geopolitics, economic change, and cultural transformation. Research on this topic varies somewhat, but among economists and workplace experts, it's generally thought that by 2030, the majority of jobs will be gig based. One such study even put the number at 80 percent.

You're likely going to be working for yourself someday, in other words, traveling from company to company, industry to industry, as your skills and expertise are needed.

Technology will surely facilitate such transitions, but it will help if you know people, especially people outside of your regular friend group, people not working at your last company, or in your last industry. When you're out looking for your next soft landing, such irregular friends are going to be your parachute.

If you have them. Do you? There's one quick way to find out, and it's with a technique called Relationship Mapping. Software for this process abounds, and some of it is even free. I highly recommend you invest the time to create—and confront—your own map. All my students go through the process, and it is always a day of eurekas.

Back in my days at Quadio, I ended up becoming good friends with the CEO of our development firm, an Irishman named Brian who lived and worked in Dublin. When Quadio crashed, he and I stayed connected. There was no reason for it. We had nothing in common, except mutual respect and nostalgia for a shared battle. But that was enough. We corresponded now and again, commented on each other's social media, and exchanged congratulations on babies (his) and new jobs (mine).

I never thought I'd work with Brian again—why would I? As a professor, I was out of the tech start-up business forever, as in foreeeeveeeer.

Yeah, then I invented two digital tools, the Values Bridge and PIE360.

Brian was my first call. We didn't need an NDA. I told him everything about the tools, and he told me exactly what I should do. His recommendations did not involve his firm—they were too busy—but he knew just the people. Thank you, my friend, I said, my irregular friend.

Now I realize that making friends with people who are unlike you can sound about as inviting as reskilling every six months. And if that's not in you, again, no shade. But that aversion suggests you steer yourself toward a career path that is firmer and straighter than one where you might need to ask for help every few miles. One with higher job security and longevity. One where a few close friends are all you really need. Or one, for instance, that is based almost entirely on skills, certifications, or training. A job that is connection-proof, and, thus, Elasticity-proof.

There's no harm in taking such a route—but you are at risk if you don't realize that's the map to follow.

The fourth and final compass coordinate is **Wonderment**, a combination of curiosity and currency.

WONDERMENT

Curiosity • Currency

Curiosity first. As is widely known, science has shown that curiosity is in large part driven by certain genetic predispositions, which suggests that just as you cannot make your eyes bluer, you cannot make yourself want to ask more questions. I mean, I'm sure you could come up with tricks to *prod* yourself into saying things like, "Really, tell me more!" but tricks are like Band-Aids. They fall off.

Thus, it is imperative that we take our true, authentic curiosity quotient into consideration when we are building our Area of Transcendence. Because some lines of work demand it, and others don't at all.

Ellen and I met each other when she DM'd me that she had grown tired of real estate sales, and she was wondering if I might look at her résumé, which she had reconfigured to land herself a job in consulting, or so she hoped.

I need to make it clear here that I do not *do* résumés. I have no special knowledge of this art form, in particular how to make résumés pop in the Age of AI. Plus, I am old school enough to think cover letters still matter, and apparently they don't. Bottom line: not my area.

But Ellen's message concerned me because I never like it when people craft a résumé without having discovered their Area of Transcendence first. You have to get existential, I like to say, before you get tactical. I told her as much, and this launched a vigorous back-and-forth about values, aptitudes, and interests. At first, I was like, "Hmm, maybe this woman is onto something with consulting, because she really values achievement. And she definitely seems like a Diagnostic Problem Solver." All good signs. Again I told her as much.

Finally, when we were just about to sign off, I spontaneously asked her, "Is there anything you're particularly *bad* at?" This is one of my shortcuts when I am doing an AOT on the fly.

A few minutes later, she typed back, "I hate research. It's boring."

I found the emoji for a red flag and sent her around thirty of them.

She sent a smiley face back, and that was that.

As many of you probably know, about 90 percent of consulting is research.

And being good at research is largely a function of your curiosity. Of how naturally you ask the next question, and the next one, and the next one. Of how authentically you want to dig a little deeper into things, and a little deeper, and a little deeper still. Either this propensity exists in you or it doesn't.

Ellen, are you still a consultant? I'm going to bet not.

Nor should you be, if curiosity is not your strong suit. The same principle holds for any other kind of job that requires a natural desire to mine for diamonds in the mountain of the unknown.

There's a second piece to Wonderment, however, that you *can* increase, and you should, if you have your sights set on a leadership role, or if you'd like to work in certain, particularly awareness-driven industries. I call it currency—being current, that is. This means having up-to-date knowledge about what's happening with your competitors, adjacent industries, and the markets. Knowing the big ideas floating around, the rising stars on the horizon, as well as the emerging tech, political movements, and demographic trends that will make a difference.

Andy was a Becoming You student who started our class as a recently discharged Army intelligence officer. He had served in Afghanistan, mainly operating surveillance drones during the US troop withdrawal, then worked as a chief of staff on a US base for a three-year stint before spending two years doing something classified in Poland. In his letter to me before the semester began, he wrote, "All I've ever known is the military. I am excited to be a civilian and enter the working world. I have no clue how, where, when, or what."

Maybe because of his long service in an institution without a lot of gray areas, Andy's values were unequivocal. Workcentrism was at 7, Achievement at 7, Belonging at 6, Agency at 4, and Eudemonia way down at 1. Andy's aptitudes made it clear why Intelligence had been such a good fit for him in the Army. He was a Specialist, a Fact-Checker, and a Future Focuser. This is an unusual array, but it made sense to me when I saw him in action. He also described himself as extremely curious, and his class participation bore that out. He struck me as self-aware, with stamina and energy that were high but appropriately contained.

As for interests, Andy had his sights on any company that might be willing and able to end his ten years of financial Spartanism. His Affluence registered at 6.

Given this data, it seemed obvious to me that Andy should parlay his MBA into interviews at any of the dozens of companies in the defense industry in the DC area, and he agreed, sending out a slew of job applications. The problem was that he was getting first interviews but no callbacks.

It just didn't make sense.

We were discussing the situation during office hours one day after class when I spontaneously decided to give Andy a mock interview. And after ten minutes, it actually did make sense.

"You don't have any opinions!" I told him. "You don't have a view, a perspective about what's going on in the defense industry—or the world. Is that really true about you?"

"I've been trained very hard not to share my opinions," he replied, surprised. "I just focus on the task right in front of me, and do it as best I can. It's not my role to have a point of view."

"Well, that makes you pretty useless to a competitive company in the geopolitical sphere," I told him. "You have to bring something to the conversation."

This was news to Andy, but it should not be to you.

Because he was in an industry—and there are so many today—where your currency is your currency. How valuable you are, in other words, depends on how in-the-know you are.

My advice to Andy was to recraft his outreach to reflect his high currency, and to show up at interviews with a narrative about why he would make any company smarter and better prepared for the future.

He did, and happily for both of us, he soon landed exactly the kind of position he wanted.

The entertainment industry is another place where your currency is your currency.

Two years ago, a friend in the TV business confided in me that she'd stopped watching TV herself. "I'm drowning in it all day. I can't go swimming in it again at night," she explained. As a result, she entirely missed two very buzzy shows on her own network. At the office, when they came up in conversation, she went along, adding comments based on what she'd gleaned from *The Hollywood Reporter* and any clips she'd seen on social media.

It wasn't enough. One day, a trusted colleague pulled her aside. "Are you okay?" she asked. "You used to have such good things to say. Now, just platitudes all the time. People are noticing."

My friend soon got back in the groove of watching everything she could on her network and all its streaming competitors. She also redoubled her reading, to stay abreast of rising actors and directors. Finally, she reinstated her practice of weekly luncheons with agents, whom she generally disliked, to keep her ears open for industry gossip.

Her relevancy campaign lasted about six months. "I just couldn't take it anymore," she told me. She felt overwhelmed by "noise and information," and compared the feeling to being sprayed by a water cannon at close range.

The wonder of her work had left her.

After a short break to regroup, my friend reconfigured her garage into a room of her own, where she's going to stay in show business in a way much more conducive to closing the aperture: writing. Her first project, she says, is going to be a piece of historical fiction set during the Italian Renaissance. No knowledge of the present—or future— required.

I love this solution.

Indeed, I love any solution that matches our level of Wonderment to the right job or career.

It's a story we should tell for ourselves.

We're now done with our round-the-dial tour of the Career Traits Compass, and my observations about how each component aligns with different jobs, roles, and even industries.

But I would be remiss if I didn't point out that, unlike PIE360 for instance, the Career Traits Compass is a self-reported assessment tool. And to repeat, one of the hardest things to know in life is . . . ourselves.

And that holds true for everyone, including Miss Becoming You.

The first year I taught the class, I decided to go through the 360 Feedback process with my students. *How fun*, I thought, *and how validating, too!* Because after all, if I didn't know myself, who did?

I am pausing here to sigh.

Following all the rules, I sent out the forms to my twenty raters, including three of my children who had worked at Quadio.

Now, this was a time in my life when things were a bit chaotic. Jack had died two years earlier, and I had only recently accepted my appointment as a full-time professor. I had also sold our old house, and bought a new one, which, oops, turned out to be a gut job. Quadio was closing down, and the pandemic was still somewhat with us. I went to bed at midnight and woke up at four forty-five every morning, and there still weren't enough hours to get it all done.

Yes, yes, my life is a Category 5 hurricane, I told myself, and yet surely everyone knows I am the calm in the eye of the storm. Surely, they were thinking, "Suzy has this!"

Suzy did not have it.

In fact, my results showed Suzy *was* the hurricane.

Stunned, upset, embarrassed, and yes, even a little offended, I quickly rounded up my kids on Zoom for an accounting. "Am I the hurricane?" I shouted at them.

There was an eerie silence. Then, finally: "Tell her!" Sophia whispered.

"No!"

"Tell her, tell her!"

"No!"

And back and forth until they finally confessed they had a theme song for me. It was a rap song by Kevin JZ Prodigy, with the grating refrain, "Here comes the hurricane, bitch!"

Ha ha ha!

I am sighing again.

Seriously, for a person who thought she knew herself, this wake-up call was hard to hear. I was not who I thought I was, or who I wanted to be.

It took a few months, but with insight and effort, I downgraded myself to a tropical storm. I modulated my Nerve, which was going overtime, and worked to increase the self-awareness and positive energy that are hallmarks of Soundness. (My Elasticity and Wonderment were fine, thank goodness.)

But the whole experience taught me something I needed to know, and I think you do, too: It is a lifelong challenge to know who we really are. But if we don't, we will never change. Which means we will never find our purpose in life, or get the chance to live it to the hilt.

On this point, I keep coming back to that haunting line at the end of F. Scott Fitzgerald's *The Great Gatsby*, when the novel's narrator, Nick Carraway, reflects on everything terrible that's just gone down among his cadre of fancy people. Wistfully, he seems to conclude that nothing really matters when it comes to getting what you want. Not wealth, not achievement, not love. We can try—but we can never really change who we are.

"So we beat on," he ruminates, "boats against the current, borne back ceaselessly into the past."

With all due respect to one of the greatest writers in the history of humanity, I just don't buy it. If I did, there would be no Becoming You.

There would be no Becoming You transformations. And there have been too many to count. Each one took the kind of self-knowledge this section on aptitudes talks about. Knowledge about how our brain works, and how our personality shows up.

We can *want* a certain life.

But our aptitudes—cognitive tendencies and personality traits together—help tell us if that life is ours to live.

10

Chloe in the Sky with Diamonds

Chloe the cloud, that's what her mother had called her. Floating and aimless, although, breaking with the usual cloud imagery, not free at all when I met her that frosty March morning over Zoom. Not free of anxiety, stress, fear, or angst. She seemed more as if she might dissipate into nothingness or burst into sorrowful sheets of rain.

Chloe longed for achievement, impact, and meaning in her life. She yearned for direction, community, faith, and a modest level of financial security. Almost every value she held dear eluded her. And yet, how to fix that problem did, too, because, as you may remember, Chloe had found herself doubting that she was good at anything at all.

How wrong she was. And how happy that makes me.

After our values analysis, I worked with Chloe on a cognitive aptitude assessment, like the one we went through in Chapter 8.

On Interpersonal Style, she was a full-blown extrovert, something I had seen with my own eyes when she was growing up. She could talk to anyone—and wanted to.

On Time Frame Orientation, Chloe was dead center, as a Balanced Focuser, able to shift from the forest to the trees and back again with relative ease.

On Visual Comparison Speed, Chloe proved to be a Visual Scanner, but I still used that as an excuse to tell the Sunny von Bülow story; I may never get over it. Then, on Inductive Reasoning and Sequential Reasoning, Chloe also tested at the midpoints, as an Investigator and a Collaborative Planner, respectively. She was also down the center in Spatial Visualization, as a Space Planner. And when it came to Numerical Reasoning, let's just say it was no big surprise to Chloe to find out that math was not her forte.

Indeed, Chloe's results only really spiked in two areas.

The first was Work Approach, where Chloe presented as the quintessential Specialist. "Why do you think I majored in Classics?" she said. She mentioned, too, her lifelong obsession with research, and how much that helped her when she was felled by Lyme. "I think I saved my own life," she observed, "because the therapy we ended up doing, the one that turned things around—I found that protocol, *I* did, in a *New England Journal of Medicine* article. I read everything. I mean, I think toward the end of my treatment, I knew more than most of my doctors." From her mother's accounts, that sounded about right. And, as if that wasn't enough evidence of a Specialist in action, Chloe then remembered something she used to do at the Lobster Shack, which was make index cards about all her regular customers, listing their names, family members, favorite orders, and other details, culled from checking out their social media feeds. "A little creepy?" she joked. "Maybe!" But turning serious, she added, "It's what made me good at my job."

Chloe's other notable aptitude result was in Idea Generation, where she was a pronounced Brainstormer. "It's true, I never run out of ideas," she said with a laugh when we discussed this result. "You'd want me to plan your academic conference," she continued. "I'd have six themes for you in five minutes. I'd have thirty activity ideas for every half-hour slot. Half of them might be ridiculous, but I'd have them." I asked her to tell me ways she was using her rapid-fire Idea Generation in her current life of gig work. There was a long pause, and finally she sighed. "I guess I'm not." Then she corrected herself. "When I'm babysitting," she said, "I can come up with a million things for the kids to do. The parents love that. Usually the kids just want to be on their phones."

We looked at each other across Zoom at that moment and sighed together.

"Chloe," I told her, "you're the most underutilized Specialist and Brainstormer whom I've ever met."

She asked me if that was good or bad, and I replied, "I'm hopeful. Let's keep going."

For personality, we turned to the Career Traits Compass.

We've already seen Chloe was very low on Nerve, impacted by her physical health, but also by her natural aversion to conflict and risk. But with Soundness, she was off the charts, with high self-awareness, positive energy, integrity, execution ability, and resilience. Her story of beating Lyme is downright inspirational, especially after being misdiagnosed for so long. I asked her if she harbored any ill will toward those doctors. "I let go of that long ago," she said, affirming my resilience formula for the umpteenth time.

Chloe and I agreed she had fairly high levels of Elasticity, based on the number of different kinds of jobs she had held and her wide variety of friends. "I've had to be adaptable," she reminded me. "I could learn how to teach chess tomorrow if it paid more than minimum wage." She added, "Everyone I meet is a friend. You know I like weirdos, right?" And finally, we agreed her Wonderment level tracked with her Idea Generation and Specialist designations: sky-high.

"I watch the news, I guess. I love hearing about the world, but more about its people than its wars and strife," she said. "Someday, I'd love to travel. Africa, Scotland, I'm obsessed. I have an app on my phone that teaches me about one new country every week."

I interrupt this chapter to say, Don't you love Chloe?

Anyway, there you have Chloe's whole aptitude profile, which is really where this entire section has been leading each one of us: to a list of aptitudes.

With Chloe's values and aptitudes in hand, all that was left to determine was her economically viable interests, and fortunately, she had just accidentally already revealed those, when she told me her attraction to event planning and travel.

And just like that, we had found our destination. Or hers, I should say. Most definitively and assuredly, hers.

Chloe has just passed her fifth year as a senior trip designer at a boutique travel agency that plans excursions for groups and individuals around the world. Her new life is, in her words: "Perfection, joy, sometimes hard, super rewarding, and all me." The company she works for is based in the Midwest, but she is able to work remotely, allowing her to take naps or lie down as her health demands.

I asked Chloe recently to describe a favorite trip she's planned. I didn't count on that answer taking an hour, but frankly, it was such a pleasure to listen to her describe her new life in all its perfect-fit glory. The custom Chloe excursion I remember best was a reunion in County Cork for thirty people who were either O'Rourkes or O'Rourke kin. Many in the group had never met IRL, but when they did, much merriment ensued, to put it mildly. ("The genes for red hair are very strong," Chloe noted, pulling out her phone to show me a few pictures her clients had sent her in gratitude.) After the clan's reunion in Youghal, they went on a weeklong walking tour of the countryside, which Chloe had crafted using every research technique under the sun. "Did you know Ireland's oldest cinema is in Youghal and it's totally refurbished in Art Deco?" she asked me.

No, I told her, no, I did not know that. But I was not surprised she did.

As Chloe went on to describe the cinema in even more detail, I could only recall the drummer from Disturbed, doing what he loved, what he was good at, in front of a crowd of cheering fans.

"Maybe you'll levitate!" I wanted to tell her—but, whatever, that would have been too weird, even for Chloe.

Now, to be totally clear here, Chloe's life is not perfect. Of course it isn't. She wishes her job allowed her to meet her clients, but that is not part of the company's business model. The steady employment, health insurance, and improved income, though, have enormously improved her day-to-day and allow her time and space to pursue other interests; she has found her way into a knitting circle with a group of women at her new church. Did I mention that along the way she also got engaged? I did not, because I thought it might begin to sound like a Hallmark movie. But darn it, she did.

The only cloud now in Chloe's life is that some of her health challenges have reemerged, as it appears that the Lyme wreaked more damage on her nervous system than previously known. She is working with a physical therapist regularly, but she also must now use a cane on occasion due to increased muscle weakness.

There is no such thing as a perfect ending—not with Becoming You, and not in life.

But how much better, how much more fulfilling, can it be if our narrative is of our own choosing and our own design along the way?

Look, aptitudes are not easy to discern. We wouldn't have needed four chapters to explain them if they were. But each one of us is like Chloe, a story waiting to be told.

Part III
Economically Viable Interests

11

Open the Aperture, Olivia

Every semester, there are students who walk through the door of my classroom knowing their values and aptitudes with clarity. But still, they're stymied by the "What should I do with my life?" question because their *interests* elude them. Especially their interests that are also economically viable. What kind of work calls them emotionally and engages them intellectually, they wonder, and is tenable as a life and a lifestyle they desire? Is it retail? Hospitality? Entertainment? Law? Teaching? Tech? Marketing? Operations? Is it in the trades, perhaps?

These seekers tend to fall into three categories.

- They find that too many opportunities interest them at the same time, and they can't bring themselves to choose. As one Becoming You workshop participant put it, "Why do I have to pick? I want to travel for a living. I want to be a therapist. I want to write a movie. I want to start a company someday. I want to be a polyglot!" My answer: "If being a polyglot meets all your wants and needs, go for it." Which brings me to an important point: Quite often, the work we do in Becoming You around values and aptitudes takes care of the "problem" of too many options, as people begin to see what's really important to them and what's really possible. But even then, there are people for whom "All of

the above" persists as they think about what exact field or industry or sector to enter.
- Two different, and usually mutually exclusive, pursuits are calling to them at the same time. Just this week, I received a long email from a Becoming You podcast listener describing his angst over which way to take his career. Would it be toward "the joy of cooking and intentional living" or "tech, AI, and automation?" This kind of either/or dilemma crosses my radar screen so often I actually have a name for it, the Cowbell Syndrome, in honor of the student who told me that some days he dreamed of being a country vet, caring for sheep and cows, and other days, he dreamed of ringing the bell on Wall Street as his tech company went public. When I asked him which of these divergent paths beckoned him with the most urgency, he replied, "Can I say both?" By the way, you are only allowed to snort at this story if you've never felt the gravitational pull of two opposing career narratives for yourself.
- And finally, there are EVI seekers for whom nothing in particular calls. This situation is rare—presenting perhaps 15 percent of the time, at least among my students and research subjects. And usually, I end up finding out something else is going on, like burnout or anxiety, which needs to be professionally addressed before further career planning can ensue. But other times, "interest ennui," as I call it, is an indicator that the student or client is looking in the wrong direction entirely. Like the former hospital nursing supervisor in one MBA section who came to business school with the intention of becoming a hospital administrator. Unfortunately, as graduation approached, jobs in the medical field were leaving him entirely cold. Then he started canvassing the pharmaceutical industry. Again, meh. Finally, he discovered—or perhaps "admitted" would be a better word—that his true passion was to become a stay-at-home dad. He was single, so

that was a small roadblock, but at least his "but it's all boring and empty" malaise found its root cause.

Regardless of which category they fall into, all of the above are in search of the same thing: an economically viable career.

Olivia was one such seeker. Mature, thoughtful, and with almost a decade of work experience under her belt when I met her as a student in the part-time MBA program, she was taking Becoming You because she knew she was ready to be done with financial services as a career. She didn't hate the work or the industry; it just carried no meaning for her. But what next? She had no idea—and that concerned her. "How can I figure out my Area of Transcendence," she asked me toward the end of the semester, "if I can't input the data for the 'interests' sphere?"

"Don't worry," I assured her, and I assure you, too. "Figuring out your interests with more clarity is usually just a matter of opening your aperture."

It's a matter, that is, of broadening your view of what kind of work actually exists. And thus in the next three chapters, we're going to take a look around, first, at the interests perhaps buried *within* you, then at the jobs, companies, and industries that *make up the world of work today*, and finally, at the *economic trends on the horizon*.

Such a survey, it turns out, can often surface the piece of data that finally alerts us to the purpose we've been waiting for, just as it did with Olivia.

Incidentally, it was the pandemic that sparked Olivia's disenchantment with financial services. She was twenty-seven and sharing an apartment on the Lower East Side with four roommates. Life was manageable, until everyone was home all day, trying to make Zoom calls at the same time. Almost overnight, work went from being a bit too slow and repetitive for Olivia's liking to being a mindless grind. Without the distractions of the office, including a few good friendships with coworkers, she increasingly found herself wondering, *What's the point?*

That question gnawed at Olivia more than you might imagine, perhaps because she came from a home where work did matter, and it mattered a lot. Her mother, who grew up in the Dominican Republic, began her life in America on an overnight custodial crew for office buildings, but within ten years, she was one of the four people running the cleaning company. Olivia's father, a former math teacher who immigrated from Haiti, had a similar career trajectory, except in private security for office buildings. He eventually managed over one hundred employees, and often spoke of his dream of starting his own business in the same space, one that would be better to its staffers and more efficient for its clients.

Because both her parents worked such long hours, Olivia was especially close to her sister, Ximena, nicknamed XiXi, fourteen months her junior. They both played volleyball in high school and, with their excellent grades, both ended up at the same college in Connecticut. Graduating Phi Beta Kappa, Olivia was quickly recruited on campus to join a company whose name produced oohs and aahs from her family and friends. A year later, her sister was recruited to a Chicago financial services firm and moved there after a jubilant neighborhood send-off.

Covid, however, ended XiXi's career abruptly. Instead of returning home to New York, though, she decided to move with her boyfriend to Denver, where they could live with his parents on a serene rural road with a view of the Rockies. He already had a remote job, and she would start looking for something in data analytics.

"Goodbye, city girl!" Olivia laughed when she heard the news. "Call me when you step on a rattlesnake." But there was no denying it—XiXi's new life intrigued her. The freedom, the flexibility, the pace, the chance every single day to go outside and *breathe*.

All it took was one visit for Olivia to say, "I'm in, too." She found an apartment outside Denver about fifteen minutes from XiXi and happily settled in. When the pandemic ended, her company agreed to let her stay remote, as long as she came to the office once a quarter.

Open the Aperture, Olivia

NYU allowed her to continue most of her studies online, but she had to travel weekly for my class and one other. Sometimes I would see her suitcase at the back of the classroom, and I would think, *That woman flew four hours to be here.* It had to be taking a toll.

It wasn't, though. When I asked Olivia about the commute, she told me it was worth it. For the first time in years, she could hear herself think. She'd learned to love hiking. She saw her sister every day. Denver was affordable, and life was simply better there. Now all she had to do was figure out work she could do locally that didn't leave her feeling numb.

Through testing in class, we discovered that Olivia was definitely on the get-it-done end of almost every aptitude spectrum. And not surprisingly, her 360 Feedback showed that her colleagues appreciated her competence and responsibility. There was one unusual spike in Olivia's aptitudes though, and that was her creativity. She was a Brainstormer, able to rapidly generate ideas without ego. As for personality, she was high on all four Compass coordinates, but especially Nerve. "No one can outrun or outwork me," she said, "and with me, let's just say decisions get made."

When it came to values, Olivia's Workcentrism and Achievement were aligned at 5. She had virtually no interest in Luminance or Radius, both at 2. Familycentrism scored a big 7 and Eudemonia a 6. As for Affluence, it came in at 4, too, neither a burning priority nor an irrelevant one.

Self-portrait complete, Olivia was ready to put down her paintbrush and step out the door.

She just needed to figure out which direction to go next.

12

Your Inner Calling (or Not)

Not long ago, I found myself doing a bit of TikTok doomscrolling.

Doom being the operative word in this case, as I was almost immediately served up a post from a young woman who was clearly on the verge of despair.

Here are her exact words:

"If you are in your late twenties or early thirties, what do you do for work? I have a college degree I'm not doing anything with that degree currently. I have experience in so many different things. But for some reason, when I think about going back into the workforce . . . I get so overwhelmed. I don't want to climb the corporate ladder, I don't want to go back to retail management, I don't want to go into healthcare. I just want to rescue dogs and live on a farm." Here she laughed sadly at the sheer impossibility of such a notion. Then she went on, "I don't even want to make a ton of money. I just want to live comfortably and be happy, and have the time to pursue my hobbies and passions outside of work. It just feels like that is not possible in the corporate America we live in. So, what do you do for work? I feel like there's got to be jobs that I'm just not thinking of."

"Help me out," she concluded, "because I know I am not alone in this feeling."

Argh! "Your problem is not *cluelessness*," I practically shouted at my phone, "your problem is *denial*."

Your Inner Calling (or Not)

This chapter is about looking *inward* for your interests.

Your *suppressed* interests, that is. And, by the way, I'm not only talking here to the people who find themselves in the third category of "interest ennui." Or the first, or the second.

I'm talking to everyone.

The phenomenon of suppressed interests happens all the time. Deep inside, we know exactly what kind of work is calling us, but *we* are the ones who won't pick up.

Importantly, such an impulse can be perfectly okay. It can be smart. It can be logical. The reason being that there are certainly times you *shouldn't* chase a passion—and to be specific, those times are when your passion collides with your values or your aptitudes. That's the whole point of Becoming You! Helping you discover a harmonious, integrated purpose, one that exists at the *intersection* of your aptitudes, values, and interests, not despite one or more of them.

I know a young man who dropped out of a fine university in Boston—where his parents were both academics, by the way—to join the circus. You couldn't make this up. He claimed clowning was his passion, and he moved to Philadelphia to attend an acclaimed circus theater training program. He managed to graduate but now tends bar. When I asked after him recently, his mother told me, "It turned out Terry couldn't juggle." Making matters worse, he'd come to discover that clowning was itinerant work, and that most people who pursued it usually had to hold down several jobs just to get by. Terry, it also turned out, valued predictability more than he'd ever realized. Which explains why he's back in school during the day while working at night. His next degree will be a master's in accounting.

When I heard about Terry, I was reminded of the professional athlete who retired in order to make movies starring herself at the cost of millions of dollars. When the first one failed to get distribution, and then the next and the next, a mutual friend commented, "Sadly, without talent, no one actually pays you to self-actualize." The operative word here is *talent*. Unless you have the appropriate skills, or independent wealth, or a huge and overriding value that cannot be denied, the hackneyed career-industry clarion call to "follow your passion" can be a fool's errand.

And yet—with that said—sometimes we *should* chase our passions. We should. We can juggle really well, for instance, and we loathe predictability.

But still—we don't go for it.

I have a friend who's a psychiatrist at a major teaching hospital who has long harbored a theory that people should reclaim their thirteen-year-old dream of a life and go live it. Then everyone would be happy, and he could retire. At eighty-four, he says he's ready.

"I think people know who they are and what they should be for the rest of their lives when they're still adolescents," he told me once, drawing on empirical data gathered in his fifty-plus years of practice. "Back in their early teens, even younger, too, they still had unfettered access to their inner lives; desires; and fundamental, deep, inborn aptitudes. They knew how their brain and soul would thrive."

"Then what happens?" I asked.

He shook his head. "They spend the rest of their lives running as far away from that knowledge, as fast as possible, until they can't even remember it anymore unless they're in therapy," he replied. "I don't know why this always happens."

Well, I know why, I told him, and so, Dear Reader, do you. It's the Four Horsemen.

You remember them, I hope: Economic Security, Expedience, Expectations, and Events. They're the social, cultural, and psychological dynamics that can so often short-circuit us on the way to dream fulfillment. And to summarize my long screed about them back in Chapter 4: the world is set up to talk us out of dreams.

Often, that "world" presents itself in the form of parents.

Your Inner Calling (or Not)

Oh, I'm not down on parents! How could I be, as a card-carrying member of the selfsame insane clown posse? But, even with the best intentions, parents have their agendas. And their limited information. And their *own* hopes and dreams. Some of which may have nothing to do with their children's values and aptitudes at all.

Parents are so often the culprit in dream killing that every semester I give the same homework assignment. It looks like this:

1. What did you want to be when you grew up?
2. Why didn't you?

Believe me when I tell you that virtually all the answers are the same. Not in their details, of course, but in their ethos. Here's an example of what I mean:

1. I always wanted to be an architect, and I was so good at it that my shop teacher in high school was really encouraging.
2. My parents told me that they worked so hard to provide us with a better life than what they had growing up and that we would do the same for our families one day. I started to major in architecture in college and loved it, but seeing the salary for an architect made me realize that if I pursued those dreams I would most likely disappoint my parents.

This student, by the way, ended up in product management for a software company. That's not a bad job, of course. But was it an aptitudes match? My guess is that it was more of an aptitudes *stretch*.

Here's another typical response:

1. I always wanted to work in a creative field. I wanted to be a director of movies and television shows. I wanted to create things and have an emotional impact on others.

2. I grew up financially insecure and both of my parents are horrible with money. I quickly saw how not having a baseline of money was not going to be okay for me. I had to rewrite the narrative my parents left me.

This student went into consulting. Sigh.

These kinds of couplets, semester after semester, were one of the reasons that I developed Six Squared, the exercise where you write the title of your current memoir, and then the title of the memoir of your story twenty years hence, *if you were able to lead the unedited life of your dreams.* It's why the Whose Life exercise prompts you to identify *other people* whose lives you want, and why Alpha Omega asks, "What would make you cry from regret on your eighty-fifth birthday?"

If you have not done these exercises yet, and your interests are what eludes you, I suggest you do them now. Or I suggest you revisit your answers with new eyes. They are all just sneaky ways of getting at the dreams you might be tamping down, because you think you should. Or your parents do.

This all hits very close to home for me.

For the entirety of my daughter Sophia's childhood, Jack and I thought she had a "problem" and it was TV, which she watched with the devotion of a pilgrim at Lourdes, sometimes even kneeling in front of the set in a state of rapture. It killed us. We tried to lure her away from her "addiction" by signing her up for sports leagues, ballet lessons, piano, pottery, painting, and volunteering for every good cause we could think of. We insisted she work every summer at one job or another so that she would be clobbered over the head with the fact that watching TV would never pay the bills. All of our efforts were for naught, as she would finish every forced activity by running to her room to watch one of her favorite shows, like *The West Wing* or *Alias*.

And school? It bored her. She put in minimal effort, and that's being generous. But ask her about what she was watching, and you would

Your Inner Calling (or Not)

hear back an encyclopedia of facts and opinions. So many opinions. About actors, and scripts, and which shows were being renewed or not.

Meanwhile, we worried frantically about what Sophia would do when she graduated.

Then one day when Sophia was a senior in college, I finally had the eureka I should have had ten years earlier. What if TV was not the problem—but the *solution*? I called Sophia in her dorm room and asked, "What would you think about going to Hollywood and trying to work in the TV business?"

She let out a small gasp.

"Would you let me?" she asked.

It still makes me want to cry.

I had almost let the Horseman of Expectations gallop away with me. I had *expected* Sophia to have the kind of career that felt familiar and "right" to me—marketing, writing, publishing—and, if I'm being totally honest, in close proximity to me, too, on the East Coast. And being young, dutiful, and loving, Sophia had almost let my expectations *happen* to her.

Luckily for both of us, she was on her way to California the day after commencement, where she began the life she was meant to have in television casting.

And fourteen years later, to her joy, still does.

I wonder if Sophia would have eventually ended up in Hollywood had she not started there? I doubt it. That's not how life works. Usually, when we step onto a pathway that's not our passion, bit by bit, year by year, promotion by promotion, we continue down the road with it. Until we're so far away, we think we can never go back, and the lid of the Velvet Coffin slowly but surely closes.

That's why it's so important not to bury our passions before we at least test them. Does this passion match my values? Does it match my aptitudes? Does it scare me because one of the Horsemen is galloping in my direction?

Or—and this is a hard question and a subtle one to confront—does it scare me because I harbor the belief that work is not supposed to feel good?

It's "work," after all.

I suspect that could have been the case with the TikToker who appealed to the world for job guidance. Because as I heard it, she knew exactly what she wanted to do with her life. She'd even stated it herself: *I just want to rescue dogs and live on a farm.*

What was stopping her? Clearly she had the values to pursue her dream; she stated as much. And while handling dogs does require certain aptitudes, like being a Present Focuser and having the traits of an Enneagram Helper type, it mainly involves skills that can all be learned. So let's consider the Four Horsemen.

As life would have it, dog rescue happens to be a field I am deeply familiar with. Not only have I rescued many dogs personally, I've served on the boards of several rescues, and I continue to serve on the board of the world's largest animal protection organization, Humane World for Animals. So let's do a little analysis, shall we? First, I can assure you that dog rescue is brimming with job opportunities. On the one hand, this is unfortunate, because it means that there are too many people doing dumb and unkind things, like abandoning their dogs when they move and backyard breeding for the fun of it. (Incidentally, the number one reason dogs are surrendered to shelters is because a new boyfriend or girlfriend doesn't like them. Yes, really.) Thus. overfilled shelters are not going away soon, and they are constantly facing labor shortages. The largest animal rescue in the Southeast, for instance, relies almost entirely on recently released convicts for staffing. This is, in some ways, a wonderful solution. It keeps the shelter running, and the dogs are cared for by people who have proven to be excellent employees over the years. It's also a service to a population that often has great difficulties reentering the working world. Of course, the biggest winners are the dogs, who, without this particular no-kill shelter existing, might meet their ends, which would make me *really* cry. I actually adopted my little dachshund, the Instagram-famous Pierre, from this very shelter, as well as the late, great Happy Welch, the gigantic, noble, and entirely aloof Great Pyrenees who was my husband's favorite person on earth besides me, but it was close.

Oops, I got talking about dogs, and off I went.

My point is that dog rescue is a viable industry, with ample job openings. If anyone, like our TikToker for instance, were to devote themselves to gaining experience in this space, they could end up running a shelter much faster than they could ever run a team or organization in the corporate world. As for affluence, you are never going to get rich in animal rescue, that's for sure. But the executives of some of the larger organizations in this space make six-figure salaries, and they deserve them. They deserve much more, trust me.

But let's put the Horseman of Economic Security aside. What about Expedience? No rescues nearby? Hmm, I doubt that. There are an estimated four million dogs in US shelters at any given time. With about fifty dogs on average in each facility, that means that there are about sixteen hundred shelters *per state.*

Then how about Expectations? Again, I'm not feeling it. Animal rescue is generally work that people admire and respect. I mean, "I work in dog rescue" is never going to prompt a mortified *"How could you?"* response. And the fourth Horseman, of Events? The TikToker's post didn't suggest there were major life changes or crises getting in the way of work. *Any* kind of work.

No, I think the utter sublimation of her interest came down to an all-too-common instinct.

When it comes to work, too many of us can feel that being able to live our dream is too good to be true. We don't deserve it, or that's not how it goes. Work needs to be hard and vaguely unpleasant.

Perhaps that's why the TikToker, urged on by thousands of respondents to her post, went on to focus her career journey on county government, data entry, and customer service from home, jobs described as having low stress and adequate benefits. In sum, "good enough" jobs.

Too bad they're missing the one passion she mentioned. The one that barks.

Amir was a student of mine who also decided his passion needed to stay closeted, for lack of a better word. He had spent four years in finance before coming to Stern with the intention of pivoting into consulting. He just didn't find anything to like about his previous job, he explained—not the research, not the analysis, not the modeling. I suggested to him that consulting might contain many of these same responsibilities, to which he shrugged. "It can't be worse."

Now, I don't want to sound inappropriate here, but it was hard not to notice that Amir had a hobby of weightlifting. It was like having a mini–Arnold Schwarzenegger in class every week, and really, not so mini. I believe the word I am looking for is *swole*.

One day, Amir missed class, and when he emailed to explain, he said he'd had a "rough night." I wrote back to suggest he produce better excuses when he entered the working world. "Oh, it's not how that sounded," he said, with a smiley-face emoji. "I was in the NYC Championships yesterday. Did not go well." He went on to tell me that he had been a finalist in a competition that he'd hoped to win, but he'd experienced muscle failure—called borking in gym slang—at two hundred kilograms on a move called the clean-and-jerk. I offered that I often "borked" at fifteen pounds on bicep curls, so I felt for him, and he laughed appropriately at the teacher's joke.

As the semester went on, Amir distinguished himself as completely disengaged with the work of Becoming You. I say this not to disparage him but because it was so unusual, thankfully. Regardless of the quality of my teaching, students tend to enjoy learning about themselves.

They come to class raring to go. But Amir always put himself in the back row, where I would spy him zoning in and out, with more out than in. Finally, I snagged him after class and asked what was up. He smiled sheepishly. He'd accepted a consulting offer, he told me. Becoming You had become a moot point.

I congratulated him. "Are you pleased?" I asked, because, despite the news, he certainly did not seem that way.

He shrugged. "It's fine."

"Just fine?"

Again, a sheepish smile, "Well, it's like you said, Professor, it's not too different from what I was doing before. Maybe it will get better, though."

"Amir," I said, "why don't you take your talents and aptitudes and go into the fitness industry? It obviously interests you and it's what you're good at—"

Talk about borking!

"Are you crazy?" he snapped, in a first from a student. "That's my hobby, that's my fun, I love it, it's not *work*," he said. "Plus, it takes years to get a gym to solvency. And people think you're a meathead. My parents would kill me. I already have a job in consulting."

I count three Horsemen in there, how about you? All but Events, right? I knew I could not fight Amir on this, nor was it my place. All I can say is, Amir, I hope you have found a way to make your sixty hours a week in the office into a life that (forgive me) pumps you up.

Seriously, it can happen. And it does—all the time. We've all met people working in their passion space, and seen and felt the glow emanating off them. Maybe we've even wondered, *Why not me, too?*

Good question!

My friend Stella spent the first chapter of her career as a medical researcher. Her parents had wanted a doctor in the family, and she got as close as she could, even earning a PhD in anatomy. At age forty-one, she finally mustered the courage to tell them that she'd never loved a single day of work. In their seventies by that time, her parents claimed they'd never even cared what she did. Knowing them as I do, I kind of doubt that, but whatever. Stella is a photography teacher now, and finally in her Area of Transcendence. (And happy, I might add.)

For Stella, the call within had started when she was eight years old, when she got her first camera as a birthday present. She kept hearing that same call all the way through college, where she took photography classes and shot pictures for the yearbook and newspaper. But all the while, she was hushing the voice that told her to make photography her life. And finally, as she sent in her graduate school applications, she was fully in STFU mode.

Advanced degrees led her to a neurology research lab at a Houston hospital, where, she would be the first to tell you, she was just putting in the hours. And her boss might add, "Not very well."

"I was a solid B when it came to performance," she recalls, "verging regularly on B-minus."

One day, word spread in the office that layoffs were coming at the hospital for cost-cutting reasons. Stella quickly booked time on her manager's calendar to give her notice and was, by mutual agreement, let go immediately.

Driving home, she could barely make sense of the emotions in her chest. She was overjoyed, relieved, and almost giddy. And she was terrified, anticipating the call she would have to make to her parents later.

Such is the grip that our dream-squashing instincts can have on us.

The call to her parents happened. They claimed that they were supportive, but it wouldn't have mattered if they weren't. Stella had reached that moment when she was ready to pick up her life's calling and begin again from scratch.

Now, as Stella is approaching seventy, her photography career is in full swing. She teaches a class online about how to write about photography; she is regularly hired to curate photography exhibits for museums around the country; she writes a popular blog about photography shows at galleries in Houston and beyond; and she judges photography contests.

Her story is actually an option that is available to all of us. Again, to stress, our values must be aligned, and our aptitudes, too. But if they are, our interests can finally speak into our lives.

And when they do, we can respond: "I'm listening."

13

All About... Industry

This chapter is going to be short, because I can't tell you about every industry, company, and job out there in the vast world of work. I can only tell you how you can find out about them for yourself.

Which you must do, if you are to open your aperture in the service of finding your economically viable interests (EVIs).

You might be amazed at what you see. Because here's a fact of life: We generally only "see" the work pathways native to our families, our friends, our social class, our location, or the ones that go along with our education or lack thereof. In business school, there's a conveyor belt into consulting and banking. Even if you arrive for your first year thinking, *Those industries aren't for me*, banks and consulting firms are on campus, calling your name in a way that's very hard to resist. Is it any wonder about 80 percent of MBAs, and not just at Stern, end up saying, "Well, if you insist"? But conveyor belts are everywhere. In Detroit, people tend to gravitate toward the automotive industry. It's where all the jobs are. Same in Miami, with tourism and hospitality. Same with energy throughout much of Texas. Similarly, I have a colleague who told me once she came from "a teaching family." I was about to say, "Wow, that's great," when her rejoinder came: "I should've been a lawyer. I just didn't know any different."

The last really robust tool designed to help people identify their

All About . . . Industry

interests and the career paths aligned with them was developed in 1970; it's called Holland Codes and it's quite good but also quite dated. Are you surprised I am attempting to update it myself? (If I manage this feat, I'll make sure to put it on my website.) But until that time, the "knowing any different" part—that's on us. And like so many things in this book, it's hard. Or let me put it another way: It's a discipline. A *practice*.

You have to develop ways to actively and regularly learn about different kinds of jobs, different kinds of companies, and different kinds of industries.

Key words: actively and regularly. This is one of the many reasons Wonderment matters and your currency is your currency. Because the work landscape is always changing.

In Becoming You, to jump-start this practice, we play bingo.

Industry Bingo, that is, which I created to help students see that there are scores of industries in the economy—scores!—containing hundreds of companies, and within those companies, dozens of types of jobs.

Here's how Becoming You Bingo works.

Every student gets a card that resembles a traditional bingo card, except instead of each little box containing a number, it contains an industry. Sometimes I throw in an MBA-friendly industry like banking or retail, but more often, the cards are filled with anything but the usual suspects, industries such as Fruit and Nut Tree Farming, Rubber, Amusement Parks and Arcades, Forestry, and Mining. (Also: Home Furnishings, Farm Equipment, and, yep, Animal Rescue.)

As per normal bingo, after everyone has a card, I randomly pick industries from a hat, and the first student who fills in a row or column wins. All in, taking in all the different bingo cards in the room, students are exposed to about 135 industries just with this little game.

Here's the twist. After a few rounds of playing, when we have seven or eight winners in the room, I break everyone into groups and give them ten minutes to speed-research one of the industries on their bingo cards. Their assignment is then to answer the following questions:

- How big is this industry in terms of market capitalization and employment? Is it growing, and if so, by how much?
- What are some notable companies in this industry, and what are they known for? Innovation? Growth? Sustainability?
- What kinds of jobs does this industry contain? What kind of individuals, with which skills and aptitudes, might find success? Be expansive in your thinking. Specialty chemicals is not just for chemists, people!
- Why would this industry be a cool or interesting place to work? What might a career in this industry feel like? Sell us on it!

This exercise is contrived, I suppose, but it's also a blast. An information explosion! Over the semesters, I've come to learn that RV parks are one of the fastest-growing businesses in the recreation industry, and an excellent fit for someone with an entrepreneurial spirit and a love for the outdoors. Forestry is also growing to the sky, and it has a booming need for people with an interest in sustainability. And how about this as a fun (and important) fact: the fastest-growing industry in the United States over the next five years, truly the fastest, is expected to be fruit and nut farming, with a 28 percent leap in revenue growth annually. There are all sorts of reasons for this trend, and I invite you to read about them online, along with information about other, similarly expanding industries, such as solar power, online gambling, 3D printing, rapid prototyping, and frozen food production.

Wait, where's tech, you're wondering? Where are Alphabet, Amazon, Apple, Google, Nvidia, and Meta? Companies that everyone knows are growing? Companies that let you say to your relatives, "Yeah, I work at—" with a nonchalant shrug.

All About . . . Industry

Those companies, friends, are not the point of the kind of aperture opening I am encouraging here. First, you already know about them. Second, everyone wants to work for them. And given their reputations, a lot of these companies can get any employee they want. In the buyer-seller equation, they are the buyer.

The thing about the more far-flung, lesser-known industries that surface in Industry Bingo is that they are the *seller*. People are not exactly flocking to jobs in the fruit and nut farming industry, okay? Who even knows about it? But if fruits and nuts *interest* you for any reason, opportunities are (here I go again) ripe for the picking.

Now, most of my students love Industry Bingo, but occasionally, I have a student who complains that the game is unnecessary for the likes of MBAs. I beg to differ. One student, Barbara, is a good illustration. She was talking herself into taking an offer in data analytics at a big clothing retailer, despite the fact it held little appeal for her, when her bingo card included a square for shipbuilding, an industry that just so happens to employ about five hundred thousand people worldwide, with a market cap of around $150 billion, and projected growth to approximately $190 billion by 2030. Some of the jobs in this field are obviously only for experts in nautical design and heavy manufacturing, but like any industry, it needs people in marketing, HR, sales, operations, project management, finance, and communications. This, by the way, is one reason why Becoming You includes all that aptitude-discovery work: so that you have a better sense of which business *function* suits you—no matter what the industry.

In class, Barbara and her bingo team ended up making quite the pitch for shipbuilding, with their report concluding, "This industry would be a cool place to work for anyone who loves travel, as it's a very international space. It's great also for people who are fascinated by geopolitics, which affects this industry more than most, and those interested in rapid career acceleration, as it has a dearth of executive talent."

I will never forget Barb coming up to me after class, almost in a trance. "I love boats. I love the sea. I love the whole idea of maritime commerce," she said. I quickly learned that her brother shared this interest and was in the merchant marine, although that kind of work—six months at sea, six months at home—held no appeal for her.

Barbara's aptitudes signaled she had everything it took to be a leader in *any* industry. She was a Future Focuser, Sequential Thinker, and Diagnostic Problem Solver. All of these aptitudes, by the way, made her an odd fit for the role she was considering in data analytics, which favors Specialists, Present Focusers, and Fact-Checkers.

Just to be thorough, I asked her about her values, and she immediately reminded me that she had scored a 7 on Achievement on the Values Bridge; she didn't just want career growth, she yearned for it. Her Workcentrism was also high, at 6. But what really caught my attention was her ranking on Scope, which also came in at 7. International travel and geopolitics, anyone? I pointed out this alignment to Barbara, at which point, teacher and student considered each other with raised eyebrows.

"Why did shipbuilding never occur to me?" Barbara asked.

Now, I wish I could say Barbara immediately went home and redirected her job search to her new industry crush, but life is rarely that neat. Instead, she did end up going into data analytics, but I have hope that when that job begins to bore her, which I suspect it will, the sea will surely be waiting for her.

If you were born after 1968, you probably know of *What Do People Do All Day?* the classic Richard Scarry board book. Having read it to my own children roughly 4 billion times, I have to assume that it's the precursor to Industry Bingo, except that Scarry's fictional Busytown doesn't include, oh, about 90 percent of the jobs in the world. No digital product managers, no audience strategists, no AI risk and safety

All About . . . Industry

engineers. It's all firemen, ambulance drivers, teachers, and bakers—the world of work you can see right before your very eyes.

I am sorry to report that, as noted earlier, there is no real, modern, adult equivalent to *What Do People Do All Day?*, which really leaves your own Wonderment. That is, your ability and propensity to say, "What else is out there? I want to know."

In pursuing the answer to that question, I want to recommend reading (or at least skimming) the newspaper every day as your best starting point, and in particular, the *Wall Street Journal*, the diary of the world economy. I realize this can be a time-consuming undertaking, but if you make it a habit, eventually you will find yourself exposed to virtually every kind of work happening in the world.

If you'd like a more immediate or more intense fix, Appendix F contains several websites, books, and newsletters that showcase industries, companies, and jobs, a list that my own website's Resources section regularly updates.

And finally, I suggest you try a technique that's not just helpful for interest identification, but for life in general. It's the practice of saying *maybe* before you say no.

Like so many of my personal clients, Paul was a recovering banker. Drawn to the industry after college because of its reputation for high pay, he was soon to discover that he made good money but not great, because he had neither the values nor the aptitudes to rise through the ranks. At heart, he was an adventurer. He loved to travel, to explore new places but also to meet new people. And with his natural warmth, humor, and empathy, people loved him back. He returned from every trip with new friends, whom he loved welcoming during their own travels to the US. As a result, Paul's life at the bank was an exercise in passing the time between vacations, and it drove him crazy that he had to cram his "happy place" into only three weeks a year. Whenever work allowed, and sometimes when it didn't, he would spend hours scrolling through social media planning his next trip, as well as keeping up with the friends he had made during his past ones.

When Paul contacted me for advice, his presenting question was, "Which industry will allow me the most vacation time?"

Instead of answering, I invited Paul to think about which industry would allow him to live his values and aptitudes on a regular basis.

I got back a hard no.

"If you're suggesting the cruise industry or the travel industry, forget it," he said. "I've looked at all those jobs, and the pay is terrible and the lifestyle sucks. You're always on, and guests are rude to you." He reported that his research showed that most people who went into travel as a profession ended up hating it.

I urged Paul—and I am urging you, too, when it comes to interest exploration—to try to stick with "maybe" for longer than you might like. Because when it comes to less familiar kinds of work, or industries with less well-known career pathways, sometimes you have to dig longer or harder for your entry point.

At my insistence, Paul set out to test his no. He sent emails to fifty travel industry professionals he found on LinkedIn and asked for fifteen-minute informational interviews, and to his surprise, three people said yes. Their conversations opened his eyes to career ideas and options he'd never encountered before. In the weeks afterward, he identified several graduate schools with hotel and travel industry programs, and he spoke at length with their admissions officers about the kinds of jobs their students landed. Using his college's alumni directory, he tracked down and spoke to a flight attendant, a pilot, and a graduate two years ahead of him who had lived around the world while working for an international hotel chain. Their careers had their downsides, as all careers do, but again and again, he was hearing about work experiences that made his heart pound with excitement.

All About . . . Industry

Slowly but surely, Paul's no evolved to maybe and then, much to his delight, to "What other kind of life is there for me?"

"I just think I didn't know enough about the industry and its opportunities," Paul told me.

It's so easy to say no to the unknown.

To learn more and make up for lost time, Paul actually decided to go back to school to get a degree in hotel administration. It would, he reasoned, ultimately unlock the most doors in an industry that had more openings than he'd ever imagined.

That imagining—that saying no to an initial no and saying yes to maybe—it's part of opening your aperture, too.

The world of work is vast and complex. It's natural to gravitate to known highways and byways.

But if your interests elude you—and even if they don't!—it never hurts to lift your eyes and explore the untrodden path, too.

14

Magnesium on Mars, and Other Megatrends

Our last bit of interest exploration shifts our focus to the far horizon—the EVIs of the future.

In doing so, we will be joining the ranks of crystal-ball readers. Sorry, that's what it comes down to. Predicting the future and its opportunities is hard, gritty, high-brain work, a mixture of art, science, data analysis, outright guessing, and assumption suspension. And even then, most people don't get it right.

Are you surprised that I'm going to recommend it anyway?

I write this chapter knowing that very few people get excited about jumping into just-emerging, very nascent industries. It feels too risky. I also know that a lot of people hate it when they realize they're working in an industry that has peaked or is, well, dying. Or that they regret the particular time, or two or three, when they passed up an opportunity to take a seat on a rocket ship, usually out of fear.

The antidote for this, at the very least, is to know what's coming—or, to be more precise, to know what's *said* to be coming. To (once again) actively and regularly stay atop the prognostications of experts. Yes, yes, even then, no one can ever really know the future. It's as the most famous line from an old TV show puts it: "Nobody expects the Spanish Inquisition." But we can still try to foresee auto-da-fés and amnesties alike, and for the sake of our learning, our insight, and our careers, we should.

Have you ever seen *The Graduate*?

The movie was released in 1967, to deserved acclaim. It stars Dustin Hoffman and Anne Bancroft, in all her rapturous thirty-six-year-old glory, and was directed by the great Mike Nichols. The plot follows Benjamin Braddock, a recent grad from what is hinted to be Williams College, who is passing time at his parents' plush home in Pasadena, California, while trying to figure out what to do with his life. Eventually, the hapless Benjamin ends up getting seduced by the "older" Mrs. Robinson (never mind that Hoffman was only six years younger than Bancroft), but that actually has nothing to do with my point here.

No, my fixation on this movie has always been related to the scene when Benjamin's parents throw a cocktail party for him with their well-heeled friends, in hopes of getting him interested in something, *anything*, in the world of work. You can tell that Benjamin hates every moment of the party, along with everyone attending it. He's just going through the motions. Because, as the audience knows, although he himself clearly does not yet, Benjamin is a guy who is not going to end up in a plush manse. He's going to be a sweet loser.

In one hilarious exchange, a woman at the party corners Benjamin and asks, "So, Benjamin, what are you going to do *now*?" To which he responds, "I was just going to go upstairs for a minute." Laughing as if this misunderstanding of her meaning is simply darling, she pushes back with, "No, I meant with your future, your *life*."

"Well, that's a little hard to say," Benjamin replies lamely.

At this exact moment, Ben is pointedly interrupted by Mr. McGuire, another guest at the party, and one of the most apt personifications of Corporate Man that you've ever seen. He beckons the graduate outside for a man-to-man talk by the pool, where we soon see Mr. McGuire essentially holding Benjamin in a bear hug so he will not run off, as he so clearly wants to.

I cannot do their exchange full justice, it's so awkward. Just try to visualize Mr. McGuire sticking his free index finger into Benjamin's chest and speaking with the authority of the world, and Benjamin answering in a monotone flat enough to iron. (Or go look up the scene on YouTube. I'll wait.)

Mr. McGuire: I just want to say one word to you. Just one word.
Benjamin: Yes, sir.
Mr. McGuire: Are you listening?
Benjamin: Yes, I am.
Mr. McGuire: *Plastics.*
Benjamin: Exactly how do you mean?
Mr. McGuire: There's a great future in plastics. Think about it.
   Will you think about it?
Benjamin: Yes, I will.
Mr. McGuire: Enough said. That's a deal.

When I saw this movie in a theater as a kid, as we did in those days, people roared with laughter. What a pompous asshat Mr. McGuire was! What a capitalist lackey! In college, watching this movie again with my friends, we also roared. What a mercenary corporate tool!

It was only much later that I found out the fictional Mr. McGuire also happened to be 100 percent right. Indeed, just about the time he was all up in Benjamin Braddock's grill, the young Jack Welch was gleefully accepting a job in the brand-new plastics division at GE, where he was excited to put his new doctorate in chemical engineering to work.

Jack got in early on one of the biggest megatrends in industrial history and rode it to the Moon. I don't think there was a day in his life when he was not grateful to plastics. And to be honest, I am grateful, too—not specifically to plastics, but to the fact that Jack had the foresight and courage to leap into what was just a glimmer of a glimmer of a glimmer of an economic opportunity. To leap into what was really just a possibility. I mean, when he started at GE, no one was even manufacturing plastics outside a university laboratory. In 1964, at age twenty-nine, Jack led the project to build the first plastics factory, in Selkirk, New York.

I once asked Jack about the Mr. McGuire scene in *The Graduate*, wondering if he, too, had found it funny. I was actually stunned by his ire. Jack was a cheerful optimist to his core. But at the mere mention of the "There's a great future in plastics" line, he became irate. "It's easy to make fun of business," he said, "but we were out there busting our asses to start something new. No safety net. No guidebooks. No clue if it was going to work out. We just believed, and we were hungry to win."

"Was it scary?" I asked him, because that was what he seemed to be suggesting.

"Terrifying," he answered.

But for the GE leaders and employees who were willing to be that scared, it was worth it.

Over the course of his career, Jack got in early on many other emerging industries. Some gambles worked, such as starting CNBC, the first-ever financial news network; and some did not, such as the ill-fated alternative football league, the XFL. In this way, he was like every participant in the megatrend merry-go-round. Sometimes you win, and sometimes you lose. But you play.

Unless you don't. And that, alas, is most of us.

Every semester in Becoming You, I endeavor to introduce my students to the best thinking about emerging technologies and megatrends.

The latter of these, megatrends, can be economic, cultural, or geopolitical. For the sake of clarity, I lump everything together and call all economically viable interests of the future "super-early potential opportunities," or SEPOs.

I have to be real here. When our section on SEPOs begins, students generally trudge along with sparse enthusiasm. I feel like a camp counselor taking kids on a hike during a rainstorm.

At first, the resistance to SEPO exploration surprised me. My first theory was: MBAs hear about new tech and emerging industries in all their other classes. Maybe I'm just being redundant. And indeed, this ended up being true about AI, which is woven into every single class at NYU, just as it is at most schools these days. So I dropped the discussion of AI from my lectures.

But that didn't really change things. I remember one day lecturing about commercialized space exploration, a SEPO based on the hope and expectation that humans will someday be able to extract minerals on other planets, like magnesium on Mars and titanium on Venus. Those who have bought into this opportunity estimate that someday, if things work out, it could be a $1 trillion industry, bigger than aerospace and mining on Earth put together.

"That's just amazing, isn't it?" I prompted my students that day in class. "I mean, imagine! There could come a time when all that mining we do on Earth, causing all that environmental damage, could be moved to planets without people and animals? If it works, the people who join the companies betting on it today will have quite the ride—literally!"

Two students vaguely chuckled. The rest zoned out.

All in, I'd say less than a quarter of my students take SEPOs to heart, but when they do, my own heart soars for them.

Hua was from the Chinese city of Chengdu and an engineer by training. She loved business, however, and was at NYU to discover how to turn her aptitudes into a career in industry, and by aptitudes, I mean an incredibly keen mind for problem solving, strategic thinking, and numbers. As for values, she was very high in Workcentrism, Achievement, Affluence, and Scope. It is rare to find a fellow 2 in Eudemonia, but I had a comrade in Hua.

Early on in the semester, I had a feeling Hua was going to gravitate toward entrepreneurship because of her hunger for success and her often unusual perspective on things. For instance, one day she mentioned that she was interviewing with a company that made clothing that dissolved, and I do not think I was alone in the room in thinking, *The reason being . . . ?*

I don't know what happened to the dissolving-clothing venture, but I do know that when Hua presented her Area of Transcendence to the class, she envisioned her future as the CEO of a company in the mobility industry, one of that semester's SEPO focus areas.

Did you know that drivers in Munich waste an average of eighty-seven hours in traffic every year, in Los Angeles that number is one hundred nineteen, and in Mumbai it's more than two hundred? Did you know that worldwide, 1.3 billion vehicles are now in use, with about 45 percent of them being privately owned? Neither did I, until my research informed me that one of the most promising SEPOs is "mobility," which might be described as the business of making getting around easier, cheaper, cleaner, and more efficient. That could mean more scooters, more trains, or even flying cars. It could mean inventions not yet out of the lab or factory. No one knows for sure yet, but some think tanks have predicted mobility could be a $250 billion industry within ten years.

That is all Hua had to hear in class. A veteran of her city's epic traffic jams, she said she knew an opportunity when she saw one. Her own research led her to a company in Sydney with a two-person electric bicycle prototype, and she was in conversations with them about coming on board as a project manager. All part of an exciting career journey, she hoped, in an industry that was on the cusp of a new beginning, just as she was.

Hua got a lot of applause for her Area of Transcendence presentation. First of all, it was insightful and well prepared. But her classmates admired her zest for the unknown and the courage she was showing by leaping into it. I know I did, too.

Now, little would give me more pleasure here than wearing you out with my ruminations on the many and sundry SEPOs people are talking about today. But I will do you one better and let you hear about them from the expert researchers, analysts, and consultants who know about them best. Thus, in Appendix G, you will also find a compendium of the forecasting websites, podcasts, and reports that I trust the most. I can't make you take a look at these resources, but to quote Mr. McGuire, "Think about it. Will you think about it?"

While I am generally risk averse, I did chase a SEPO once, and it was with Quadio, which was in the music tech space. Even though we didn't make it, those few years were among the most exhilarating of my professional life.

Exhilarating *and* petrifying.

During that period at Quadio's helm, especially when it all felt incredibly fragile and I feared I was steering us into yet another hurricane, I often thought of the Magnificent Seven, as I called them in my mind. They were seven classmates of mine at Harvard Business School who did the craziest thing upon graduation in 1988.

They moved to Silicon Valley.

We all thought they were insane. Please recall that back then, we didn't even use personal computers. Silicon Valley was just an area near Stanford University with a few start-ups situated along Sand Hill Road. That address means something special now, but at the time, it meant nothing at all.

I recall asking someone why the guys in the Mag Seven were "dropping out," as it seemed. Any of them could have gone into banking or consulting, like the rest of the class. After all, they were the best of us. Great personalities, fabulous résumés from their previous lives at the likes of Goldman and BCG.

"I think they really love golf," was the answer from a classmate.

No lie. That was the answer.

Anyway, a few of them are gazillionaires now, and the rest are doing just fine, thank you. At reunions, they all seem to have the nicest tans. Maybe they did like golf, after all.

Or maybe, they were the anti–Benjamin Braddocks of our time who, somewhere along the way, heard our era's version of "Plastics. Enough said" and, instead of trying to run away, ran straight for the cliff and leaped boldly for the future.

SEPOs are not for the faint of heart. They never have been and never will be. But to truly identify our interests, we must look inward, around, and then outward. Only then is our Becoming You journey complete.

15

Olivia, Eyes Wide Open

Olivia had told me she was worried about ever identifying a new direction for herself post–financial services, and I had assured her not to be. Looking back, I think my hope had been that Industry Bingo would spark a new "Oh, that's cool" awareness in her, and off she would go.

But in class, it was easy to see that Industry Bingo left her unmoved, and my hard labor trying to make megatrends come alive similarly seemed not to impress. I won't say I saw Olivia's eyes flutter closed when I started talking about quantum technologies, but I saw her eyes flutter closed.

Thus, it was with great anticipation (and trepidation) that I awaited her final presentation to the class. I was confident she knew her values with clarity, and her aptitudes, too. Her perfect EVI was still a mystery to me, but I hoped it wasn't to her. Especially given the fact that she had traveled back and forth to Colorado a whopping twelve times to discover her Area of Transcendence.

When at last the big reveal came, it took me by happy surprise, and Olivia, too, it seemed. She presented her project with a smile on her face as bright as Colorado's big sky.

"Co-Founder and Co-CEO, Sisters Office-Staffing Solutions," the center of her Area of Transcendence chart read.

As the class listened intently, Olivia described how she finally came up with the kind of work that called her.

Olivia, Eyes Wide Open

"I was hiking one morning with XiXi," she said. "That's the way we like to start the day, and usually, to be honest, we don't talk that much." But that day, she went on, the deadline to come up with an AOT for class had her brain churning, and as they sat on a rock ledge atop a small mountain they'd just climbed, she asked her sister, "What could we do *together*? I mean, I just want to work with you. I've known that for years and years. But I've always been afraid to say it. Because it's crazy, right? Or maybe it's not?"

XiXi burst into laughter. "I thought you'd never ask!" she said. She had grown tired of her freelance jobs in data analytics, which paid well but left her feeling enervated by their lack of connectivity and impact. She, too, had long dreamed of working with her sister, but had pushed the thought away as impractical.

For the next hour, the sisters watched the sun rise and started to form the idea for a company in the sector they knew best, office cleaning and security staffing. The industry was screaming for improvement, they knew from almost three decades of observation, as it is rife with logistical inefficiencies that hurt both employers and employees. They began to imagine a web-based application that would take out the two layers of middlemen that, in their estimation, added very little value at a very high cost. Their conversation was filled with what-ifs, and as they brainstormed with each other, the sisters were so excited they practically ran down the mountain to start getting their ideas on paper.

True to the Becoming You process, Olivia and XiXi also took the time to do a values check with each other. They were aligned, both wanting an entrepreneurial venture more bent on making change than going public. Both women strongly desired lives of flexibility and self-determination. Both rated Familycentrism a 7. When it came to money, Olivia was satisfied with a 4, XiXi a 5. As you might recall, Olivia scored 5 on Workcentrism. XiXi had discovered by taking the Values Bridge that she was a 6. Neither had any interest in Luminance, but Non Sibi was a shared value at 7.

They then did a survey of both of their aptitudes and discovered more good news. Olivia's adeptness at execution, along with her non-ego-bound creativity, were a perfect match for XiXi's bent toward future focusing and strategic thinking. Both women were extroverts, filled with the Nerve and Elasticity that every entrepreneurial venture requires.

That evening, notes in hand, the sisters called their parents to run their idea by them. The conversation lasted two hours as they added a plethora of suggestions and improvements and cheered their daughters on. "We need you to do this!" her father said before their goodbyes. He and their mother would be Sisters Office-Staffing Solutions' first investors.

At long last, Olivia knew what it felt like to have purpose.

And she could see in her sister's eyes that she was not alone.

All of that hopefulness shone through as Olivia presented her AOT to the class, along with slides illustrating the business's rollout, first in the Denver market, and then Colorado Springs, and then Albuquerque.

When she was done, a classmate asked when she planned on getting started with the venture.

"I gave my notice when I was in the office today," she said, to a round of applause. She added that her boss wasn't surprised and noted that her heart hadn't been in the work for a while.

"Understatement!" Olivia added for effect. Then, more seriously, she thanked her group for putting up with her during its Industry Bingo presentation and its SEPO report project. "You were all looking outward, and I was looking in," she reasoned. "I appreciate your patience."

There were nods of understanding all around. And that's how it often goes for those seeking their EVI. Until they find their direction, all are lost.

And then, at last, with eyes wide open, they're found.

Part IV
Conclusion

16

A Forever Kind of Thing

I hate the last day of Becoming You, and, not gonna lie, I hate writing this conclusion, too. Because as a methodology, Becoming You is meant to be a forever thing, a way of thinking and sorting things out that you return to at every crossroads, time and again. What are my values? My aptitudes? My interests? And what does that make the Area of Transcendence at the intersection of all three? Ah, yes, I get it. Understood. That's why this new direction, or this next step, makes the most sense. I'm ready.

The Becoming You–forged path you take at first might change with time, a little or a lot. It probably will. Life happens. But when it does, and you reach another crossroad, Becoming You awaits you. That was, and is, my intention with this book.

It is not intended as a prescription, a one and done. It is a companion—dare I say it, a friend. I will never apologize for the cringe!

I hug a lot of my students goodbye on the last day of class. We've been on an important journey together. I am hugging you now, too.

And I will do so with these words: We really have just two ways to live our lives. By default or by design. We can be the editors of our lives, or the authors.

And I, living my own purpose to the hilt, my heart filled with love and hope, have been the author of this book in hopes that you can and will be the author of yours.

The final slide in every student's AOT presentation on the last day of class is supposed to depict their AOT-guided life thirty or forty years in the future. It should answer the question we begin class with, played out to the nth degree: *Tell me, what is it you plan to do with your one wild and precious life?*

For Olivia, that had meant finding a way to show what Sisters Staffing would look like when she and XiXi were in their sixties. For that, she had turned to the magic of AI for help, and the result was an illustration of her and XiXi kicking back on the front porch of a ranch along a Colorado riverbank. "We're happy because we've just sold our company for $30 million," she narrated, adding they'd used some of their windfall to create a scholarship in their parents' names at their alma mater. She also drew our attention to the scene in the picture's background: horses, chickens, mountain bikes, and grandchildren.

There is a reason Becoming You is called the class where everyone cries. Although sometimes, and maybe a lot of the time, the biggest crybaby is me.

There were other presentations that day, of course, many of them also heartrending, filled with confirmation again of what can happen when we do the demanding work of excavating our values, identifying our aptitudes, and finally figuring out, one way or another, the kind of work that fills our hearts, minds, souls, and bank accounts, all in the right amount for us.

There were also presentations by students who did not reach a "perfect" AOT, and who did not narrate their future lives filled with voices of hope. That happens. Of course it does. The searching involved in Becoming You sometimes does not fit neatly into a semester. Indeed, sometimes all we hear on the last day is a field report from our fellow travelers who are still on the journey, though not for lack of trying. They are still seeking answers to some of the most profound questions we will ever ask ourselves, about who we are and what we should do with ourselves with the days we are given.

I love both the seekers and the finders. In the end, because the Becoming You journey does not end until we decide it should, we are one and the same, forging onward.

Borne ceaselessly into the future.

Appendixes

Appendix A
Six Squared

Six Squared is a two-part challenge.

First, think about the story of your life to date, as if it were a memoir. Now, write its title using only six words. I realize that summing up your life in six words is not easy, sorry. And yes, just six words. Because somehow that number of words is a magical catalytic mechanism. No, I don't know why.

It's interesting. I've facilitated this exercise countless times now, and there's a vast range in how long it takes. Some people nail it on the first try. Fifteen seconds and they're done. Others agonize and take the full fifteen minutes I usually allot. Still others can't complete the assignment until they have a few hours to contemplate and revise and revise again.

All I can say, as you do this part yourself, is take the time you need. It's worth it.

_____ _____ _____ _____ _____ _____

Now for the second part. I'd like you to imagine your life twenty-five years hence. Your *perfect* life, that is. The one you would have if you could live by your values, achieve your hopes and goals in every sphere of your life, and do what you want to do.

This is the story you would tell if you were the *author* of your life, not the editor.

Go ahead, allow yourself to imagine *that* life in all its glory. Imagine waking up in the morning, the hours afterward, the first activity, the next, the afternoon, the evening, the bedtime. Where are you? With whom? Doing what?

Let yourself do this. I mean it, *let yourself*. Maybe for the first time. We almost never give ourselves permission to indulge in this kind of dreaming. Because it all seems so impossible.

And maybe some of it is. But why cut yourself off before you've even started? The world will edit our dreams soon enough. *Let's have them first*. Let's go there in our minds.

Done? Do you see it?

Now, write the title of *that* memoir:

_____ _____ _____ _____ _____ _____

Finished? Great. But are you feeling a bit . . . overcome? Uncomfortable? Confused? Exhilarated? I've seen all of those reactions and more. I've seen people finish this part, put their pens down, and cry.

And the reason is that I don't usually need to tell people there is one last step in this exercise; they can see it coming.

Compare your first memoir and your second.

Sometimes these two titles are remarkably close in nature, suggesting you're definitely going in the right direction with your life. That can feel very validating. Hey, I'm on the right path! But other times, the comparison portion of this exercise shows you just how far you are from living the life of your dreams, literally.

So ask yourself:

Is the distance from your current life to your perfect life short or long? Would it require a tweak or a reinvention? And, given your answers, which values do you seem to be living by right now—and which do you want to be living by as you move forward? Are they the same, or different?

Now, to be clear, I did not invent this exercise; I adapted it from the Six-Word Memoir phenomenon launched in 2006. That was when Larry Smith, a writer and editor, joined forces with a brand-new thing called Twitter, and issued a challenge to Internet users to submit their life story in six words. The contest was supposed to last a month, but that idea evaporated when literally a million-plus submissions poured in. Publicity ensued, and before you knew it, schools and communities started holding Six-Word-Memoir-athons. In 2012, Oprah asked her followers to share their Six-Word Memoirs, and the exercise officially became a thing. (Oprah's Six-Word Memoir, by the way, was, "Seeking the Fullest Expression of Self.")

While he launched it into the popular consciousness, Larry Smith would be the first person to tell you that he did not invent the idea of the Six-Word Memoir either. No, that would be the literary giant and (very unfortunately) giant alcoholic Ernest Hemingway. As the story is told, and it could be apocryphal, Hemingway and his writers' posse were at a Key West bar in 1937, and in a drunken revel, Hemingway ended up proclaiming that one could write a novel in six words. His friends vigorously disagreed, at which point Hemingway grabbed a piece of paper and a pen from behind the bar and scribbled, "For sale: baby shoes, never worn."

Ernest Hemingway, you genius, you.

The six-word *novel* idea was altered, obviously, when Larry Smith and Twitter brought the idea to the world, in favor of something more personal, a nano-autobiography. Let me suggest you spend a lazy afternoon (if you ever find one) scrolling through the zillions online. They are provocative, poignant, and pointed, and sometimes all three at once.

"Abandoned at five. Learning to thrive."

"Went to Harvard, married a crackhead."

"Found true love, married someone else."

"I should have stayed in Europe."

"Old too soon, smart too late."

And then perhaps the most famous of all: "Not quite what I was planning."

I love that one, don't you? Because life never is what we expect. Even with Becoming You! Although Becoming You exists to mitigate and optimize life's surprises, and to steer us away from having too darn many of them.

For those struggling with this exercise, or just anyone who would like to hear more about it, allow me to provide a few Six Squared examples from the field, starting with one of my favorites, from a young man who was getting his MBA part-time as he held down a middle management position at a small insurance company. He was also married, with two toddlers. Amazingly, however, he was also an A++++ student, thoughtful, dedicated, and serious. Sometimes his classroom contributions were so wise, it would make me wonder, "Wait, is Robert actually Yoda?" It perplexed me, as an aside, why he seemed to be on such a tamped-down career trajectory.

I was soon to get a clue. His present-day Six-Word Memoir was, "Okay, Let's See How This Goes."

Here was a person who was living tentatively, for lack of a better word. I don't know why he lacked self-belief. All I knew was that his doubt was ill founded.

But when Robert allowed himself to dream his dream of a life with the second part of Six Squared, here's where he landed.

"Thank God I Did Not Listen."

Wow.

Robert had used this exercise to look into the future and decide, *I am muting the voices of doubt in my head, and when I do, it is going to be so much better than I ever imagined.* Maybe those voices were his own. Maybe they were from his parents or a teacher along the way.

Voices carry, as the song goes. But so can dreams, if we let them.

Robert spent the rest of the semester allowing himself to reclaim his deeply held values of Radius and Achievement, and planning a new career accordingly.

Here's another paired example. It was written by one of my quietest students, who frankly always appeared somewhat miserable.

Because she was.

Beatrice had been a professional dancer, and during the pandemic she took a job as an administrative assistant at a nonprofit arts-funding organization. There, much to her anger and shame, she found the "real" team members assumed she was unintelligent and "overly emotional." Her ideas were ignored, and occasionally even greeted with sighs and eye rolls. Finally, in what even she would call a fit of spite, she decided to apply to business school. When she got in, her sense of validation trumped the little "Uh-oh, what did I just do?" voice in her head.

Once enrolled, it only got louder. Macroeconomics, corporate strategy, digital marketing, finance. Beatrice loathed it all, and her current-day Six-Word Memoir explained why: "I Kept Running. Should've Been Dancing."

But then came her future memoir:

"Too Sensitive? The World Needed That."

Beatrice had allowed herself to imagine a life where she could be her authentic self in a world that fully rewarded it. Basically, the exercise led to the epiphany, as she told me later, that "as a life-organizing principle, spite is about as stupid as it gets."

Incidentally, when Beatrice eventually presented her Area of Transcendence report to the class, at the center of the circle, there was one word: Rockette.

Heck yes, Beatrice! For letting yourself dream, seeing the path forward, and embracing that it is a journey paved with your authentic values, the loudest ones being Voice, Agency, and Eudemonia.

I will leave you with one last pairing.

It was written by the kind of student who almost never self-selects into Becoming You, a finance bro, and I mean that with all due respect. The world needs people who devote their every waking hour to the smooth operation of the world economic system so that money goes where it is supposed to go, when it is supposed to go there. I mean that.

This particular student had two characteristics, however, that made him an unusual member of the finance folk: he was African American and gay. Not to generalize, of course, but any bank in the world will tell you they are not yet where they want to be in terms of diversity.

But there was Tim, the spring before graduation, with a job waiting at one of Wall Street's behemoths.

I was not surprised, nor will you be, by his present-day Six-Word Memoir: "Grind, Grind, Just Don't Look Up."

"Well, that's how it goes," was his explanation. Finance has its upsides—like money and prestige—but it comes with lifestyle costs. Everyone knows that.

Tim, as it turned out, was one of those students who did not exactly breeze through the second part of this exercise. In fact, I could see him in the back row literally squirming in his seat. At one point, he even stood up, walked across the back of the room, and walked back, as if he might even leave. *What is up with that?* I wondered.

What was up was his second entry: "Fuck It All! Why Not Me?"

At the time, all I could think was, *Well, someone is on a journey here.* I didn't have a chance to think more, because class was over, and Tim was the first one out the door.

A few weeks later, more was indeed revealed. During his AOT presentation, Tim told us that it was when he compared his two memoirs that he literally decided to ditch finance and pursue his true lifelong dream of joining forces with his brothers to build a worldwide nightlife juggernaut—bars, restaurants, and clubs, all united under one insanely cool brand.

"I cannot give up my whole life for values I do not have," he explained. "This," he said, pointing at the company's logo, which he had designed himself, "is where we're going." If he had asked for unpaid interns at that moment, I think he would have gotten a small army.

The class cheered. People loved Tim's dream.

But the only dream you really need to love is your own.

Again, the world will edit that dream. There are skills you don't have. There are resources that are hard to come by. Life happens. Reality is, well, real.

But you must have your dreams first, before the editing sets in. You must. They will show you your values, if nothing else, and often, much more.

Appendix B

Whose Life Do You Want Anyway?

Sometimes necessity truly is the mother of invention, and by "necessity," I mean, "a hysterical screaming fit in one's kitchen."

That's exactly what I had one day in September 2011, when my shiny recent-college-graduate son told me that he could not, after four years of classes, coaching, cajoling, and, ahem, *tuition*, figure out what to do with his life.

Somewhere in the middle of my invective-laden response, I managed to shout, "Whose life do you want anyway?"

Unexpectedly, that prompt was so effective in changing the trajectory of my son's life that it eventually gave rise to one of Becoming You's most popular values-excavation exercises.

It comes in the form of a chart:

Whose life do you want anyway?	*Here's what I love, like, or otherwise covet about this person's life.*	*"Um, no thank you."*
Person 1		
Person 2		
Person 3		
Person 4		

The work of completing this exercise is as straightforward as it seems.

In the first column, list the four or five people whose lives you love, like, admire, and/or covet enough to think, *If I had to trade lives with someone, this person would definitely make the cut.* Don't get too analytical, okay? Each name should pop up pretty naturally.

Your selections can be people you know personally or not; they can be living or not; they can be historical, fictional, or your fifth-grade teacher. Just make sure to list four or more. My own list contains Oriana Fallaci, a firebrand Italian war correspondent who died at seventy-seven in 2006; Hoda Kotb and Martha Stewart, who need no introduction; Mary Erdoes, the vice chairman of JP Morgan; and a woman my age whom I'll call Sally—a wonderful mom, devoted grandmother, and golf partner of mine—who once explained her less-than-stellar performance on the course with the unforgettable line, "I don't do golf, Suzy, I do golf skirts."

In the next column, your job is to identify the elements or factors that prompted you to select each person. Is it their fame? Their impact? Their wealth? The more honest you are in this step the better. Because as I have mentioned roughly seven thousand times already, when it comes to Becoming You, the old saying holds: "Quality in: Quality out."

Thus it is in this column, for Hoda Kotb, I wrote, "So much positive impact. Huge Scope! Everyone loves her. Beautiful inside and out. Perfect person. Fabulous arms!" For Oriana Fallaci, my box contained the words, "World-changing, brilliant, fearless, independent." For Mary Erdoes: "Sets economic agenda for the world. Fierce and brilliant. Famous for her leadership. Very good legs!" And Sally: "Joie de vivre. Perfect marriage. Throws the parties no one wants to miss. Sexy and funny."

My point: Say what you really feel. Don't hold back.

In the final column, because no one's life is perfect, and because this exercise would be impossible without this step, you get to record which aspects of each person's life you would like to leave out, if you had your druthers. An estranged child, for instance, might show up here. Or a lack of financial security. Or a stint or two in rehab. Just identify whatever it is that makes you think, as the chart notes, "Um, no thank you."

For me, I took pause with the immense, unshakable weight on Mary Erdoes's shoulders every single day and night, which surely she feels as a top leader at one of the world's biggest banks. For Sally, I wrote that I would opt out of her decision to opt out of a career. I loved her life, except for the "no job, like ever" part. Really, really, no thank you to that. In fact, in this column, my exact notation for Sally was, "No career, just could not handle."

When all the boxes on your chart are filled in, the most important part of this exercise begins: the identification of patterns, for in those patterns lie values.

To illustrate, let's look at two charts from students of mine.

The first was created by Maxine. In college, Max (as she liked to be called) majored in math, without much idea where it would lead. After graduation, that meant she ended up being a business development associate at a big commercial real estate firm in New York, where she analyzed data and built spreadsheets. She'd come to business school "to pivot."

To what? Well, anything but real estate. "I couldn't make the case to myself that selling space in high-rises made the world a better place," she once told the class.

Here's her chart.

Appendixes

Whose life do you want anyway?	Here are the key factors that make me love the life this person leads.	"Um, no thank you."
Elon Musk	*Incredible entrepreneur who leads companies driving market solutions to the climate crisis.*	*Public feuds. Twitter takeover. Political views.*
Barack Obama	*Inspiring leader. Realistic about what is achievable. Healthcare reform!*	*No privacy. Can't trust people.*
Raya (friend)	*Very well-balanced life. Strong relationship and career. Tolerant, open-minded.*	*Nothing.*
Nate Pettit	*Inspiring teacher who is showing what it really means to lead. Pushing innovative teaching practices. Overcame tough upbringing.*	*Professor salary.*

The first values pattern that struck me was that three out of four of Max's selections were individuals with enormous impact: Elon Musk, President Obama, and Nate Pettit, a Stern professor beloved for his innovative approach to experiential learning and his big, appealing personality. Indeed, all these folks are larger-than-life types; they have what the Values Bridge would call high Radius and Luminance, influencing issues much larger than themselves.

Might that be one of Max's values, too?

I was going in that direction when another pattern began to emerge by my reckoning, one that suggested the trade-offs Max would be willing to make—or not.

Elon Musk, she had noted, had too much noise around him. President Obama couldn't trust anyone. And, as for her professor, well, you don't teach to get rich.

Appendixes

But her friend Raya, Max's chart seemed to say, kind of had it nailed. Happy relationship. Excellent job. Peaceful life.

The values calculus presented in Max's chart was a life of meaningful but not outsized impact and wealth, with the upside of allowing privacy and predictability. A few weeks later, that profile was to pop up almost exactly in Max's Area of Transcendence, which she pinpointed as "an executive at a climate change and healthcare policy consulting firm."

A second example is the chart created by Tim, whom we met in the Six Squared discussion in Appendix A; he was the finance bro who, over the course of the semester, realized he wanted to ditch Wall Street to build a nightlife empire with his brothers.

Whose life do you want anyway?	Here are the key factors that make me love the life this person leads.	"Um, no thank you."
Dad	*Lives his passion. No one questions if he's a good person. Physically attractive. Principled. Never had a boss. Humble.*	*Conflict averse. Emotional. Money problems.*
Mom	*Intelligent. Hardworking. Not afraid to be the "bad guy." Moral compass. Physically attractive. Entrepreneurship.*	*Doesn't have a lot of friends. Unclear professional purpose. Not universally liked by people. Paused career for family. Money problems.*
Roger C (leads the Mission Investments team at a major non-profit foundation)	*Intelligent and accomplished. Can call anyone in NYC and they will pick up. Super well connected. Purpose-driven work, but still white collar. Doesn't have to worry about money.*	*Doesn't seem to have a family. Didn't take risks professionally. Has always worked for other people.*
Tyler Perry	*Accomplished. Doesn't worry about money. Iconic. Well connected and respected. Unapologetic. Generous. Entrepreneur.*	*Too many rumors surrounding personal life. Work-product sometimes known for the wrong reasons. Uber-capitalist. Questionable if truly respected by peers.*

Some of Tim's values are quite clear, aren't they? There's financial security (Affluence) and physical attractiveness (Beholderism). But

255

that's not all. I see a yearning for Agency with the line "Never had a boss." I strongly see Scope and Radius with Roger C and Tyler Perry.

Perhaps I am being abetted by twenty-twenty hindsight, but Tim's chart is like John the Baptist of his Area of Transcendence. It's out there shouting, "Look what's coming! You won't believe it! It's going to be big!"

Values, when we listen to them, are exactly like that.

Perhaps by now you're wondering about my poor son who launched this exercise, whom we last saw being screamed at in the kitchen.

In my defense, he had just been fired from his job in consulting.

And further in my defense, my husband and I had just spent weeks *warning* him he was going to be fired from said job in consulting.

Why? Because he wasn't trying.

We knew because he was living with us.

Yes, yes, cue the scary music.

Every day, Jack and I would watch in horror as Roscoe rolled out of bed at eight a.m., getting to the office, we estimated, around nine. Then he'd roll back into the apartment at around six, which, by our estimation, meant he'd left the office a bit after five. On the weekends, he would take off for adventures with friends, perhaps spending, we estimated, no more than an hour over the course of two days preparing for the upcoming week.

We were doing a lot of estimating in those days, watching our son prepare to get canned.

Which, of course, we told him repeatedly. Every other new graduate, we informed him, was arriving at the office as the sun rose, to beat the partners who were, like us, doing a lot of estimating that summer. And certainly no one left before dark. Most of them spent the weekends at their desks.

Every time we openly fretted, our ever-dutiful Roscoe tried to calm us down. "Don't worry," he assured us with an air of confidence. "I got this!" Years later, I was to learn that Roscoe was actually shaking in his boots about his inevitable demise at the firm but afraid to let on for fear of hurting our hopes. Oh, sigh. It makes me sad, remembering it, for all of us.

Anyway, one Friday after about eight weeks on the job, Roscoe got home at five p.m. He also mentioned that the partners had given all the new college grad hires an assignment due Monday morning at ten. He would knock it out maybe Sunday night.

"This is a test," Jack sharply interrupted the reverie. "Every single one of your teammates is going to be in that office all weekend long, working their asses off—except you."

"Don't worry," Roscoe said as usual to placate us. "I have enough time."

He did not.

On Monday, Jack and I were sitting in the kitchen when Roscoe popped his head in at eleven thirty a.m. Estimated time of firing: ten fifteen.

"You won't believe what happened . . ." were his first words to us.

At which moment, Jack stood up and exited the kitchen faster than you can say "Incoming."

You know, my friends, you love your children very much. You do; it's perhaps the one common thread of all humanity. And when you have a kid as promising as Roscoe from such an early age—star student, star athlete, star everything—it is so easy to pour yourself into them like a spigot gushing madly, to let your hopes and dreams of their life run away with you, like an untethered raft in Class 5 rapids.

I had done that. Guilty as charged.

And here the recipient of all that love was trying to show me that my dream of his life and his dream were not the same thing.

He was trying, as I said. I was not yet receiving.

Instead, I was screaming. "How could you do this to us? How could you let us down? How could you not listen to us? How could you waste all your potential? How could you not want the same things we want for you?"

As I let loose, Roscoe got smaller and smaller in size, as if my words were a battering ram. He dropped his head, stooped his shoulders, and finally slumped in a chair. And there, as he sat, I stood over him, still shouting. "I just don't get you. I don't get what you want to do with your life, where you want to go, what you want to achieve. I mean, you can't tell us any of those things. So just tell me, whose life do you want? Whose life would make you happy?"

I stopped because suddenly Roscoe was no longer looking small. He had somehow unfurled, and he was looking at me intently.

"Mr. Grady. I want Mr. Grady's life," he said with precision.

"You must be kidding."

"No. I am dead certain."

Kevin Grady was—well, let's just say he was not what I wanted to hear. But he was *something*. A hint, a clue, a first glimmer of insight. He owned and ran the summer camp in Maine where Roscoe had been a camper for years, and then a counselor. I knew him as a good guy, obviously content and comfortable in his skin, openly besotted with the little northern nirvana he had built. In the off-season, the camp converted into a community program teaching leadership skills and team building to vets and local Maine students, using hiking challenges and rope climbing.

"Go work for Kevin Grady, then!" I cried. "Whatever!"

This was the moment when Jack deemed it safe to return to the kitchen, and I filled him in. "Go, go!" Jack echoed me, although possibly because he had determined disagreeing with me that day would not be advised.

Look, here's what happened. Roscoe did indeed go work for Kevin Grady. He loved it, and he excelled. He ended up meeting his wife there, too, and stayed for two years, during which time he realized his life's work had to be somewhere at the intersection of helping people, play, creative design, and the outdoors.

WHO KNEW?

I certainly did not.

But I knew that the moment of epiphany for us both occurred when I asked him not *what* he wanted to do, but *who* he wanted to be.

Just as this exercise does.

Roscoe is thirty-five now, a husband and dad. He's very happy in his job in the world of games, and indeed, he is living out his values of Non Sibi, Belonging, and Voice. He and his wife embrace their low-Scope life in Maine. I like Maine, too, one month a year.

But here's the thing.

I've learned over the years that how much *I* like Maine does not matter when it comes to Roscoe living the life of *his* dreams.

All that matters is what Roscoe likes. For instance, Maine.

And that's the thing about values. They're entirely personal. The world does all sorts of things to mute them or change them. And that is why, sometimes, we have to discover them in the most oblique ways.

Like asking not what life you want, but *whose*.

Appendix C

The Proustish Questionnaire

I've done challenging things in my life, but few as daunting as my attempt, during the pandemic, to read the longest book ever written, Marcel Proust's *A la Recherche du Temps Perdu*, which is famous for, well, being 4,300 pages.

I'm pretty sure no one has ever finished *A la Recherche du Temps Perdu*. It's not terrible, it's just utterly undisciplined, with tangents and digressions on every other page. Somewhat ironically, the translation of the title is *In Search of Lost Time*, and after throwing in the towel at page 2,095, all I could think was, *Tell me about it*.

Now, in point of fact, Proust did not create the Proust Questionnaire. He merely popularized an *unattributed* collection of piquant queries that, he claimed, could divulge a person's true character. He was not wrong. The original version of questions, while seemingly simple in their phrasing, prompt those answering them to divulge their truest feelings about what they love, hate, yearn for, and fear. They nudge you to identify who you want to be, what you like to do, when you can do anything of your choosing, and how you'd like to be remembered.

With the Proustish Questionnaire, I have shortened and modernized Proust's namesake survey, and added four of my own fill-in-the-blank prompts. Yes, you might say it's audacious to edit, parse, and otherwise put my fingerprints all over a universal classic, but there you go.

I've also added an assignment. Along with answering each question, I ask you to reflect on what value or values each response might suggest. This is where the Welch-Bristol Values inventory comes in very handy or, frankly, you can use any other values that may have emerged from previous Becoming You exercises.

As you compose your two-part answers to the Proustish Questionnaire, take your time but don't overbrain it. Your gut reaction to each prompt is usually your most authentic.

Have fun.

Appendixes

1.	Where would you most like to live?	
2.	What is your favorite virtue?	
3.	What is your idea of perfect happiness?	
4.	Who are your real-life heroes?	
5.	What character trait do you most abhor?	
6.	What is your greatest fear?	
7.	What talent would you love to have?	
8.	What person, living or dead, do you most admire?	
9.	What is your greatest achievement?	
10.	What is the lowest depth of misery?	
11.	What is your favorite pastime?	
12.	Who or what is your greatest love?	
13.	What is your mantra?	
14.	I have to . . .	
15.	I will never apologize for . . .	
16.	I'm never sad when . . .	
17.	In life, I'm most grateful for . . .	

And now for some examples and reflections:

Where would you most like to live?

As I've mentioned, it never ceases to amaze me that people omit location as a value when, in many cases, it is the precise desire that can most influence, or even control, our lives. I've had students conduct their entire Area of Transcendence analysis, only to let it slip out at the end that everything has to happen in Iowa because that's where their family is, or Tulum, because that's where their "spirit animal comes alive." And I'm like, "Did you think that location part didn't matter? In your case, it happens to drive *everything*."

And I'm not just talking about Iowa over Manhattan, or Tulum over Texas. I'm talking city versus suburbs, near family or far, among a community or off the social grid. Eventually, we all go home to where we want to be; we all go home to what *feels like home*. Neglect to factor this value into your Area of Transcendence analysis at your peril.

Which is your favorite virtue?

The virtue you pick with this prompt—because you can pick only one—is a proxy for your most valued way of showing up in the world.

Did you answer authenticity? *That's Voice.*

Generosity? *Non Sibi.*

Courage? *Agency.*

Beauty? *Beholderism.*

Faithfulness? *Cosmos.*

All values.

I had a student whose reply to this question was grit. "I never take no for an answer and I'm very competitive with myself," she went on to explain. "I like to push myself in every aspect of my life." Later her value of Achievement showed up loud and clear in her Area of Transcendence—where she had her sights set on being an entrepreneur in the newly emergent immersive tech space.

Appendixes

What is your idea of perfect happiness?

I once had a class of thirty midcareer executive MBA students, and even after an hour of trying, three of them still could not answer this question. I still ponder that, and with a kind of sadness. Because this query is just another way of asking, "If you could have it all, what would 'all' look like?" For whatever reasons, those three students couldn't let themselves go there.

For decades, the last page of *Vanity Fair* magazine featured the Proust Questionnaire with a celebrity, including Snoop Dogg, who answered the prompt this way: "Everybody around me is happy, my spirit is right, and just nothing but peace and tranquility is in the building."

I'm sensing Belonging, Beholderism, with its love of orderliness, and Familycentrism in there.

Consider also this, from a fiftysomething business executive who took a Becoming You workshop: "I look up, and the ticker says $100, +12.5."

Um, hello, Affluence and Achievement.

I love the vast difference between these two answers, and what they tell us about the uniqueness of our values.

Who are your real-life heroes?

I have a friend who will drive eight hours to save a pregnant mutt from being euthanized. In listing her as my hero—she was the first person who came to mind—I became starkly aware of not just my love for animals, but my value of Radius. I ardently want to be part of the movement that ends animal cruelty.

Other answers I've heard over the years are similarly revealing.

Michael Jordan: *Achievement and Scope.*
Malala Yousafzai: *Radius.*
Elon Musk: *Affluence and Achievement.*
My mother: *Belonging and Non Sibi.*

Your answer here—and importantly, its underlying reasons why—can speak volumes about the behaviors or traits you most value, and perhaps wish you had more of yourself.

What character trait do you most abhor?
This prompt asks you to rate, quite simply, your very-most least-favorite human idiosyncrasy.

I'll go first. I abhor—I detest, I revile—pompous asshatery. And I object to it because one of my top values is authenticity, or as the Values Bridge would codify it, Voice.

That, in a nutshell, is how this particular prompt works, kind of backward.

For instance, if you name selfishness, you probably value Non Sibi or Radius. It you hate slovenliness, you likely value Beholderism. If you hate meanness, you probably value Belonging. You get the idea.

What is your greatest fear?
I'm convinced this question works because buried inside every fear is a desire, and desires are usually values.

For example, many parents reply to this prompt with something regarding their children. As a friend once answered with poignant candor, "My son dying and being scared, and me not being there. I would die myself for that not to happen." I don't need to tell you what this says about her level of Familycentrism.

Of course, some people don't have children or, even if they do, list other fears. Remember Deidre, the free-spirited woman struggling with her family's and society's expectations of her? Her answer to the question was simply, "Jail." The implied desire? I would suggest it was to live her nonconformist life without punishment. The implied value? Nearly unlimited freedom of movement, self-determination, and independence. Or in a word, Agency.

By contrast, consider the answer from a social activist I know. She'd been arrested for her protests over the years and, as a result, was often without work. She sometimes made her rent by donating blood. You might think her greatest fear would be homelessness. Instead, she answered, "That this is the way the world is, and must be, and we can never change it."

Her desire was for change, and her value was social justice, seen in Radius.

Peel back your answer to this question to find the value inside the desire inside the fear.

What talent would you most like to have?

"To speak any language." "To be amazing at tennis." "To not care about other people's opinions of me."

Values, values everywhere.

Fluency in any language might mean you value a life of travel, e.g., Scope. Or it could mean you value Achievement; after all, in some global companies, to be bilingual is human, but to be trilingual is divine. Context matters.

To be a master of the tennis court might mean you value social mobility. Or impressing others. Or Beholderism's physical fitness. Or all three!

And to be able to shrug off the haters? This answer could mean you value self-love and self-confidence in and of themselves. Or it could mean you value the kind of risk-taking in business or life that such qualities would unleash, if only you had them.

Your longed-for talent has a message for you about the person you want to become, and in this way is often an excellent values proxy. Who knew? Well, Marcel Proust, apparently.

What person, living or dead, do you most admire?

I'd estimate that about 75 percent of the answers I've seen to this question are either "Mom" or "Dad." That's why the "why" here is so important.

"Because he was so humble and worked so hard."

"Because she fought to show the world how capable she was."

"Because he always puts our family first, before work and even his own happiness."

I've also heard Barack Obama and Oprah mentioned countless times. Also: Condoleezza Rice, Queen Elizabeth II, and Dolly Parton. Tom Brady and Steph Curry. Cher and Hillary Clinton.

The actual names here matter not. The answers' power lies in *why*, from the 40 zillion options before you, you picked the one person you did.

A student, for instance, once listed Mother Teresa as her reply.

I'd expected to see Radius as her reasoning, or perhaps Cosmos. Instead, I was surprised to see Belonging.

"I've secretly always wanted to be a nun," she explained later. "That way, you're never alone."

Again, when it comes to values discovery, your *why* on this one matters more than your *who*.

What do you consider your greatest achievement?
You might assume that Paul Newman would list his Oscar to answer this question, and that James Brown would list his Grammys.

Instead, you have one of the greatest actors of all time saying, "Being number nineteen on Nixon's enemies list," and the Godfather of Soul replying, "Going to church and belonging to a faith."

Values, again.

I'll never forget the time I did this exercise with a bunch of buttoned-up Scandinavian businesspeople. I was in Copenhagen to give a speech about organizational culture, and I started off with the Proustish Questionnaire for fun, and to familiarize the group with the concept of values overall.

One member of the audience did not seem to be loving the exercise very much; I could tell from the grim set of his mouth that the questions might be landing a little close to home. And I was right, because when the discussion for this particular prompt came around, he raised his hand to volunteer his answer, and then stood to read it:

"My greatest achievement is breaking the cycle of alcoholism and abuse which has destroyed my family for four generations. That story stopped with me."

Apparently, this man's colleagues were not unaware of this feat—and it was a feat—because his words were received with warm, prolonged applause.

The desire to break a family narrative is a mighty value indeed, one of Agency and Voice. And pride in the achievement of it—*or of any value*—is what is captured so elegantly in this question.

What do you consider the lowest depth of misery?

It can be sweet sometimes to hear my students answer this query, as they are young, and for many, misery is still a stranger. This allows their answers to be as abstract as "sadness," and "being alone." But occasionally I get a zinger, like from our friend Vivaan, the wallpaper enthusiast, who said, "Being ordinary." Defining value: Voice.

Vivaan wanted to be extraordinary, which, happily, he most certainly was headed toward.

More seasoned Becoming You students tend to answer this prompt with the wisdom of their years: "My cancer coming back and me with so much more life to live," "Nothing to show for all the work," and "Realizing none of it was worth it."

Proust's own answer to this was "Being separated from Mama," and from all reports, his mother, Jeanne, was the organizing principle of his life. Indeed, estrangement from loved ones, or the loss of a loved one, often shows up in the answers to this prompt, demonstrating the prevalence of Belonging and Familycentrism as important values. No surprise there, but if your answer is something altogether different, if only for its deviation from the norm, it's probably a value worth noting.

What is your favorite pastime?

Imagine all the possible answers to this query! The writer Joan Didion named gumbo making. Kareem Abdul-Jabbar replied, "Writing. A well-turned phrase is as satisfying as a slam dunk." David Bowie came up with "Squishing paint on a senseless canvas."

From my own classes and workshops, I've heard "Gardening with Vivaldi on blast," "Driving around to nowhere with Michael on Sundays," and "My work is my life and my life is my work, so the answer is working."

That last one, by the way, was not from a Fortune 500 CEO or Wall Street banker or tech entrepreneur. It was from a nurse who travels to some of the world's most dangerous war zones for Doctors Without Borders. Her favorite pastime, it turns out, is saving lives. That's Non Sibi on blast, with Radius right alongside.

Who or what is the greatest love of your life?

Let the record show, please, that when *Vanity Fair* published the Proust Questionnaire with my husband in 2005, his answer to this prompt was "My wife, Suzy." Thank you still, sweetheart.

A person can indeed be your top organizing principle. It happens all the time. In fact, I had a student once who blew up his plans to go into consulting because, after all the Becoming You exercises, he realized his girlfriend was his top value.

Reader, he married her—and they started a business together.

But, Achtung! This question doesn't restrict you to answer with a person—it's "who or *what*." Thus, I've heard wide-ranging answers, including these: "The company I created," "My family's farm," "My garden," "My boat, for its freedom," and "My dogs." (That was not me, by the way, but definitely no shade.)

Any answer to this question will provide you with data on a critical value, and at the risk of sounding like a broken record, I will leave it there.

What is your mantra?

In the real Proust Questionnaire, this prompt is worded "What is your motto?" Other adaptations record it as "What is your favorite saying?" I kind of smushed "motto" and "saying" together and came up with "mantra," which can be anything from a sacred utterance to a personal slogan. Either way, it's a thought you consider so true, you live by it.

A quick study in contrasts:

I once had a client who answered this prompt with "I'll sleep when I'm dead." His values were Scope and Achievement, and he lived that way—that is, with gusto, risk, and occasional recklessness.

Another client gave the answer "Everything in its place." She happened to run a small art gallery, and Beholderism, with its appreciation for aesthetics, was clearly a top value.

Finally, a student once boldly announced to the class that his mantra was "Eat, drink, and be merry, for tomorrow we all may die." That famous exhortation is often attributed to Shakespeare—my student himself claimed as much—but actually comes from the Bible, in several books of the Bible. Regardless, it's about as good a signal as any of pleasure and well-being, aka Eudemonia, as a value.

I have to . . .

When I posted an Instagram Reel about this prompt a year ago, little did I know that two million people would watch it and hundreds would reply with answers such as these:

Sit, and drink coffee, and have some time to myself.
Pray.
Go outside every day.
Have an uninterrupted shower.
Dance and listen to music.
Write at least three times a week.
Clean my kitchen.
Protect public money with my integrity.
Find a way out of my marriage.
Forgive myself.

I love these answers so much. Their diversity. Their humanity. Their laser-like ability to illuminate our hearts and souls.

I don't know your answer, of course, but whatever it is, I do know it is telling you a value, because desires, again, have an uncanny way of doing that. Especially when they come to you with a just simple nudge like this one.

I will never apologize for . . .

Consider a few of the hundreds of answers I got when I took this particular prompt to social media:

> Being a polite Canadian. It's baked into our DNA.
> Being extremely detail oriented, I've honed it over a looooong time.
> Holding my son's hand.
> Playing tennis five hours a day.
> Asserting boundaries.
> Putting integrity above loyalty.
> Going back to school late in life.
> My belief in God.
> Helping others, even though I'm often told I am too nice.
> My optimism.
> Going to bed early.

In just a few words, so much data. Not Pure Proust, true, but another Proustian poke with more aha to it than you might expect.

I'm never sad when I'm . . .

The full version of this prompt—the one I use in class—goes: "I'm not sure what happiness is, but I know I'm never sad when . . ." The first clause is technically not necessary, thus the shorter version above. But I do like the full setup a lot; maybe it just gives people more runway for an answer.

Regardless, here are some of the responses I've heard in recent years:

> Talking to people.
> Advocating for animals by scaling cultivated meat innovation.

Traveling.
In Italy.
Serving others.
Golfing.
Buying new clothes for me and my kids. Just being honest.
Dancing. It's all I ever wanted to do.

That last line—"It's all I ever wanted to do"—kind of says it all with the prompt. Isn't that just another definition for a value?

In life, I'm most thankful for . . .
Finally, here are some of the many answers I've heard to this prompt:

My family.
My marriage, which almost didn't make it.
My health.
Laughter.
My resilience.

I added this final question to my adaptation because I suspected the source of our gratitude might tell us something about our values. And it does, probably as directly as any of Proust's original questions. I wonder what he would think of it, and how he might answer it himself.

Maybe, just maybe, he was grateful he finished writing that book of his.

Appendix D
Alpha Omega

When I first started using this exercise in 2009, I called it "the Big Three." But as time went on, and my appreciation for it grew, I changed its name to Alpha Omega—the Greek phrase often used to refer to the totality of things—to reflect how much information it somehow manages to generate. And in just three questions, too!

Let's consider them in turn.

First: *What do you want people to say about you when you're not in the room?*
Believe me when I tell you I have heard every answer to this question.

That I'm not crazy like my mother.
That I'm CEO material.
That I'm rich.
That I'm hot.
That they'd invest in me.
That I don't give a damn.

Quite a spread there, right? And each one, a values clue.

Take the first answer. It came from a woman named Carrie who was trying to make a reputation for herself as a funeral director in a small town. Her parents had divorced when she was young, and she moved in with her dad, apprenticing with him, starting in high school, at their third-generation family-run funeral home. But her mother was never far away. She was widely thought of as the town crank, possibly schizophrenic, in and out of institutions. Brief periods of lucidity increasingly gave way to stretches as a disruptive homeless person in a town that prided itself on peace and quiet.

Once Carrie had returned home after college and stepped in as her father's second-in-command at the funeral home, she sometimes found herself resenting her mother to the point of anger. Everything her dad had worked for, she thought to herself, and everything she hoped for, too, could be lost in a moment if her mother did something in town to damage the family's hard-earned reputation for propriety and reliability.

That moment had not yet happened when I encountered Carrie at a workshop for my decision-making methodology 10-10-10, but the fear of it shaped who she was. All her life, her mother had been the specter of chaos, making Carrie yearn for stability, predictability, and respect. In the parlance of the Values Bridge, she wanted a life of low Scope and high Belonging. Her answer to this Alpha Omega question revealed both plainly.

Consider also the aforementioned answer "That I'm hot." It was spoken by an author, famous for her Gothic-flavored novellas. I'd never seen her wear anything other than shapeless linen dresses, her face without makeup and her graying hair in a bun.

"Am I superficial for saying that?" she said, laughing, after she told a small group of us doing the Alpha Omega together for a workshop. We were all too surprised to answer, but I finally did by reorienting us to the point of the exercise.

"Do you value being sexy?" I asked her.

"I value *sex*!" she replied. Her husband, seated beside her, said, "So do I!" and we all laughed.

My friends, sex is indeed a value. It falls under Eudemonia in the Values Bridge inventory, in case you missed it, and you may go adjust your answer now if you did.

I told you the Alpha Omega questions prompt us to think about our values in new ways.

Second: *What did you love about your lifestyle growing up and what did you hate?*

Let me jump to the chase with this one. We often replicate what we loved about our upbringing in our own lives. Summer trips, opening presents on Christmas Eve, family dinners on Sunday. The problem is, we often replicate the stuff we hated, too. And because we do that, it can blur our vision about our true values.

Over the years, I've heard a wide range of answers to this prompt, too.

> I loved the pasta all the time. I *hated* being picked on for my weight.

> I loved the warmth and unconditional love. I *hated* the fighting about money and the fact there was never enough of it.

> I loved my dad's job because I was so proud of him. I *hated* the travel and always making new friends. I was lonely.

> I loved our house, our dog, and my grandmother's cooking. I *hated* my brother's drinking.

The last answer came from a fifty-year-old banking executive named John whom I met during a Becoming You workshop. When he volunteered to expound on it for the group, his face fairly lit up as he described the old Victorian house that he called home from his birth. It was rambling and quirky, filled with comfortable couches and the aroma of his nana's specialties. He and his three siblings had their own bedrooms, making him the envy of his friends. They also envied his wonderful father, who, he told us sadly, died of heart failure while John was away at college.

When I asked John about his brother's drinking, his reply surprised me. He described the captain of the high school football team, an outgoing BMOC type with lots of friends, and a great student who went to a far better college than John was able to attend.

"When did his problem begin?" I asked.

"Seventh grade. He'd swipe bottles from the bar off the kitchen, bring them upstairs to his room. Everyone knew it. No one said a thing." His parents, John said, silently kept the supply going. "No one wanted to ruin the picture," he said.

I asked John to ponder what that negative experience made him value in his own life.

"Open communication. Honesty. Telling it like it is." His answer was immediate and firm to me; it suggested a high value on Voice.

John sensed the next question before I even asked it. "I need to be better at those things in my life, I do," he said. "I definitely hold things in. Hold back. I shouldn't, but they're familiar to me."

Here's my point. We hate things for a reason, and usually a *values-based* one. In answering this question, the hard work is finding the value within our ire, and making sure we are living it the way we truly want.

Third: *What would make me cry at my eighty-fifth birthday—from regret?*

This question is meant to get you to think about your legacy. The mark you want to leave behind. It prompts you to imagine yourself in a room, blowing out a ton of candles on a cake, too many to count. It wants you to imagine the unfinished business that would make you sad enough to burst into tears.

Earlier, we met Greg, who (sadly and unrealistically) replied that he wanted his obituary on the front page of the *New York Times*. But here are some other answers I've heard.

Realizing I was never going to reconcile with Sandy.
Knowing that I wrecked the family business.
Seeing that there was no one there to celebrate with me.

I once did Alpha Omega on a long car ride with my best friend, Sue. As I've related, we've been through a lot together.

"You're going to make it to a hundred and five, and I hope I'm by your side," I told her as I steered the car along I-95, "but tell me, what would make you cry from regret at the end?"

"Losing you again," she said.

Usually, Sue and I are big jokesters, but we have our serious moments, and this was one. My heart surged with love for her. I knew exactly what she meant.

"You value friendship," I said. "I do, too." I did not add that on the Values Bridge, this value falls under "Belonging," because that would have been really nerdy and kind of rude.

"I value *you*," she corrected me. In my mind, her answer shifted from "Belonging" to "Familycentrism," because over the decades, that's what we have become.

But at that moment, exact labels were unimportant.

Understanding mattered so much more.

And that's the goal of Alpha Omega.

Appendix E
Welcome to Your Enneagram

I strongly urge all Becoming You travelers to pause their journey long enough—twenty minutes, thirty max!—to take the Enneagram, a personality test with ancient origins and timeless insights. You can easily find it online. There are many free versions, but if it's within your budget, I recommend the RHETI (Riso-Hudson Enneagram Type Indicator) version because its questions are the most scientifically validated. After you get your results, I further urge you to probe your Enneagram personality type indicator with the many videos and podcasts available. Knowing how you see the world, as well as understanding your core needs and fears, is crucial information as you work to create your most accurate Area of Transcendence—and purpose.

There is no one better in the world to introduce you to the Enneagram than Rasanath Das, the world's leading expert on the tool, whose interview with me follows. But first, Ras's story in brief.

Growing up in bustling, commerce-centric Mumbai in the 1980s, Ras caught the movie *Wall Street* with friends one day—and, with it, its definition of success. College in India led to a job at Deloitte in New York, then to a Cornell MBA, and then, as he had long dreamed, to investment banking with Bank of America.

He had arrived, he thought, but life had other ideas. A near-death health challenge impelled Ras to reexamine his paradigm for success and his chosen path. As he explored those questions for two years, he somehow managed to live and work as a monk at a monastery on New York's Lower East Side while continuing to toil on Wall Street by day. There he met fellow monk Hari Prasada. Eventually, the friends left the monastery to start Upbuild, an Enneagram think tank and consulting practice.

In recognition of his contributions to the Becoming You curriculum, and his illuminating lectures each semester, Ras was appointed a Visiting Fellow at NYU Stern's Initiative on Purpose and Flourishing in 2024. Our conversation follows:

Okay, let's imagine I've just received my Enneagram results, and I'm, like, "Whoa, what does this all mean?" What would you say, Ras?

> First, I would explain the test. Very broadly, you could call the Enneagram a personality typology, but unlike so many of the Jungian typologies, like Myers-Briggs or the DiSC Styles system, the Enneagram looks at the hard wiring behind how we see the world. And what I mean by the hard wiring is that we all have a sense of identity that we want the world to validate, which we call the ego. The Enneagram codifies nine very distinct "ego lenses"—nine very distinct ways of seeing the world. Each ego lens brings with it a unique set of gifts and a unique set of insecurities. Much of the time, we are not aware of these gifts and insecurities, but they are unconsciously running how we see the world. But when we become aware of them, we grow as human beings.

Scholars say that there is evidence the Enneagram was invented by the Assyrians in 900 BC, and I will admit I was first concerned about the validity of the tool because of its links to mystical Judaism, Christianity, Islam, Taoism, Buddhism, and ancient Greek philosophy. It just felt very woo-woo to me.

> The Enneagram's roots are very old, but in the 1960s, modern social science "reclaimed" it, if you will. Oscar Ichazo and Claudio Naranjo, academics who had extensive training in psychology, got very involved, and started to give more rigorous shape and form to the nine types. That work was further inherited by the people whom I personally studied the Enneagram with, Don Riso, a Stanford-educated scholar

and author, who came upon the Enneagram when he lived with the Jesuits for a number of years, and Russ Hudson, also a renowned author and scholar. Together, they created a modernized version of the Enneagram that is named for them, the Riso-Hudson Enneagram Type Indicator (RHETI), which is scientifically validated.

What's the first thing you should do when the Enneagram tells you your "type?"

Make sure it's right. Your results are a type *indicator*, not a type. You should take your top three results and ask, "Okay, which one am I *really*?"

I will jump in here to say a quick way to do this is to go to Upbuild.com and listen to the brilliant podcasts about your top two or three results to see which description resonates the most deeply. It's quick and totally free!

Thank you. I will say that the podcasts also explain that each Enneagram type has a healthy and unhealthy presentation. It's often in hearing about the *unhealthy* presentation that we start to recognize our own behaviors very clearly, and are able to say, "Okay, it's clear, I'm this or that type for sure."

You've said that we can start to grow when we become aware of our Enneagram type. Explain what that means.

When you can see which of your insecurities, which of your fears, are actually in the driver's seat, you can begin to not react on impulse or by habit. You can slow your decisions down, or prevent behaviors, or stop patterns that are actually your fears doing the thinking. I must add that this change can take time, because we have often lived with a note that we are more healthy than we think we are. It can first come as a shock to our system that we may not be who we think we are. But in time, acceptance transforms itself into humility, and humility becomes the container through which we actually grow into becoming more healthy.

Sometimes when I start this practice of learning and changing with someone after they get their results, they ask, "How many days until this is fixed?" People want a button where suddenly I press this button and I'm free. I should be free. But it's forever. The Enneagram test sets you off on a life practice of awareness, acceptance, and growth.

Do certain Enneagram types track with certain jobs? For instance, should all leaders be Achievers?

I think anybody can be a leader. But the *kind* of leaders that they will be, depending on their Enneagram type, will be significantly different. A Helper, Type 2, is a significantly different type of leader than a Challenger, Type 8. A leader who is a Peacemaker, Type 9, is going to be seeking consensus. Each Enneagram type has a different orientation to leadership, a different approach. To me, the much more important question is how healthy you are.

And remember, the power of the Enneagram is not just to understand yourself but to understand the people on your team, or your family members.

The Enneagram essentially highlights each person's gifts, but also the suffering that each person carries, which can be so silent. They are suffering, you realize, and I am, too.

And then what?

And then you take full responsibility for your suffering. You start to break the patterns of unhealthy behaviors. You also start to bring a certain quality of empathy into your relationships, and that empathy then creates a fertile ground for working together.

When everyone on a team is in the healthy part of the spectrum, you can disagree creatively and respectfully. You're in a place of awareness and understanding. It's absolutely magic. It's a joy.

And it all starts with awareness, and the journey is toward a life you build and live deliberately.

Appendix F
Relationship Mapping: A Primer

Relationship Mapping is a well-honed technique used to visually represent and analyze the relationships and connections between various entities within a system, organization, or context. It's commonly used in project management, for instance, to understand how, when, and where different individuals interact with one another.

For the purposes of Becoming You, however, Relationship Mapping is a bit too much, and I prefer the concept of building a **Relationship Inventory** instead. The point is to create a picture of who you know—in order to make sure that you have "irregular friends," people outside your immediate circle, as discussed in Chapter 9.

Irregular friends make your mind a richer, more interesting place, and broaden you emotionally, culturally, and intellectually as a human being.

They are also much more likely to be able to bail you out when your job evaporates, because one of the dirty little secrets of business is that when companies and industries go down, they typically go down together.

In class, we are very straightforward when it comes to this exercise, and I literally ask students to fill out a simple, one-page diagram that groups their friendships by various categories, such as school, work, internships, and family.

But if you're looking for a more sophisticated approach, there are several software applications I can recommend. Some are free; others are free and have premium versions as well:

- LUCIDCHART: An online tool that allows you to create various types of diagrams, including relationship maps. It has templates and a user-friendly interface.

Appendixes

- MIRO: A collaborative online whiteboard that can be used to create relationship maps and other visual aids.
- XMIND: A mind mapping tool that can be used to create visual representations of relationships and connections.
- MICROSOFT VISIO: A powerful diagramming tool that can be used to create detailed relationship maps and process diagrams.

Appendix G
The World at Work: Resources

This appendix contains resources for learning about the world of work today, and tomorrow.

Today first.

Along with staying on top of the news through the usual suspects, such as the *Wall Street Journal*, CNBC, *Fast Company*, *Forbes*, and *Fortune*, a few sites aggregate important information about current trends in the workplace. The first and foremost of these is LinkedIn, which has access to billions of pieces of data about hiring. It releases several reports a year that contain a wealth of information about emerging jobs and in-demand skills. Its annual "Workforce Report" tracks numerous industry and company trends, and I am not alone in considering it a must-read.

I also recommend regular visits to the website of the **Bureau of Labor Statistics (BLS),** which provides detailed reports on employment statistics, job outlooks, and industry growth trends in the United States. Similarly, **Statista** provides market research reports on a wide range of industries and job sectors. And finally, while technical, **IBISWorld** offers industry reports and analysis on market trends, growth, and competitive landscape.

And now for some websites and resources where you can explore and stay updated on megatrends:

1. WORLD ECONOMIC FORUM (WEF): The WEF provides extensive reports and articles on global trends and challenges, including economic shifts, technological advancements, and environmental issues. Look for its key annual reports: "Global

Appendixes

Risks Report," "Future of Jobs Report," and "Global Gender Gap Report."

2. MCKINSEY & COMPANY: McKinsey offers research and insights on a wide range of megatrends affecting business and society. Their reports cover topics like technology, globalization, and shifting demographics. Check out the Insights & Publication section on their website for the latest reports.

3. DELOITTE: This professional services firm provides in-depth reports and articles on emerging trends in various sectors, including technology, finance, and healthcare. Look for their annual reports called "Global Human Capital Trends," "Tech Trends," and "Global Economic Outlook."

4. GARTNER: Gartner offers research and analysis on technology trends and their impacts on various industries. Their reports often include predictions and strategic recommendations. I often visit the Research and Insights sections of their website for the latest trends.

5. THE BROOKINGS INSTITUTION: Brookings provides research on economic and social trends, including demographic changes, globalization, and policy impacts. The Research section of their website is a treasure trove of reports and analyses on megatrends.

6. PEW RESEARCH CENTER: Pew offers data-driven insights into social and demographic trends, technology adoption, and global issues. Look for their annual reports on "Social Trends," "Technology & the Internet," and "Global Attitudes."

7. TRENDWATCHING: This group focuses on identifying and analyzing consumer trends and innovations across various industries. Explore their "Trend Reports" and "Innovation of the Day" for the latest insights.

8. THE ECONOMIST: The smartest platform around is also quite

Appendixes

costly, but it can be worth it if you are a megatrends acolyte. Look for their regular articles on innovation and technology.

9. MIT TECHNOLOGY REVIEW: A scholarly journal, yes, but it often provides insights into cutting-edge technologies and their future implications.

Acknowledgments

I don't think I've ever read a book without flipping to this page before diving in. The reason is that I've written a couple of these things, and I know that no one does it alone. Far, far from it.

Like everything in my life, nothing would be possible or worth it without my children and their spouses, Roscoe and Michelle, Sophia, Marcus and Eva, and Eve, the last of whom took it upon herself to tell me I had to write *Becoming You* for the people who needed it but might never be able to take the class itself. I love you all, and I also love your children and dogs.

Every step of writing this book, conducting my research, and teaching the Becoming You methodology has been aided and abetted by a team that is second to none. That list is topped by the inimitable Hallie Reiner and includes the fabulous Aleeza Zinn, Tanya Jojy, Dustin Liu, and Madeline Paul. I owe deep gratitude also to Rosanne Badowski and Barbara Pritchett, for all the while making the world go around, and perfectly, too.

I am grateful for the bright and beautiful insights of my editor and publisher, Hollis Heimbouch, a dear friend and conceptual genius. My writing was made altogether better by the superb handiwork of Susannah Kemple and Rachel Kambury. Many thanks also to my literary agent, the famous (and wise!) Bob Barnett.

Now for the academics. Becoming You could have never happened, and would have never happened, had it not been for the kindness, enthusiasm, and encouragement of the universally beloved Raghu Sundaram, who was the dean of NYU Stern when I popped up into his life out of nowhere. (Raghu is now the university's senior vice chancellor.) My course, and thus this book, would likewise never have flourished had it not been for the guidance of my professorial posse, brilliant NYU Stern professors Steven Blader, Nate Pettit, and Sonia Marciano, who taught this rank amateur how to teach. Finally, so much of my thinking about values, and indeed the Values Bridge, which is at the center of this book, owes great credit to the organizational behavior scholars Graham Abbey and Robin Holt, my PhD thesis advisors at the University of Bristol. That university's vice chancellor, my lifelong friend Evelyn Welch, has also been a radiant guiding light for me.

As noted in the text of this book, my ideas were made far better and the Becoming You methodology made immeasurably more effective by the insights of Rasanath Das; Enneagram expert and the CEO and founder of Upbuild; and Betsy Wills, business leader extraordinaire and coauthor of *Your Hidden Genius*. I am also indebted to research conducted by clinical psychologist Dr. Alexis Kenny.

A few final thanks, and very important ones. My NYU Stern students have inspired and encouraged me beyond measure. I want to thank them again here for sharing their lives and stories with such honesty and vulnerability. I need to thank as well the students from around the world who have attended my Becoming You Intensives and Workshops; I've learned so very much from you.

My sisters, Elin Kaufman and Della Spring, are the unconditionally loving cheerleaders everyone should have in their lives. I thank Sue Jacobson for letting me share our story, and forever being a part of my story, and immense gratitude too for my dear friends Linda Tullis, Elaine Langone, Jane Reiss, Jackie Welch, Pieter Estersohn, and Beth Willams.

Finally, about the dogs. I don't want to thank them. They made me happy every day that I was writing this book, but please. They contributed nothing to my writing process but aggravation, panting and

Acknowledgments

whining at me on cue every time I entered a creative flow state. Instead, I need to thank Charlie Blanch and Katie Blanch, the amazing brother-sister team who babysat these same said dogs all summer. Without them, I'd still be writing. You two are iconic.

And so is everyone I just listed. I love you. I thank you ardently and profusely. And I promise not to do this again, until I do.

ONE PLACE. MANY STORIES

Bold, innovative and empowering publishing.

FOLLOW US ON:

@HQStories